SHELTON STATE COMMUNITY
COLLEGE
JUNIOR COLLEGE DIVISION
LIBRARY

DISCARDED

W9-BWY-412

BL
2480
.T27
H37

Harris, Grace
    Gredys, 1926-

Casting out anger

DATE			

© THE BAKER & TAYLOR CO.

Cambridge Studies in Social Anthropology

General Editor: JACK GOODY

21

Casting Out Anger

OTHER TITLES IN THE SERIES

CASTING OUT ANGER

RELIGION AMONG THE TAITA
OF KENYA

GRACE GREDYS HARRIS

Professor of Anthropology
University of Rochester

CAMBRIDGE UNIVERSITY PRESS

Cambridge
London · New York · Melbourne

Published by the Syndics of the Cambridge University Press
The Pitt Building, Trumpington Street, Cambridge CB2 1RP
Bentley House, 200 Euston Road, London NW1 2DB
32 East 57th Street, New York, NY 10022, USA
296 Beaconsfield Parade, Middle Park, Melbourne 3206, Australia

© Grace Gredys Harris 1978

First published 1978

Printed in Great Britain by
Western Printing Services Ltd, Bristol

Library of Congress Cataloguing in Publication Data
Harris, Grace Gredys, 1926–
Casting out anger.
(Cambridge studies in social anthropology; 21)
Bibliography: p.
Includes index.
1. Taita (Bantu tribe) – Religion. I. Title.
BL2480.T27H37   299'.6   77–80837
ISBN 0 521 21729 6

CONTENTS

v

PLATES

Plates 4 and 13 were taken by the author. All the other photographs were taken by and are the property of Alfred Harris. They are reproduced here with his permission.

FIGURES

PREFACE

Anthropological fieldwork is at once a professional activity and a profoundly personal experience. The process whereby one's presence becomes familiar to members of another society, one's inquisitiveness tolerable and one's personal foibles recognized as such has by now been documented many times. The corresponding experience of growth in knowledge of the language and etiquette, the feeble and then more full (but never complete) grasping of the social order, has also received attention. But anthropologists tend to say little of the way in which the fieldwork experience later becomes a part of the life of the one who, year after year, struggles to understand the 'data' against a double background of academic concepts and personal memories.

It is now a long time since we arrived in the Taita Hills to begin research lasting from July 1950 to August 1952. Since that time, concern with Taita has been woven into daily living. But the Taita are not today quite the same as they were in 1955, when I completed my PhD thesis on their ritual system. Major political events in Kenya have involved the Taita in a variety of ways as have economic trends both localized and world-wide. Another generation has grown up. Accordingly, I have declined to use the tense of the 'ethnographic present' even where, as in discussing language, the past tense is rather awkward, and even though much of the traditional society and culture is still alive. The picture given here is of Taita religion in the middle of the twentieth century, as we observed it during fieldwork.

In the course of trying to grasp the nature of Taita religion I have found both social structural analysis and exploration of cultural form indispensable. The discussion therefore attends to the connections between religious action and social relationships, and also to the ideas and beliefs that inform social life while being partly independent of social structural specificities. I have been more concerned with Taita religion as a mode of acting in the world than as a way of thinking about the world apart from action. Partly for that reason, the first chapter provides (among other things) the general background necessary for understanding what the later chapters propose respecting the social dimension of religious activity. The chapter also contributes to the effort to show how Taita religion functioned as one of the means by which, in action and thought, an environment was transformed into a world, psycho-biological individuals into persons, and human aggregates into communies.

Analysis and presentation have been guided by a number of convictions, some of them long-standing, some more recently acquired (the anthropologist also changes after the fieldwork). I mention only a few here. First, I remain convinced that relations of kinship and descent were culturally and structurally basic to Taita life as I observed it. The Taita concepts of *βupaga*, kinship (literally, blood-ship) and *βundee*, agnation, did not merely mask relations that were 'really' economic and political. To say this is to reject some of the views put forth at a time when the politicization of a large part of our own social life has coloured our judgement of peoples and periods with different experience. It is also to reject a methodologically unsound view of what is 'real' in social life. A second conviction is that the anthropological study of ritual symbolism has suffered, (1) from overuse of semiotically-inclined searches for meaning;[1] (2) some social structural reductionism;[2] (3) a view of symbolism as representing what somehow 'really' exists outside the rituals. My own attempt is to show the forms making up rituals as *presenting* realities that are lived in ritual itself. The latter point touches on a third conviction that, while social anthropologists ought to avoid the facile psychologizing that too often overcomes academics talking about non-literate societies, we must nevertheless deal with the fact that religion as a social creation meets with basic psychological formations as shaped by particular societies and cultures.[3]

It is my hope that in writing this book so long after field research I have not distorted the data but have brought to them more understanding. A good part of the 'purely descriptive' material (insofar as there is any such thing) comes from my PhD thesis. So does the central argument of Chapter 4 where I deal with the Taita doctrine of angry hearts in the context of domestic rituals. I have changed some of the terminology while retaining the central propositions in a modified form, and some errors have been corrected. Chapter 2 shows the influence of certain developments in ethnographic methodology. Chapter 3 has been shaped by a growing concern with religious rituals as lived by persons as they go through the life cycle, as personhood undergoes transformation and as actors experience different facets of a religious system that has wholly unfolded only for the aged.[4] Chapter 5 is old. Chapter 6 has the most new material. The idea of 'sets' of symbols I proposed in a paper presented in 1969 to a faculty–student seminar in the Department of

Anthropology, University of Rochester. It also appears in a published paper.[5] The discussion of speech in Taita ritual emerges out of an interest in performative utterances going back to the publication of J. L. Austin's book *How to Do Things with Words*.[6] That part of Chapter 6 is also related to a series of four lectures on the language of ritual given in the Department of Social Anthropology, University of Cambridge, in Lent Term 1976 and to a paper given at the Monday Seminar of the Department of Social Anthropology, University of Manchester, in March 1976.[7] Comments on the lectures and the paper have contributed to revision of the chapter.

Research among the Taita of Kenya was carried out with my husband, Alfred Harris. Each of us had a grant from the Colonial Social Science Research Council whose generous support also provided pre-fieldwork studentships at Oxford and writing-up time at Cambridge. While we were in the field we received much helpful advice and kind hospitality from the late H. E. Lambert and Mrs Lambert; from Peter and Ayesha Walters; from members of the CMS mission at Wusi, and from the Holy Ghost Fathers at Bura. George Mwakalamu Jocelyn and Amon Kinusa Rofasi were invaluable field assistants and kind friends whose understanding of our anthropological concerns and personal dilemmas saw us through many difficulties.

The book was written during a leave of absence from the Department of Anthropology, University of Rochester. Jack Goody, the staff, emeritus staff, and students of the Department of Social Anthropology of the University of Cambridge were gracious hosts during the year. Assistant staff were all kind and helpful. Edmund Leach generously lent an office. The helpfulness of Peter Gathercole, Curator of the Museum of Archaeology and Ethnology, and John Pickles, Librarian of the Haddon Library, added much to the pleasure of working again in the building where as a graduate student I spent many hours. Karen Stringer, Secretary of the Faculty of Archaeology and Anthropology, typed the manuscript, which was given a final checking by Jane Harmon, Editorial Assistant in the Department of Anthropology, University of Rochester; I thank them both.

Taita said that every person has three parents: a mother, a father, and a mother's brother. To my three anthropological parents I hereby express gratitude that can never be adequate to what they have given me of their wisdom and friendship: my two principal teachers, Fred Eggan and Meyer Fortes, and also I. Schapera, who first set us on the road to Taita.[8]

To one of my colleagues, the late Gerald E. Williams, I can no longer speak of my appreciation, but must tell others that I owe much to his

ability to build bridges between linguistics and social anthropology. Sally
Chilver, Charles Morrison, and Audrey Richards have my heartfelt thanks.
So have the many graduate and undergraduate students in my course on
comparative religious systems whose questions have influenced what I have
written.

Very special debts of gratitude are owed to my sister, Adelaide Gredys
Winston, for her continuing support of my endeavours; and to my god-
parents, John and Patricia Paliouras, whose hearts' kindness has sustained
me. I cannot express sufficiently my thanks to Al Harris, my husband,
colleague and friend, with whom I have 'talked Taita' for so many years
and whose insights and encouragement have contributed so much. Finally,
to the Taita, *Chaβucha na ndigi βoruβu*; Thank you very much indeed.

G.G.H.

NOTE ON ORTHOGRAPHY

1. The symbol β stands for a phoneme with two allophones:

   (a) a voiced plosive bilabial stop, following *m*, as in *kumβona* = to see him (her);

   (b) a voiced bilabial fricative, in all other positions, as in *Kuβona* = to see, to perceive.

   This phoneme contrasts with *b*, a voiced implosive bilabial stop, as in *kumbonyera* = to cause him (her) to do.

2. The symbol *ŋ* stands for a voiced velar nasal continuum, as in *ŋombe* = cattle.

   This phoneme contrasts with *ng*, a voiced velar nasal continuum released with a voiced velar stop, as in *ngoma* = shrine.

To the memory of my parents

LOUIS AND GUNDA GREDYS

'Let the mountains and hills
bring a message of peace for the people.'
Psalm 72:3

I

INTRODUCTION

The tension between 'insider' and 'outsider' points of view creates problems for all anthropological studies, especially those concerned with religion. The degree of explicitness with which the two viewpoints are distinguished varies; but the analyst must always find a way of coming to terms with the views of those for whom 'beliefs and practices' function as truths and necessities to live by and act upon. This introductory chapter begins by presenting that outsider's view which places the Taita Hills, the Taita people and their way of life in an ethnographic context. Attention then shifts to include the Taita's own view as presented in speech and action. The first part of the chapter provides information on location, physical setting and ecological relations, historical associations and linguistic affinities. The latter part is based on the Taita picture of themselves and their homeland in relation to non-Taita, and to their internal divisions. Like other peoples, the Taita constructed a world of human meanings. They followed a map of social topography on which contours were marked in part by ritual beliefs and practices. In sketching the social contours and locating their ritual markers, I here provide background for the later chapters on religious thought and action. The Taita view of themselves took account of ecological, demographic, linguistic, and other internal differences. As they saw it, their internal differentiation could not cancel out their oneness. In this respect the anthropological outsider's view of the Taita social and cultural system as an appropriate object of study meets with the insiders' view of themselves as one people over against all others.

As one journeys from Mombasa by road or rail to the interior of Kenya, the narrow strip of green lowland bordering the coast soon disappears. A vast, gradually rising plain lies around one, a plain of red soils covered with thorny bush, dry and rough, with here and there some barren rocky eminences standing like huge pebbles scattered on a great beach. About fifty miles inland come the last settlements of the coastal peoples and the traveller arrives at the eastern boundary of Taita District. Past the former military barracks of Mackinnon Road come two more stopping places on the railway. Fifty miles further on, Voi township, a junction on the railway, was for many years the district headquarters. Following the railway on from Voi westward towards the Tanzania border for another fifty miles, one passes through country occupied by the Wataveta people. The main Uganda line to the north and west crosses uninhabited bush and then, leaving Taita District, passes through Kamba country to the south of Mt Kenya, to Kikuyu country, Nairobi, and beyond.

The Taita Hills, jutting up sharply from the plain, dominate the scene at and around Voi. The road into Voi from the southeast carries the traveller near the foot of Sagala Mountain, an isolated ridge separated by about ten miles from the main massif of Dabida. Further back towards the coast, to the south and between Voi and Mackinnon Road, the great isolated Kasigau Mountain will have been passed. Dabida, Sagala, and Kasigau are the homeland of the Taita people.[1] To the lowlands surrounding them, the Hills occupied by the major portion of the Taita people stand in great contrast, especially after the rains when the slopes rise bright and green. Within the Hills there are contrasts too, for they rise steeply from the plain (which itself lies between 2,000 and 3,500 feet above sea level) to a maximum of 7,000 feet reached by the highest rocky peaks of Dabida.

In order to reach the heights one passes through three ecological zones.[2] First come the dry foothills with the parts of the plain adjoining them; there the rainfall (coming in two wet seasons, from March to May and from October to December) is only 15 to 20 inches per year. Above, with an upper limit at 3,500 to 4,000 feet, a second zone receives 20 to 40 inches of rain per year; this zone has grasses, light bush and trees in the few uncultivated spots. Here small, occasionally flat-bottomed valleys alternate with ridges that often are sharp and steepsided. Numbers of small streams, intermittent and perennial, run along the valley bottoms and plunge down the steep hillsides. Still higher, the country becomes more rolling, with some relatively large upland valleys, greener than below on account of an annual rainfall of 40 to 60 inches. To the east and north in Dabida and also on Sagala, the higher portions do not receive this high rainfall and there the slopes rise steeply, often knife-backed, craggy, and dry. During the dry season mists surround and winds buffet all the peaks.

In the topmost zone, scattered clusters of houses extended downwards from about 5,500 feet. The upper zone also included a number of densely packed villages of up to several hundred houses. Dispersed settlement in clusters of two to a dozen houses characterized the middle zone which carried the bulk of the population, totalling about 53,000,[3] and the most intensive cultivation. There, particularly in the central portion of Dabida and in Teri Valley on Sagala, little forest remained on a landscape largely domesticated, if rough. Further down the settlements continued more sparsely. A few compact villages occupied the shelf adjoining the plain, both on Dabida and Sagala, but they did not rival in size those of the upper zone.

Out on the plain a band of cultivation dotted with intermittently inhabited dwellings surrounded a large part of Sagala and also the northern, western and parts of the southern side of Dabida. In a few places these bands extended several miles out. Cultivation intensified only where streams running down from the Hills or across the plain provided the necessary water. Here and there on the uncultivated portion, single herdsman's shelters stood, while several miles out in a few places such as Makitau in the west and Mariwenyi in the east, clusters of houses and stock enclosures marked the places where prosperous herdsmen had moved more or less permanently to look after their animals. The former Colonial government facilitated the alienation of five blocks of land for sisal growing from the strip surrounding the Hills. Indeed, alienation and the draining of swampland, especially the latter, cost the Taita much of their most valuable plains-border land. Otherwise the plain, given over formerly to Crown lands in the south and to game preserves around the other sides, stretches on to the heights of Kamba country in the north and of Pare and Sambara country in Tanzania. Nearer, a few of the low, small, rocky eminences were inhabited intermittently in the past. Otherwise the bush lies rough, dry, and game-ridden. It can be crossed on foot if need be, but without irrigation it defies settlement by cultivators.

The surrounding plain never isolated Taita completely. Other peoples sometimes received Taita in time of famine and in turn sought refuge in the Hills. Kamba also raided in the vicinity of the Hills, though it is recorded that in the early days of European penetration into East Africa the Kamba, instead of following a well known route across the plain via Maungu and the Voi River, used an alternative route for fear of encountering Taita.[4] According to their own traditions, Taita raided into Pare and Sambara country and less frequently into Ukambani. Certainly trade with these other people took place, but determining its scope poses difficulties.

Contact with Arabs and 'Swahili' from the coast may well have occurred early; memory and tradition did not yield information about a time when Taita did not trade hides for Arab beads and cloth. One of the caravan routes (though a relatively late one) passed into the interior near Mbololo peak, and some Arab families in Mombasa still remembered during the fifties having had Taita slaves. Krapf and Rebmann, the first Europeans to reach the Hills, visited Kasigau in 1849 and 1847 respectively, and after them came a series of travellers, explorers and missionaries.[5] In 1883 Mr Wray of the Church Missionary Society founded a

station in Teri Valley, Sagala. The French of the Holy Ghost Fathers who
founded the Roman Catholic mission at Bura were succeeded largely by
Irish priests. In 1885 the Hills were annexed in the name of the Sultan of
Zanzibar, but shortly thereafter they came under the Imperial British East
Africa Company. The activities of British Colonial government expanded
gradually. After two moves, administrative headquarters were set up in
Voi in 1914 and another move was made during the fifties to Wundanyi,
now a substantial town, in central Dabida. Today Taita are citizens of the
independent African nation of Kenya.

Considerable inter-change of population appears to have taken place
among the Bantu and non-Bantu people of Kenya and Tanzania. Most
peoples considered that they have absorbed populations from elsewhere,
attributing this commonly to movement during famines caused by
droughts. Certainly some Taita sought refuge in the recent past among the
Taveta (from Dabida) and in Giriama country (from Sagala). Movements
stimulated by famine may well account also for the export of population
from Taita to Taveta, Pare, Sambara, Kamba, Chagga and perhaps also
for reverse movements into the Taita Hills.[6]

One language was spoken by everyone on the main massif, but four
main dialects coincided with the four main valley systems along which
the population oriented themselves. These main dialects had a low degree
of differentiation and, correlatively, a high degree of mutual intelligi-
bility.[7] The main dialects in turn divided into a great many sub-dialects
which did not bar communication. The speech of the Kasigau people
probably should be considered a dialect of the language of the main
massif. Teri, the long and narrow valley lying about 3,500 feet up on the
western side of Sagala, carried the bulk of that mountain's population.
The speech of the Teri people comprised a language not mutually intel-
ligible with that of Dabida and Kasigau, but some of the remaining
Sagala population spoke variants of the latter.[8] Teri adults, especially men,
tended to be bilingual[9] and also considered their own language closer to
that of the coastal Giriama than to the language of Dabida and Kasigau.[10]

During our fieldwork (1950–52), British officers complained that the
Taita were not really 'one tribe'. They noted how much difficulty Taita
encountered when seeking food and shelter outside their own localities.
To the Colonial officers every African was supposed to belong to a 'tribe'
within which mutual aid extended to all. Taita, while making the same
observations about the state of affairs, seemed never to tire of character-
izing themselves as βandu βamweri, 'one people'. I shall show grounds
for accepting both the Colonial officers' view of the Taita as a collection of
social fragments and the Taita insistence on their unity. Thought and
action revealed both aspects.

Mlungu, Creator, made all human beings: *βandu* or *βaadamu*. The latter term, derived from Swahili and meaning 'children of Adam', itself points to relations between Taita and non-Taita. Stressing as it does the similarities among groups of people, it conferred on those relations something of a positive value in contrast to some other ideas. However it linked to nothing in Taita ritual as such; the analyst must seek elsewhere for the ritual significance of *Mlungu* (see Chapter 5). The concept of *Mlungu* through a creation myth brought to a focus Taita recognition of major cleavages in the society of Colonial Kenya. *Mlungu*, working as a potter, moulded all human beings of clay. Europeans were formed and fired between dawn and mid-day, Asians from mid-day until dusk, and Africans between dusk and midnight.[11] There might be some doubt about attributing an African origin to this myth, associating dark people with night, since for Taita, as for so many African peoples, the night was associated with secrecy and illicit activity, especially sorcery. Yet it is the case that Taita, again like many other Africans, used the same word for the darkness of a deep brown skin, for the darkness of night, and for the darkness signified in English by the colour term 'black'.[12]

The myth condenses several convictions economically: that all men, being the creatures of *Mlungu*, are alike in substance and form; that the divisions between Europeans, Asians, and Africans are significant and as 'natural' as dawn, mid-day, dusk, and midnight; but that these divisions connect with skin colour in a complex way, for given the fact that skin colours occur along a continuum, the points of division are in another sense 'unnatural'. The myth also serves as a means by which Taita identified themselves as 'Africans', although few Taita during the Colonial period exhibited any concern with 'African unity'. The British were well-known as *βaingereza*, whites in general as *βazungu*; many Taita offered the opinion that all *βazungu* were just varieties of *βaingereza* who all knew each other in their homeland, *βulaya*, variously England or Europe. The felt opposition between Taita and white Colonials appeared in ritual prohibitions that identified the latter as one sort among many sorts of outsiders, non-Taita. The need for protection against outsiders of all kinds furnished a ritual marker of Taita identity, the Defender shrines, discussed further on.

Another myth accounts for the differentiation of Taita from two other groups. In it the progenitors of the Masai, Kamba, and Taita peoples figure as three brothers or half-brothers whose different responses to a paternally imposed ordeal result in different skills and their concomitant ways of life. Masai become expert herdsmen, Kamba expert huntsmen, and Taita expert cultivators. It would be misleading to see this myth as representing the social separation of three closely related peoples or even as meditating upon cultural similarities and dissimilarities fairly accurately portrayed. Masai, fearsome as raiders who skirmished about the plains-borders of the Hills, were indeed envied as owners of large herds. Kamba, however, followed a mode of subsistence not so very different from that of the Taita, although hunting probably continued into the Colonial period to be more important in Kamba country than in Taita. A myth concerning social separation and cultural divergence might be expected to include coastal people such as the Giriama to whom Taita reckon themselves connected in varied ways. Rather, the myth associates Masai pursuits with domesticated animals and Kamba pursuits with wild animals, making the Taita those living most fully a life of humanity and domestication.[13] The contrast between the Hill homeland and the plains, as a contrast between the safety of domesticated life and the dangers of the wild, provided an important theme in Taita ritual.

That theme, embracing but not limited to cultural and social separation from Masai and Kamba as two special kinds of outsiders, found expression also in topographical imagery. According to some Taita, the earth has the shape of a crescent moon. Taita lived on the horns of the moon and all others lived in the hollow. Since Taita had long known that some other peoples lived in hill country (on a clear day the top of Mt Kilimanjaro can be seen from part of Taita), we are not facing a bit of topographical naiveté. The formulation filled out the significance of the Taita name for themselves – People of the Hills, a people apart.[14] All others had to approach the Taita or be approached by them across the plains, and so were figured as 'plainsmen'. To say that all Taita recognized each other as People of the Hills is not to deny significant internal differentiation. The main portion of the population, living on the main massif, considered themselves somewhat different from those of Sagala, whom they called βasaga, while feeling more akin to the βakasigau of Kasigau mountain. The Wasagala, as the people of Sagala mountain called themselves, referred to the people of Dabida, the main massif, as Wateta and to those of Kasigau as Wakasigalu. Despite linguistic variation and some differences in custom, and despite also acknowledged diversity of origin, the inhabitants of all these mountains insisted they were 'one people'.

It might well be argued that Taita reiteration of the 'one people' theme signalled a desperate effort to deny the internal fragmentation that so disturbed British Colonial officers. But in fact Taita did *not* deny internal differentiation; they pointed to bonds which were supposed to overcome differentiation with something positive. To be 'one people', People of the Hills, meant more than to stand apart from plainsmen. It meant to know and follow the way of life known as Kidaβida. That way of life did not differ entirely, in the Taita view, from the ways of life followed by other peoples known to them: for example, the Pare of Tanzania (then Tanganyika) were mentioned frequently as following similar ritual practices. But as a totality, as a complex of practices, *Kidaβida* was supposed to be unique. Someone could not be said to know and follow *Kidaβida* merely by having acquired an ethnographer's familiarity with Taita ways. Taita assumed incorporation in a mesh of relationships with other Taita and of loyalties focussed on a local community within the Hills. Persons so incorporated had rights and obligations of a Taita kind to which they adhered whether or not their forbears were thought to have entered the Hills as immigrants. *Kidaβida*, as a way of life, was taken therefore to have social as well as cultural significance.

Residents of a few parts of the Hills spoke of themselves as descendants of recent immigrants to Taita. Such were one group of villagers in Teri, Sagala, who claimed Kamba descent within two or three generations. Usually various groups were described as being 'from the side of' or as having come 'from the direction of' the Sambara, Giriama, Kamba, and so on. A few people claimed descent from supposed autochthones called *βanyamba*. Others said that their remote ancestors were the so-called *βambisha*, variously identified as original inhabitants and as mysterious and formidable trading people 'from the north'. Another small group who entered the central Dabida area three generations ago from the slopes of Mbololo peak proudly claimed descent from King Solomon, perhaps as a response to their rather precarious position in their new local community. Sometimes claims about immigration were defended by calling attention to small stone cairns dotting the plains and supposedly containing the bones of ancient immigrants to the Hills. Whatever the particular external connections claimed, Taita took the position that diversity of origin was compatible with being 'one people'. Descendants of King Solomon, autochthones, descendants of Kamba or of the children of an in-married Pare man, all were supposed to be one people following *Kidaβida*.

The peculiar complexities of Taita unity-in-diversity nowhere appeared more strikingly than in the system of Numbers which I now describe.

In traditional Taita society everyone belonged to one of the categories of persons called Numbers (*Mtalo* = Number; *kutala* = to count), with membership being transmitted from a man to his sons and daughters. Not everyone of the same Number belonged to a single descent group, nor did Numbers regulate marriage in any way whatsoever.[15] Since patri-lineages (see below pp. 15–17) were localized, local concentrations of the various Numbers were coextensive with one or more of the lineages in a given neighbourhood. The Four-people (*βanya*) and Six-people (*βasasadu*) had the most numerous memberships, including patrilineages in many parts of the Hills. The Three-people (*βasadu*) accounted for fewer persons. Though some Taita claimed that Ten-people (*βaiḵumi*) occupied parts of the country remote from their own, we never located anyone who identified himself as a member of that Number.

The Numbers functioned mainly in the two kinds of divination: one by casting *Saru* seeds (for 'small affairs' or 'affairs of the homestead') and the other from entrails (for 'important' or 'public' matters). Both kinds of divination were numerological, employing the numbers one through ten. Each number carried several possible meanings in a code variously interpreted according to the configuration of signs under particular circumstances. Divination sought to identify the source of a misfortune or threat of misfortune with the activities or feelings of human and non-human agents so that the correct ritual action might be taken. In that process, the Numbers could provide a first approximation by eliminating persons whose Numbers did not appear in the configuration of signs, or by directing attention to the local members of one or another of the lineages carrying the Number. But interpretation conjoined any *Mtalo* sign with other signs.

The signs regularly labelled as One, Two, and Three helped also to identify agents according to genealogical generation relative to the individual being divined-for, and so provided more refined information. All information was taken to refer to male agents unless (1) the subject of the divination was female or (2) the sign for Nine displayed special features, indicating a woman's involvement. In this way women constituted a marked category, the Nine-people, and men an unmarked category, in addition to their membership in their fathers' Numbers (pl. *Mitalo*). Those Five-people who were Taita permanently residing on the plains-border also retained their fathers' Numbers. But they had moved part-way into another category that included everyone and everything foreign to Taita that reached or threatened them from the plains wilderness. Kamba, Pare, Giriama, Asians, Europeans, Arabs, all were 'people of the plains wilderness' (*βandu βa ḵireti*). All were considered real or potential enemies. In accord with that view, beasts of the plains as well as cattle rustlers and sorcerers, whether Taita or non-Taita, counted as Fives.

Identification of Taita as Three-, Four-, and Six-people therefore occurred as part of a wider system sorting out persons as (1) Taita or non-Taita, (2) male or female, (3) in ego's own generation, the first ascending generation or the first descending generation, (4) belonging to one or another lineage within a given locality. Given that, the intervals of the patrilineally transmitted Numbers, Three, Four, and Six, look a little less strange, and the absence of descent or marriage functions is more understandable. Most of the numbers from one to ten had multiple meanings that contributed to the ambiguity of divinatory configurations.

That ambiguity provides a clue to the elusiveness of the 'Ten-people' postulated by some Taita. That number commonly indicated 'an affair of livestock', more particularly of cattle. Not surprisingly, those localities supposed to be especially rich in cattle were singled out by other Taita as the home of Ten-people. On arrival in those localities the anthropologists found only the same Numbers as occurred elsewhere in the Hills.

The Numbers were linked to traditions of diverse origins, but not in a simple way, since a single Number could include lineages purported to have diverse ethnic origins. The Four-people dominant in Teri valley on Sagala mountain were considered to be of (fairly remote) Giriama origins, but the Four-people of other parts of the Hills were sometimes spoken of as being (even more remotely) of Kamba descent. Some of the latter denied the claim, countering that they and the Six-people were the 'real' Taita autochthones while Three-people and the alleged Ten-people were of foreign origin. Some of the Three-people in central Dabida claimed to be 'from the side of' the Masai, while others posited ultimate descent 'from the side of' the Sambara. People in any one part of the Hills carried only a rough sketch of the Number affiliations in areas remote from their own. Therefore a different overall picture emerged depending on the source of the information. An accurate mapping of the local distribution could result only from questioning members of each lineage about their Number.

Whatever their Number and ultimate origin, all Taita faced common dangers from the humans, animals, and influences of the plains wilderness as marked by Five. In the ritual system, the apartness of Taita from all others was marked by the need for defence secured by the powerful medicines known as *Figi* (*figi* = stopper or barrier; *kufigika* = to stop up, to forbid passage). The protective influence of these Defender medicines manifested itself in the illness, paralysis, or even death they could bring to animal and human enemies in their vicinity. Even acting like an enemy in the neighbourhood of a *Figi* endangered Taita. The latter therefore had to observe the taboos peculiar to each protective medicine, a require-ment bearing on Taita unity and diversity. For example, a great *Figi* protecting the plains lying in the direction of Kamba country especially 'disliked' persons wearing traditional Kamba clothing or acting like Kamba. Taita, including any supposed to be of ultimate Kamba descent, had to avoid being mistaken by the *Figi* for Kamba; they had to behave and look like Taita for their own safety. The great *Figi* then supported uniformity within Taita, insisting from within the ritual system that all who claimed to be Taita must act in accordance with the Taita way of life. The diverse origins of those belonging to various Taita Numbers had to be cancelled by their opposition to all the ways of the foreign Fives.

In pre-Colonial times, cattle-raiding parties (according to some Taita) drew men from many parts of the Hills, especially when a raid was ordered by a Seer (see below, pp. 26, 135). In that case the Seer's instructions included the order in which men were to march according to their Numbers. If such ordering did take place, it must have created an explicit link between the cooperation of diverse Taita groupings and their opposition to all non-Taita. Opposition to whomever and whatever was non-Taita was an important aspect of Taita concern that they be recognized as 'one people'. More positively, Taita called attention to a fundamental unity of cultural and social forms, a unity overriding acknowledged diversity of origins and summed up in the term *Kidaßida*, their way of life, the Way of the Hills. Myths, the system of divination and *Figi* regulations were prominent ritual markers emphasizing that unity. Consideration of the ritual specialists concerned with the *Figi* medicines shifts attention to the social divisions so deplored by Colonial officers. All Taita looked to *Figi* medicines to guard the uplands against the evil influences of the plains. But, characteristically, no national shrine or ritual office took up the defensive task. That was done by ritual specialists attached to the local units here called neighbourhoods. In the relatively closed nature and self-sufficiency of neighbourhoods, Colonial officers could find the basis for their conviction that Taita were not a 'tribe'. They were looking for a political unity not encompassed by the Taita's own conception of 'one people'.

Taita local groups and descent groups were not related to each other as members of a continuous series of adjacent and interdependent units. The social landscape was marked off into discrete, highly independent neighbourhoods. Usually a community – for such a neighbourhood was – had its own name. Always its members said that they occupied 'one country' (*izanga jimweri*) and were 'one people'. The term 'neighbourhood' does justice to the fact that their boundaries, though neither wholly rigid nor eternally stable, defined far more than a mere vicinage.

Certain aspects of neighbourhoods call attention to ecological relations. Despite turning to cash-earning activities, Taita continued through the Colonial period to live largely by cultivating foodstuffs and herding relatively small numbers of cattle, goats and fat-tailed sheep. Major ecological zones differed from one another in respect to the balance between cultivation and herding, settlement pattern and other aspects of land use. In the middle altitudes of the Hills the bulk of the population lived in small villages whose residents were 'food rich and livestock poor' relative to others.[16] This middle zone is better watered than both higher and lower zones and it had the largest number of irrigation ditches.[17] Sweet potatoes were grown on hillside fields while drier slopes were given over to maize and a great variety of legumes, cassava, and cucurbits. Dry fields at lower altitudes carried maize, grams, and peas, making use of the long rains. However, the main crop of maize on which the residents of the middle zone depended ripened after the short rains of December to January. On the slopes above or between cultivations some of the livestock grazed, kept at night in the houses or in special shelters and enclosures. Larger aggregations of livestock were kept on the plains in shelters and stockaded corrals built against hyena and leopard.[18]

In the upper zone, large settlements grew up at the less numerous places of good water supply. Here there was valley cultivation, and in a few places 'European' vegetables could be grown for sale. Mists and overcast skies meant that maize and millet did poorly and so the inhabitants of this zone could not count on getting their main crop from the home fields. The same uses were made of the different kinds of fields, but farmers concentrated on stream-bordering land on the edge of the plains. Such neighbourhoods were 'fodder rich' and 'food poor', relative to others. The settlements on the plains-bordering shelf, the lowest zone, were those of people who had moved there in order to be near plains-border fields or herd enclosures. No doubt the cessation of raiding encouraged such movements, but water supply remained crucial.[19]

Every neighbourhood known to us followed a single pattern of land use respecting hills and plains-border. That is, some neighbourhoods had their population concentrated in a few large villages whose residents got their main crop from below. Others had dispersed populations whose upland fields provided the main crop.

Each ecological adjustment presented its own problems in the management of resources for herding and those for cultivation. Towards outsiders a neighbourhood presented an almost united front, strongly resisting the sale or even the loan of a plot of a resident of another neighbourhood. Should someone be willing to give up residence in his original neighbourhood and move to another (as in rare uxorilocal marriage) he could get land-rights in his new home. But no one could be a resident in one neighbourhood and have land-rights in another. Conversely, the sale, but more especially the loan, of land to members of the same neighbourhood was extremely common. Neighbours were bound together by a multiplicity of land transactions. In effect they formed a wider land use unit within which members had to satisfy their need for arable land and for pasture. Heritable rights over arable land as property belonged to men who, ideally, transferred them from father to son. Women dominated as holders of use-rights, primarily in their capacities as wives and mothers growing most of the household food. Within the confines of a neighbourhood heritable rights in land as property concerned patrilineages especially (see below p. 16). But the intricate network of loans, by means of which persons satisfied their need for land of varied kinds, followed the lines of affinal and matrilateral ties.[20] Such arrangements facilitated and, in the Taita view, made it desirable for most people to marry within the neighbourhood. Up to 80% of neighbourhood men in fact took wives from within the local group. Endogamy therefore contributed importantly to the operation of the neighbourhood as a land-use and land-controlling group.

In most respects neighbourhoods were not so exclusive with respect to livestock as with respect to land rights. Any independent male householder had the right, always allowing for claims of kin, to enter into livestock transactions wherever he chose. Two uses of livestock kept many animals within the neighbourhood. The first involved giving livestock as bride-wealth. Since the majority of marriages united members of neighbouring large lineages, most bridewealth livestock circulated within the neighbourhood. The second was the sharing of the meat of beasts slaughtered for divination, religious offering or festival. Those activities commonly brought together members of one neighbourhood and so largely restricted the consumption of meat to the local group.

Genealogies show that the patterns of marriage preference have not always remained the same over the generations. A nearby large lineage once excluded for marriage purposes may have been drawn in, or changes in the composition of a neighbourhood may have taken place because of population shifts. Sometimes a lineage gradually withdrew from a part of its area, or migration left a rump group to be assimilated into another neighbourhood. Stability could be long term. In the latter cases neighbourhood boundaries were virtually never crossed for marriage purposes, even in the absence of natural barriers to interaction and movement.

The marriage pattern affected the composition of a neighbourhood and, from an individual's point of view, the extent of the area containing most of his kin. For any one person, a considerable range of kin was likely to be close at hand. A man's married daughters and their in-laws were nearby and so also his matrikinsmen if his own father 'married close'; he may have taken his own wife from among his matrikin or his daughters may have gone to them as brides. Clearly the people of a neighbourhood were related to each other in many ways.

Against this background of multiple ties and the interaction they entailed, Taita often said of their neighbourhood that its people were 'like one lineage' (*sa kichuku chimweri*). They went even further and, taking into consideration intra-lineage marriages, said that 'we are like one lineage *because* we inter-marry, and we inter-marry *because* we are like one lineage'. Agnation, matrifiliation, affinity and local propinquity for Taita were not mutually exclusive, but entailed one another. From one point of view a neighbourhood was an association of patrilineages, with the members of each sharing *βundee* (fathership, agnation). From another point of view a neighbourhood was a group sharing *βupaga* (blood-ship, i.e. kinship).

Taita summed up the complexities by saying of their neighbourhood, 'we understand one another' (*dasiḳirana*). If asked why they did not inter-marry with people just as close physically, they answered that somehow they and those others had not come to understand one another. In this way Taita aptly described the neighbourhood as a highly autonomous political unit bound together by ties of kinship and marriage and by control over land resources. This context clarifies the usage by which a traitor was described as *mja ḳuβi*, an 'eater in two places'. Preventing an outsider from having access to land, was explained as not so much being stingy about the land but of not wanting people around who really belonged elsewhere.

Exclusiveness of the neighbourhood was manifested not only in preventing non-residents from gaining land rights but in taking care about who was admitted as a resident. True, it was meritorious to give refuge to a stranger in trouble, perhaps fleeing famine. A proverb says *mugenyi ni vua, na vua ni mugenyi*, 'a guest (or stranger) is rain, and rain is a guest'. But refugees sometimes stayed on to become land-debtors and, consequently, political supporters of their host, their descendants marrying locally and giving rise to new lineages in the neighbourhood. Therefore a man had to be circumspect enough to consult at least formally with his neighbours before giving freely of his hospitality.[21]

Anyone offering hospitality to a stranger would have had to be an elder, standing at the apex of the system of age-statuses. In the briefest terms, males had higher status than females; initiated youths and maidens counted as higher than non-initiates; married people were superior to the unmarried; those with children to the childless; independent householders to those who were under their fathers' supervision. Old men as independent householders with sons and grandsons, with large herds, and with fields to lend to younger men ranked highest of all. Ritual knowledge and possession of personal shrines (see pp. 34–6) accompanied their wealth and legitimized their influence.

Within a neighbourhood the achievement of elderhood proceeded in the context of household and lineage membership, but required eventual validation by elders of other constituent lineages as well. A pool of neighbourhood elders provided a governmental body. They heard disputes and acted as witnesses, assessors, and repositories of knowledge concerning customary practices and relevant events. They formed *ad hoc* councils differently constituted depending on circumstances. In disputes relationship to one of the parties might bring elders into cases, but it was primarily high status as elders that gave them an authoritative voice. Elders had few legitimate secular means of backing their decisions with force, but they wielded considerable power through their administration of the juridical rites: conditional curses, oaths and ordeals, and participating in the Executioners' Society (see p. 40). Juridical rites counted heavily in disputes between intractable parties and between men who were themselves elders. Otherwise, moral authority, control over resources in land and livestock, and their religious functions enabled elders to exact a large measure of conformity. The same attributes allowed elders to establish cattle-keeping arrangements, mutual-aid partnerships, patron–client relationships, and extra-neighbourhood marriages not available to non-elders.[22]

Peace, *sere*, was one of the great desiderata of Taita life. Indeed, the word *sere* sums up all well-being, physical, social, and what we would call psychological. Physical violence seldom broke the peace both because self-help was not part of the legal system and because Taita were genuinely committed to a non-violent way of life. However, any neighbourhood was the scene of numerous internal disputes, mostly concerning livestock debts outside bridewealth. In the wider world, neighbourhoods could seldom come together in opposition to other like units. Massive land encroachment was the affair most likely to unite groups, and in the past some feuding (*βuda*) certainly took place.

For the most part elders appear to have maintained a considerable degree of Hill-wide as well as inter-community peace through the network of blood pacts called *mtero*. Created by means of juridical ritual, *mtero* pacts guaranteed the settlement of quarrels and cemented alliances. Facilitating trade, mutual-aid partnerships, and extra-neighbourhood marriage, a blood pact protected partners against double-dealing, gaining for each access to another otherwise closed local community. Richer and more influential elders established correspondingly more numerous personal allies outside their neighbourhoods. Inroads into neighbourhood solidarity resulted.

Some Taita claimed that at the time of British arrival unification of all the inhabitants of the Hills was proceeding under the alliance of elders of two neighbourhoods, Mwangeka of Mwanda and Mgalu of Mbale. Perhaps the alliance might have led to new developments had not Mwangeka been killed.[23] Whatever the potentialities, Taita remained politically decentralized. In the ritual sphere, decentralization was marked by the attachment to neighbourhoods of the two entities supposed to bring public benefits: the Defender medicine, *Figi*, and the groves and medicines of rainmaking.

The protective influence of *Figi* medicine and its associated taboos extended over the combined portions of the plain in which members of neighbour lineages had their herder's houses. Its custodian was *mundu wa Figi*, man of the *Figi*, or *Mfigiki*, the Defender, whose closest partner in the religious affairs of the neighbourhood as a whole was the *mundu wa Vua*, man of rain, or Mnyeshi-vua, Rainmaker. The latter position belonged, in some cases hereditarily, to a lineage other than that of the Defender. Prospering the neighbourhood as a whole consisted of guarding against enemies and ensuring the rainfall without which crops and grass, men and livestock would not thrive. The conduct of neighbours affected what Defender and Rainmaker contributed to the maintenance of neighbourhood peace.

Certain religious performances presided over by Defender and Rainmaker were decreed by shades of the 'people of long ago' through a Seer known as *Mlodi* (pl. *βalodi*; *kuloda* = to dream, have visions). Every neighbourhood acknowledged at least one Seer as authentic. Every neighbourhood also had diviners expert at throwing the seeds in *Saru* divination. Neighbours joined one another in haruspication, for every elder had learned how to read entrails in *βula* divination. People usually went to a diviner in their own neighbourhood, while Seers more commonly competed with one another in such a way as to gain for some a measure of influence in neighbourhoods other than their own. Diviners were all men, but a few women became Seers.

The Defender, Rainmaker and Seer dealt with religious matters pertaining to local communities as such. Religious performances centring on members of constituent lineages often drew in neighbours through ties of matrilateral kinship. Further, elders of different lineages, by virtue of being matrikin, affines or friends acted as one another's religious assistants. In these various ways, members of a neighbourhood were involved together in religious events of many kinds and on innumerable occasions. Religious ritual showed each neighbourhood facing out towards other like units and performing the tasks vital to the survival of Taita as a people standing over against all others. Neighbourhood ritual also faced inwards to the maintenance of peace within a community of kinsmen who were at the same time members of separate agnatic lineages.

The Taita word *kichuku* was used for a body of kin related to each other by a network of agnatic, matrilateral, and affinal ties and characteristically co-extensive with a neighbourhood. The same word also stood for patrilineage, but only in this usage occurred with modifying words indicating variable span and depth. By legitimate birth every Taita gained membership in a *kichuku kibaha*, great lineage, within which all shared *βundee*, agnation in addition to *βupaga*, kinship. The genealogical boundaries of a great lineage set the limits for inheritance by male members

of rights in land and livestock as property. They also provided under-
pinning for the residential rights of male agnates who anchored the great
lineage spatially within a neighbourhood. The great lineage was *not*
exogamous.

Male members of a great lineage claimed a portion of Hill country as
their upland home where most of them lived and held rights in arable.
In the areas of dispersed settlement each lineage had from one to three
square miles, but the size of territories claimed by lineages occupying
concentrated villages was more difficult to ascertain. Most lineages claimed
a stretch of plains-border land also, sometimes adjacent to the upland
centre. A tract of uncultivated plains wilderness or bush below the dwelling area provided grazing.[24] Depending on the part of the Hills occupied,
members of a lineage had a Hill homeland differing in resources from
others. In their exploitation of it, Taita employed land use and property
rules permitting the use by individuals of varied lands. As noted above,
those rules distinguished between men as owners of property rights and
women as primary holders of use-rights. Male householders and their
wives, trying to secure access to plots suited to many different crops, made
use of patrilineally inherited rights and of loan, pawn, and even purchase.
The distribution of fields among neighbouring lineages bore witness to
the partial breakup of lineage territories by the last three means. However,
resistance to the alienation of much land to non-agnates acted as a constraint. Land left by a man without sons was not allowed to pass out of
the great lineage except in extraordinary circumstances, an heir being
sought among the deceased's close junior agnates. Ritually the system of
land use and land rights was important in throwing great emphasis on the
jural relations of father and son, brothers and close agnatic cousins.

Residential changes, an important feature of the land use system, were
related to the quest for satisfactorily varied holdings. Since rights were
held by individuals and since householders moved independently, the
male members of a lineage distributed themselves in complex ways. Small
villages or sections of large ones grew by accretion and then vanished as
people moved away again; but the retention of rights in a deserted spot
might make it the place of a new village or hamlet in later years.[25]
Clearly, the actual occupancy of lands within a great lineage territory at
any one time represented a temporary distribution of and adjustment to
variable resources.[26] The extent of such adjustments was limited by the
nature of neighbourhoods. Each constituent great lineage in a neighbourhood sought to maintain the cohesion of agnates as holders and occupants
of land while their members tried to exploit the widest possible range of
matrilateral and affinal ties for land transactions. All great lineages in a
neighbourhood stood out against granting rights to people outside the local

community. The result was a contained movement of right holders and occupants within a neighbourhood, with considerable but incomplete maintenance of the territorial integrity of any great lineage. Not surprisingly, pressure of population on the land brought about increasing numbers of land cases. The claims of agnates and of neighbourhood kin and affines began to be hotly disputed.

Men owned livestock and passed it, if possible, to their sons but, as was the case with land, a wife's claims could not be ignored, especially her right to a milch cow.[27] Livestock never passed to someone in the same generation as a deceased owner, but to the closest agnates in the next generation. Beyond a certain point stock could be allowed to pass out of a great lineage, for agnatically remote potential heirs might be unwilling to assume those responsibilities for daughters and widows which inheritance of livestock entailed. Furthermore, many livestock transactions were, by comparison with land transactions, untrammelled by considerations of agnatic claims. As with land, so with livestock: the lineage functioned as a property-transmitting unit; but in the case of livestock there was nothing resembling the lineage-dominated territory. Perhaps cattle pedigrees provided some parallel in asserting the superiority of 'our' cows. The glory of cows, however, lay in their calves and these often went by means of transactions of various kinds to members of other lineages.

In practical affairs a great lineage did not divide into a continuous series of nesting segments although segments of some orders were identifiable. The legal descendants of any male member of the lineage could distinguish themselves by using the name of their nearest common agnatic forbear, just as members of the entire great lineage called themselves after their apical ancestor. The ancestor's name would in any case be preceded by the word *βeni*, meaning 'the people of [so and so]'. For example, all the members of the great lineage descended from Shako were *βeni Shako*; the agnates descended from Shako's sons Mwamodo and Mwaluala were *βeni Mwamodo* and *βeni Mwaluala*, those from Mwamodo's brother Keke, *βeni Keke*. The word *kichuku* was also used for a segment of any span and depth.

Often a great lineage encompassed two to five segments consisting of people who traced their descent through males to a common male ancestor placed genealogically in the fourth generation from living senior men. These segments sometimes were localized or partly localized in the sense that the homesteads of male members dominated a portion of the large lineage territory. Just how they were connected genealogically with the common ancestor (who might be several or only one generation further back) was a matter for argument. No major practical significance attached to such argument because within the large lineage, the four-generation 'small lineage', *kichuku kitini* (pl. *vichuku vitini*), had the greatest functional importance. In that unit members traced their descent through males to a common male ancestor who was the great-grandfather of the most junior generation. Sons of the founder, a set of brothers and half-brothers, were themselves each the founder of a three-generation line called 'little house', *kinyumba* (pl. *vinyumba*). In any one generation, men sharing a common agnatic grandfather (i.e. the junior generation of a little house) comprised an 'inheritance [group]'' *ifwa* (*kufwa* = to die). These men finally settled the estate in land and livestock inherited from their common grandfather through their fathers. The most junior generation of a small lineage was, then, made up of a number of genealogically adjacent inheritance groups. Figure 1 shows the inter-relations of the various named segments.

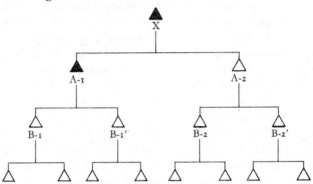

X and his agnatic descendants = a small lineage
A-1, A-2 = founders of adjacent little houses
B-1, B-1', B-2, B-2' = one inheritance group
grandsons of A-1
grandsons of A-2 = two adjacent inheritance groups

Figure 1.   The structure of the small lineage

The small lineage defined the limits of strongly enjoined mutual aid as well as accurate genealogical knowledge. Within the small lineage in which he was a member of the fourth generation, a man needed to know with whom he shared an agnatic grandfather; those were members of his inheritance group. Otherwise he only needed to know the other inheritance groups from whom (if they were to die without male issue) he and others of his inheritance group might inherit. Beyond this he had to know only whether someone was or was not a member of the same great lineage. Old men, of course, had a wider range of genealogical knowledge, for they knew the relationships within the small lineage of which they were the junior generation, while knowing also those within the little houses or the small lineages which they themselves had founded.

Marriage ties as well as property relationships were important within the great lineage and its parts. That was so in particular because *great lineages were not exogamous* either by rule or practice. Marriage prohibitions, defined by degree of consanguineous and affinal kinship, added to the functional importance of the small lineage. It was the only group of agnates whose members could not marry without special ritual precautions, and then only if they were no closer than second cousins. The choices of non-agnatic kin were perforce similarly governed since no first cousins of any sort could marry. Still, the arrangement was especially significant for members of a small lineage, since it set limits on the extent to which the property interests of males as potential co-heirs could be complicated by the exchange of women and bridewealth.

In practice, up to a third of the men of a great lineage married women of their own lineage. It was a rarity for a small lineage not to have entered into the network of marriage ties binding members of a large lineage. That network bore the mark of the rules forbidding two sibling groups to establish more than one marriage bond.[28] The resulting dispersion of marriages within a great lineage meant that most, if not all, members were ultimately related to each other affinally and/or matrilaterally as well as agnatically. Taita spoke of the practice of marrying kin as 'returning the seed' (*kuβunja mbegu*) and saw in it one of the bases for calling a lineage 'one people'. The oneness of a non-exogamous great lineage as a body of kin and affines provided the model for the assertion, mentioned earlier, that the endogamous neighbourhood was 'one people'. Yet the agnatic relationship was singled out as special: agnates were distinguished from all others as *βandee*, 'father's people'.

The political relevance of the great lineage, as of the neighbourhood, linked to the system of age-statuses. No descent groups held a higher status than others whatever parochialism might produce by way of rhetoric. But in the sense that men came to social maturity as founders of their own small houses, the great lineage provided the initial setting for elderhood. Every lineage included men who achieved that eminence, not only within their own agnatic groups, but in the local community at large. The elders of a great lineage together had a voice in ordering members' affairs, but not as representatives of segments in balance and opposition. A pool of elders functioned for the great lineage in something of the same way as the wider group of elders conducted neighbourhood affairs, though certain critical differences held. In their capacity as lineage seniors, elders carried the weight of authority deriving from fatherhood and agnatic seniority, shown in their mediation between agnatic juniors and patrilineal ancestors. They could seldom act as a closed group, however, even in disputes

concerning agnatically transmitted property rights. Taita law recognized
the right and duty of a person's maternal uncle to enter on his behalf into
any dispute in which the sister's child was involved. Observance of that
rule alone sufficed, in the endogamous neighbourhood, to involve elders in
the affairs of each other's lineages. In this and other ways, the lineage pool
of elders merged with that of the neighbourhood.

In the neighbourhood, particular lineages supplied the Defender and
the Rainmaker.[29] A Seer might come from any lineage and, as noted
above, might extend his or her influence beyond the neighbourhood.
Saru diviners, likely to draw clients from their own lineages, also attracted
members of other neighbourhood lineages. In religious ritual, the contours
of the great lineage were marked by the ancestral skull repository and by
the great shrine assemblage.

Taita exhumed the skulls of the dead, storing them in places called
Ngomenyi (*ngoma* = shrine; see p. 32 and pp. 83–4). Every large lineage
had a skull centre containing the skulls of those adult males and their
wives who left a legitimate son behind them. Usually a little grove of trees
surrounded the spot where the skulls were placed on the ground, preferably in the shelter of a little rocky ledge, the most recent ones fully
visible. No custodian tended *Ngomenyi*, nor did any priest make offerings
to the ancestors there on behalf of all members of the large lineage. The
place itself was not the scene of any religious performances other than
those in which the skulls were ritually established after exhumation or
replaced after disturbance (e.g. by a wandering goat). But the skull place
provided the focus for offerings to the ancestors when participants faced in
its direction for the performance of certain key actions.

Each great lineage also had an assemblage of shrines known collectively
as *Mlimu*, in the custody of an elder approved by the elders of the lineage
as their *primus inter pares*. Other elders, rich in worldly goods and ritual
prerogatives, assisted him. The lineage shrine assemblage, housed in the
homestead of its custodian, was resorted to by lineage members for ritual
attentions to the shrines. During the later part of the Colonial period,
lineage members attended on the shrines individually, most of the
collectively oriented rituals having ceased. In spite of that, Taita spoke of
visitors to the lineage shrines in such a way as to present them as a
congregation visiting what some referred to as 'the Taita church'. Such
lineage congregations in fact had overlapping memberships: a person's
matrilateral ties sometimes required attendance at a shrine centre other
than his lineage's own, just as they might require ritual attentions directed
to a non-agnatic ancestor. Once again, ritual action moved along the network of bilateral and affinal ties within a neighbourhood, bringing
together members of associated lineages.

Nonetheless, *Ngomenyi* and *Mlimu* truly marked out the great lineage. The skull repository belonged to the lineage as a group of *βandee*, 'father's people', not otherwise, enshrining those men who left agnatic descendants, and the mothers of their sons. As for *Mlimu*, it was known also as 'medicine of people and of wealth', guaranteeing the continuity of the lineage and the prosperity of its members over against others.

Villages were composed of homesteads occupied by households under male heads. Small villages (of two to ten or twelve homesteads) usually contained agnates who had built near one another along a little ridge or on adjacent hillocks and knolls. (In large, dense villages the space between such features was almost filled up with dwellings.) Such agnates might be to one another father and son, brothers, members of an inheritance group, or quite remote agnates. Even where close agnates lived together in a village or village section it was highly unlikely that they constituted its total membership or that they would remain together permanently. Not all of a man's sons built near him, while if some members of an inheritance group built together, the others were likely to congregate later in life, in the early years of their independence from their father or fathers.

Since land rights could not be gained in a neighbourhood other than one's own, a man could engage in transactions with his affines only if he married locally,[30] a matter of no small importance for the neighbourhood. The conjunction of male ownership rights with female use-rights was also important for villages. Women of a village normally held at least some of their current cultivations near one another. They had to respect each other's boundaries if the village were to remain at peace, and they were supposed to help with farm work when one of them was ill or had recently given birth. 'Agreement' among women was cited as one of the reasons for 'marrying close'. In practice, village women were very often kin to one another and to some of the male residents other than their own husbands. If men who lived near one another had wives from the same lineage, they knew the *chia*, way, of that lineage. Wives from neighbour lineages knew the customs of the country, *mizango*. Knowing each other's ways and customs was supposed to make for friendliness.

In spite of the fluidity of villages and their sections, it would be wrong to say that villagers had no sense of unity or that they were in no wise regarded as a group by outsiders. The familiar phrase, *βandu βamweri*, one people, was heard of villagers as of agnates and neighbours. There was no office of village headman, but fellow villagers were expected to keep the peace and to settle village matters under the direction of the senior or most dominating man or men. Kinship, generation, wealth in livestock, land rights and personal ability were all factors that influenced the exercise of authority. Where two or more elders resided together affairs were settled, in theory, by the consultations of householders, and the elders formed a peer group dominating others. When such elders were really approximate equals in wealth, age and their concomitants, the separateness of their own sections of the village was sometimes stressed by each, even though they continued to say that theirs was *muzi gumweri*, one village. In other cases, one elder dominated.

Villages as such were not brought into opposition. Enmity might persist as a result of a faction-forming dispute that had split one village into two. But any affair of importance was sure to draw in people who were members of several villages, given the fact that co-residence was only one basis among many for the alignment of parties to a dispute. In everyday life villagers often helped one another. Especially important was the informal exchange of foodstuffs among women. Both men and women lent each other tools and utensils. Men and boys were responsible for keeping the paths clear. Though building a new house or livestock corral brought in many non-villagers, fellow villagers had a special obligation to attend and help. Whereas a kinsman living far away could be excused for pleading pressing business elsewhere, non-attendance by a fellow villager was an open insult.

In religious affairs the village was not marked by any offices or by possession of shrines or other medicines. (Members were often concelebrants of religious rituals, but by virtue of other connections.) Medicines placed by the Defender at crossroads between villages protected all the innocent by endangering all the wicked, and individual homesteads also had their protective medicines. Working against thieves and sorcerers, protective medicines shielded a householder from dangers within the village itself. Undoubtedly fear of sorcery should be entered in the list of reasons why village composition varied and changed. In a more positive way, the festivals, *ndima*, which Taita did not consider religious, brought village people together. Girls' initiation rites and weddings were especially important, with women as prominent participants.

Taita dwellings seemed to rise from the earth they stood on, with mudded walls over post and wattle frames. Roofs were thatched or, less commonly, made of corrugated iron. The round house, of older style, displayed a variety of interior designs. Some others were square and many rectangular ones with several rooms were patterned on one old missionary house in central Dabida. Outbuildings sometimes included a small building housing livestock (and adolescents) and granaries. However, many homesteads consisted of but one round house, perhaps with interior divisions, having above the fireplace a storage rack that took the place of a granary. A dwelling, *nyumba*, and its outbuildings were surrounded by a smooth, swept courtyard, the *βaza*. In many cases the latter was marked off by a ring of small boulders, or partly surrounded by a hedge, the opening in which was blocked by a gate that could be firmly secured at night. Many other homesteads simply stood in the midst of a clearing. In the areas of dispersed settlement, there was usually a kitchen garden to one side, as well as a bit of waste land where refuse was thrown.

Since relevant features of the composition and cycle of domestic groups are treated elsewhere (see pp. 93–5), I note briefly only a few major points. Members of a family, at one stage occupying a single household and homestead, were concerned with the personal shrines owned by male householders and their wives (see pp. 62–3, 66). The domestic family and their circle of close kin participated, over and over again, in offerings to ancestral shades. Family members, whether in one household or many, were also the people who performed the religious rites in which the 'hearts' of living persons were purged of anger and placated. In these ways, family and close kin were the focus of ritual in which action was linked to the concept of individual human persons as possessed of and affected by the mystical anger central to Taita religion.

The social topography of Taita had, then, the following features: the distinction of Taita from all others as 'People of the Hills'; the internal unity-in-diversity manifested in the Numbers; local communities or neighbourhoods, made up of two or three inter-marrying great patri-lineages and functioning as land use and political units; non-exogamous lineages that were territorial, land use and political units not exhibiting continuously nesting segmentation; an age-status system that provided the apparatus for the political functions of both neighbourhoods and lineages; villages whose variable constitution and fluidity reflected the land use and political systems; homesteads occupied by domestic families; and individual persons whose life careers were mapped to a large extent by the above social groupings and differentiae.

In marking the contours of the social topography, ritual performances as such ignored the unity of the Taita people as a whole. However, the Numbers, functioning largely in divination and haruspication, gave form to the recognition of Taita unity explicitly emerging from diversity of origins. Neighbourhoods were marked by the religious offices of Defender and Rainmaker, some of whose cooperation proceeded under the direction of a Seer. Lineages appeared in the religious system as those groups possessing ancestral skull repositories, *Ngomenyi*, and shrine centres, *Mlimu*, the latter in the custody of a senior lineage elder. Villages were the focus of non-religious festivals. Homesteads were religiously important as the loci of domestic families who, with their close kin, were concerned with private shrines, with the placation of ancestral shades, and with rituals focussed on the angry 'hearts' of living persons.

Throughout this chapter, 'religion' and terms related to it have been used without definition. Now, the major connections between religion and the social order having been outlined, the discussion turns to another question: what kind of an entity was 'Taita religion'?

2

THE DOMAIN OF TAITA RELIGION

The term 'Taita religion' is used here for what the Taita themselves referred to as *ßutasi*, a bounded domain within their total way of life. To describe and analyse *ßutasi* then is to do more than to explicate an anthropologist's construct.[1] Taita spoke of their traditional religion also as *malago ga ķutasa*, the words or affairs of *ķutasa*, the latter being the verbal form used to signify the basic religious act. In this manner, religious matters or affairs could be treated as paralleling other bodies of knowledge and action such as farming (*malago ga ķulima*) and trade or business (*malago ga biashara, malago ga pesa*). Looking outwards to the world of non-Taita, they sometimes used Swahili and English terms to facilitate comparison of their ways with those of foreigners. As they sometimes called lineage shrine centres the 'Taita church', using the Swahili word *ķanisa*, so they used the word *dini*[2] to compare Taita religion with others. Christianity as understood from missionary teachings and from observation of Europeans, was *dini ya Kristo*; Islam was *dini ya Islamu*; Judaism, understood as the religion of the Old Testament was *dini ya ßayehudi*. Seen as comparable to and coordinate with those religions, Taita religion was *dini ya Kutasa* or *ßutasi*. Of Africans, some were believed to follow a body of practices like the Taita one in having the act of *ķutasa* at its centre. On account of this the Pare were said by some Taita to 'have' *ßutasi* or to be practitioners suitably called *ßatasi* (sing. *Mtasi*). The features reckoned to be part of Taita practice but not followed by other Africans could be specified as part of *ßutasi gwa Kidaßida*, that is *ßutasi* according to the Taita way.

Internally to *Kidaßida*, Taita religion was marked off by the centrality to it of the act of *ķutasa* and also by its differentiation from other areas of ritual. *Kutasa* was usually performed in a squatting position with the arms held loosely across the knees, one hand holding a container of sugar cane beer, unfermented cane juice or water.[3] Spraying out mouthfuls of liquid, the performer uttered phrases, exhorting or supplicating a mystical agent or agents and calling down blessings on one or more living humans and on what pertained to their welfare. At some point the utterances explicitly or implicitly rejected the angry feelings of the performer himself.

As an act believed efficacious, ḳutasa was asserted to have an inner aspect of which spraying-and-speaking was the outward and audible form. The state of the performer's 'heart' (ngolo) was intrinsic to the performance, since only from a heart 'clean' and 'cool', freed from anger and resentment, could the necessary sincere utterances issue. Kutasa in itself provided the means both to effect the final casting out of anger and resentment from the performer's heart and to turn away the anger of the agent(s) addressed. Some elaborate occasions of βutasi included ḳizongona, animal offering, and ḳuvoya, placatory gift. Of those, Taita would give summary descriptions taking the form, 'We kill a goat and ḳutasa with beer', or 'We kill a chicken and ḳutasa with beer'. Many traditional religious performances consisted of ḳutasa alone.

Within ritual, religion was set apart from other domains. Its clearest opposite was sorcery, βusaβi, the use of spells and medicines intentionally to harm others. Acts of explicit anti-sorcery formed the appendages of many religious performances and, in a sense, all acts of ḳutasa had an anti-sorcery dimension. Religion was also distinguished from a body of juridical rites by a way of speaking similar to that allowing real and classificatory siblings to be set apart. Speakers would distinguish between 'true religion', or 'primary religion', βutasi tiḳi, and those rites of which it was said that they were 'a sort of religion but not primary religion', ni sa βutasi, ela si βutasi tiḳi.[4] Despite such explicit distinctions, some of the concepts and practices of βutasi as a whole overlapped those of other areas of ritual. At a later point it will be profitable to explore some of the overlapping in order to throw light on the nature of βutasi itself.[5]

Traditional Taita religion was not one of worship and praise regularly performed. It was a body of responses to the intervention in everyday life of agents conceptualized as person-like in varying degrees. These agents are here called 'mystical' since although their reality was manifested in common events, their mode of operation and, above all, the occasions of their intervention were not knowable until after the fact. They were part of the 'occult', not of the 'patent' aspect of the world; they were not 'supernatural' but part of the fabric of the universe.[6] Some rites, notably those of rainmaking and crop-prospering, though seasonal, occurred at the time and in the manner directed by a Seer's visions. Otherwise, most religious occasions followed on divination at the time of misfortune or bad omens. Divination identified the mystical agent whose intervention was responsible for misfortune or its threat. Then the diviner or diviners, alone or in consultation with other elders, prescribed the ritual remedy. Occasionally, in moments of extremity, the mystical source of danger was sought introspectively by 'searching the heart'. (Hereafter the word divination is at times used for both Saru divination and βula haruspication).

Before the influence of Christian missionaries, all Taita practised
βutasi as part of Kidaβida, the Taita way of life. Even during the late
Colonial period only a core of Christian converts and children of converts
totally refused involvement. We never heard anyone speak disparagingly
or ashamedly of the traditional religion outside the walls of the churches.[7]
One reason was that βutasi was intimately connected with the social system
in which Christians as well as βatasi continued to live and act. In the
main, the forms and processes of traditional social action held during the
pre-Independence years. Taita Christians, like their βatasi fellows, lived
and acted as members of neighbourhoods, lineages, villages and households, bound to others in their community by a network of kinship,
political and economic ties. In the absence of total social segregation of
Christians, they had to remain within the orbit of βutasi as it interpene-
trated those other fields of social life.[8]

A second and related reason for the relatively positive view taken by
Christians was the continued prestige of the elders who supervised and
performed the rites of βutasi. Elders had, in Taita idiomatic speech, real
knowledge of religious and other ritual affairs, not mere acquaintance.[9]
Furthermore, theirs was the knowledge without which one could not
claim to be truly versed in Kidaβida. The political role of elders, sanc-
tioned by possession of personal shrines, put them in a strong position
vis-a-vis Christians. The latter, largely because of their literacy and schooling, became Government chiefs more easily than βatasi during the pre-
Independence years, appearing to βatasi as useful intermediaries with the
Government. Internally, Christian chiefs often found their efforts balked
by influential elders to whom they were 'mere children'. (Missionaries
were needlessly mystified by the frequency with which their prize trainees,
some of whom were elected as Government chiefs, became backsliders by
establishing polygynous marriages. To do so was one of the ways in
which a non-elder of wealth and literacy could try to approximate the
standing of a traditional elder.)

A third reason for the continued pervasiveness of βutasi in the pre-
Independence years was its embodiment of a view of reality that Christian
teachings were considered not to contradict wholly. That view held that
the working of the universe included mechanism but was not limited to it.
Mystical agents, including those lying within human persons, were subject
to anger and that anger could be manifested in the sickness and death of
human adults, their children, and their livestock, or in plague and drought
affecting humans in the mass. The ideas of causation entailed do not seem
very different from those of many 'religious' persons in Western societies
willing to give a mechanistic explanation of events while holding to a
metaphysics in which the intentions of Deity ultimately determine which

of two or more potential courses natural processes will actually follow. A Taita example is that of the man who assured the British hospital doctor that he did indeed understand the explanation for his wife's difficulty in labour: the woman's pelvis was small and the baby's head was too large for her. The question that still plagued the Taita, he insisted, was 'Who caused this baby's head to be too big for the mother?'.

Taita expected people to age and die, to be subject to injury and disease. But in their view a person did not develop a serious illness or die in a particular way, at a particular time, from mechanistic causes alone, nor did he survive only by medical treatment. Death and sickness beyond passing indisposition were not merely changes in the state of the body; they were moral events as well. Taita action was consistent with this view. In times of illness they would use whatever secular medical means were deemed appropriate. They would also divine in order to identify the mystical agent responsible for the illness as it occurred within a particular life history, a moral event within a moral career. Where Taita traditional beliefs differed most from missionary teachings was in attributing quasi-personal sentience and agency to certain materials and objects as well as to non-material entities.[10]

Prescription of religious action followed divination, that action always centring on the performance of *ƙutasa*. In *ƙutasa* the casting out of anger from performers' hearts was signified and effected; also in *ƙutasa*, the anger of other mystical agents was turned away and converted into beneficence. Taita religion was therefore the means of restoring *sere*: peace, health and general well-being. In realizing its primary aims, getting rid of anger, *βutasi* used special versions of the ordinary Taita means of maintaining and re-establishing amicable relations between those in a long-term relationship: the giving of gifts, especially gifts of food, and commensalism.

Taita religion though not co-extensive with Taita world-view, was a domain within which the latter emerged in ritual action. In the world as understood and lived in by Taita, the human self, the community and the physical environment were inter-connected parts of a universe both 'natural' and permeated by values and feelings. In many respects, the human self functioned as a model for the understanding of society and the non-social environment. But the human person was seen in the light of his social development and relationships and as having necessary bonds with the non-human world. Qualities recognized in humans were read into the world at large; but qualities of the world were also read into human persons. It is important to bear this in mind as I move on to discuss the mystical agents whose anger required religious rituals.

The conceptualization of mystical agents covers the range of their operation as well as the qualifications for approaching them. Including these in the discussion fills out the picture given in Chapter 1 of the relation between mystical agents and the social order; it looks forward to discussions of particular religious rituals and their components, and facilitates comparison with non-religious ritual.

The universe, according to Taita, was created by *Mlungu*, who was therefore also known as the Creator, *Mbonyi*. Active in the world as its maintainer, *Mlungu* was manifested particularly in life-giving rains and in death-dealing droughts and plagues. Having power of life and death over living creatures, *Mlungu* was also appropriately called *Mdimi*, the Powerful-one (*kudima* = to be able, to have power; *idima* = liver, will; *yadimikaga* = it is possible, it can be done). Connected with rain, *Mlungu* was also associated with the topmost peaks where the first rain falls, but not in the sense of dwelling there. Nor did *Mlungu* dwell in the sky despite an association with the above (*aigu*) from whence rain falls. *Mlungu*, indeed, had no dwelling place and could not be seen, nor was the Powerful-one knowable or approachable by individual human beings. Seasonal rituals of crop-prospering and rainmaking were supposed to be addressed to *Mlungu*, with the offering of a sheep used also in the medication, forming part of the rites. Those rites occurred at the direction of the neighbourhood Seer, under the direction of the neighbourhood Rainmaker, and needed neighbourhood-wide participation for their efficacy. As members of a neighbourhood, people could suffer from drought and plague sent when *Mlungu* was angered by the moral rottenness of a community that failed to root out its sorcerers.

A degree of personalization may be seen in the attribution to *Mlungu* of a propensity to respond angrily to evil in a community and also willingly to accept offerings. A quite different aspect of *Mlungu* appeared in statements treating that agent as the ultimate ground or cause of all processes, irrespective of moral significance. For instance, one Taita woman said when discussing sorcery, that 'if you are made ill by *Mlungu*, all you need is a little [non-ritual] medicine; but if a sorcerer is at work, then you need a very great [ritual] doctor'. In such statements, Taita seemed to conceptualize *Mlungu* as the hidden but assumed cause of the mechanistic order in which minor illnesses were to be expected. This being so, *Mlungu* would not enter into diviners' diagnoses in the search for the mystical agent responsible for an individual's misfortune. But causation was not limited to mechanism in the Taita world, made by *Mlungu* as Creator and maintained by *Mlungu* as the Powerful-one. Sorcery was both sin and crime. A sorcerer violating fundamental morality transgressed against human decency. A neighbourhood full of undetected sorcerers was on the verge of ceasing to be a viable moral community. Its condition would arouse the anger of *Mlungu* in the latter's person-like aspect. Also in the person-like aspect, *Mlungu* was supposed to 'hear' the wishings for rain and well-being that were central to rainmaking and crop-prospering rites.

That there was a personal aspect to *Mlungu* receives some additional support from linguistic facts. The form of the word *Mlungu* could place it either in the class of nouns for (mostly human) persons or in the class including non-personal but animate beings. The plural form *βalungu*, appropriate to the class of personal nouns, did not occur; but the plural form *milungu*, appropriate to the non-personal animate class, was in use. However, *milungu* were not many *Mlungu* and did not 'add up to' *Mlungu*; they were mystical agents, some of which were based in *human* personhood. There was *no* plural form of *Mlungu*, as Creator and Powerful-one. The person-like aspect of the latter was attested rather in the use of the pronominal forms appropriate to persons. Taita said, '*Mlungu wabonya huβu* [*Mlungu* does thus]', paralleling such sentences as, '*Uja mundu wabonya huβu* [That man does thus].' Had the word *Mlungu* belonged to the non-personal but animate class the pronominal agreement would have yielded '*gwabonya huβu* [it animate] does thus'.[11]

Running somewhat counter to the personalizing tendency was the form of utterances central to those religious rites concerned with *Mlungu*. In those utterances, speakers wished for the good things of life created and controlled by *Mlungu*, but they never addressed *Mlungu* as 'you' and they never urged or exhorted *Mlungu* to accept offerings and extend beneficence to them. This feature of religious action seems, indeed, to make a bridge between the personal aspect of *Mlungu* and the ultimate cause aspect. It supports the view taken here that, for Taita, *Mlungu* was neither entirely personal nor entirely non-personal, but *supra-personal* Creator.

Mlungu's ultimate unknowability might appear to be linked to the notion of non-personal ultimate cause. Yet it is not incompatible with personhood as seen in human beings who, in Taita thought, were ultimately inscrutable. The inscrutability of *Mlungu* may in turn have contributed to the usage by which Taita said of any unusual object, especially one unfamiliar to them, '*Ni mlungu* [It is *mlungu*]'. No evidence indicated that Taita employed a concept of an impersonal, pervasive force inhabiting strange-seeming objects or creatures. A camera, a nylon stocking, an unusual rock or a hitherto unobserved living creature could call forth the remark, '*ni mlungu*'. But it could not be said of such things that they were *Mbonyi* or *Mdimi*. Though having the word *mlungu* applied to them, they were things or non-personal creatures. They played no part in *βutasi*. Especially if they were items of European manufacture, they might one day turn up among the 'wonders' shown on the last night of girls'

initiation, a non-religious festival. It was never suggested that strange
and unusual things were special manifestations of *Mlungu*.[12]

The plural *milungu*, though belonging to the noun class for non-
personal animate creatures, referred both to mystical agents inherent in
the human person and to those inherent in animals. An incorporeal but
sentient aspect of any living creature was *mlungu*. The *milungu* of men,
unlike those of animals, continued their existence after death, for a
human being could become an *mrumu*, one of the *βarumu* or shades of
dead ancestors.[13] Living persons, ancestral shades, and living animals
shared this characteristic: that they had the capacity to affect the health
and well-being of living persons by means of their anger. In this they
resembled *Mlungu*.

Use of the form *milungu* rather than *βalungu*, the form appropriate
to the personal noun class, might well have served two purposes. *Milungu*
allows for attending to what animals and humans share, an incorporeal
but sentient component functioning as a mystical agent in the world.
At the same time it kept animals out of the class appropriate to human
beings, since their mystical component did not continue after death; they
had no survival personalities. The form *milungu* also created distance
between the mystical agents inherent in animals and men on the one side,
and *Mlungu* on the other. *Milungu* were not parts or duplicates of
Mlungu, who did not encompass any or all of them. *Milungu* were
personal, not supra-personal mystical entities.[14]

Much concerning the Taita conceptualization of *milungu* is better left
to a later discussion of the human person and his moral career (see
Chapter 3). Two aspects are relevant here. One is the general nature of
the occasions for arousal of the anger of mystical agents inherent in
humans or animals. The second is the inter-connections between the anger
of those mystical agents and the anger of *Mlungu* as speculated upon by
some Taita. As to the first, the dangerous mystical anger of humans and
animals was supposed to be aroused by ignoring or transgressing their
rights, or simply by callous, inconsiderate behaviour. More particularly,
the rights of persons as members of families and narrow circles of kin,
and the rights of domesticated animals as quasi-members, could not be
transgressed without mystically endangering the wrong-doer. When such
transgressions occurred, the offended one's heart, the locus of the sentiments, became 'hot', or he was 'injured in the heart' (*waβaβwa
ngolonyi*), that is, the wronged person or beast became angry and resentful. There followed, as divination would later reveal, suffering of the
transgressor. The second point touches on the speculations engaged in by
some Taita concerning the mechanism by which the anger of hearts could
do such damage. It was held by some that 'the anger of hearts goes to

Mlungu and it is *Mlungu* who sends misfortune', a view that brought *Mlungu* into involvement with the affairs of everyday life. Other Taita refused to take those speculations seriously, saying only that such things were beyond knowing. The first point of view was defended partly on the grounds that occasionally divination indicated that someone's behaviour had been so generally offensive that *all milungu* were angry and had removed from him their beneficent aspect. In that case the prescribed ritual required the placation of all *milungu* and, it was said, of Creator as well. The various Taita comments indicate that the precise relationship between *Mlungu* and *milungu* was not a subject for orthodox doctrinal pronouncements. As in other areas of *βutasi*, differing views were tolerated while many people considered speculation futile.

Some of the above remarks require amplification. Ancestral shades, like living humans, became angry at the transgression of their rights which included the enforcement of proper kinship behaviour among their descendants. Angry *βarumu* were spoken of and also addressed as the possessors of hearts that could become hot, yet an ancestor's heart could have no specifiable connection with the physical organ. A dead person who was legitimately the parent of a son usually passed two or three years without ritual tendance apart from the funeral and post-funeral observances. Then, by a message in the form of misfortune visited on the survivor(s), he announced that he wished to have his skull disinterred and installed in the lineage skull centre, *Ngomenyi*. The skull so installed was not again approached unless it became displaced from within the repository. Although offering ought to be performed 'in the direction of' *Ngomenyi*, ancestral shades did not inhabit the skulls. The latter provided material *loci* for the *βarumu*. Skulls did not house ancestral shades, they enshrined them.[15] Skulls were *ngoma*, shrines, belonging to a set of things called shrines and thereby being associated with mystical agents of non-human provenance.

Ngoma, shrines, included: the Great *Figi*, the neighbourhood assemblage of Defender medicine; the lineage shrine assemblages; the individually owned major shrines; and minor personal shrines. If anything enshrined (without containing) *Mlungu*, it was the mountain peaks where the first rains fall and from where some of the rain medicines must be plucked. Tabooed groves in every neighbourhood also constituted places associated with rain. Some groves were used for the performance of the main portion of rainmaking rites in which offering and supplication were implicitly addressed to *Mlungu*. The medicines prepared by the neighbourhood Rainmaker for use in those rites did not constitute an *ngoma*. Nevertheless, rain medicine qualified as a Great Medicine.

Entailed in the previous statement is the fact that the category of *ngoma*, shrines, overlapped with that of medicines, of which some were Great Medicines, *ßuganga ßubaha*. Among *ngoma*, the skulls of ancestors were not medicines; and among the Great Medicines, that of rain was not a shrine. Other entities that were both shrines and medicines were treated as likely to become angry if they did not receive proper tendance, including offering, if their taboos were broken, or if they had not yet been physically created.

The Defender medicine (Great *Figi*) and the medicine of rainmaking were community medicines whose beneficent effects depended on the co-operation of the two ritual officials controlling them. Together, these two Great Medicines protected the local community from without and brought positive benefits within. Defender medicines were 'hot', matching the heat of the plains wilderness, while the ingredients of rain medicine were 'cool' like the damp coolness of the highest peaks. In the same scheme of complementarity, *Figi* were extremely fierce while *Mlungu*, with whom rain medicine was associated, was seen as slow to anger. A *Figi* benefited a local community by threatening with misfortune all external enemies. But a *Figi* also turned its anger on Taita transgressing its taboos, which included fighting among themselves in its vicinity. *Figi* also disliked the presence of a menstruating woman because her blood was like the blood of wounds inflicted in fighting. When a rampaging *Figi*, angry because Taita had transgressed its taboos, threatened not only the culprits with illness but the entire community with overwhelming drought, the Rainmaker had to join with the Defender to 'cool the plains'. The Defender had no equivalent role to play in the seasonal rainmaking and crop-prospering rites bringing life-giving rains and the fertility of crops, domestic animals and human beings to the community.

Each lineage shrine centre contained an assemblage of objects, each with its own name, together described as 'Great Medicines of people and of livestock' (*ßuganga ßubaha gwa ßandu na mifugo*). The total assemblage was *Mlimu*; the overseer of its affairs was *mundu wa Mlimu*, the man of *Mlimu*. Housing the shrine assemblage and supervising the presentation of sacrifices and offerings of beer were his tasks, but his fellow elders participated in ritual performances. The group of persons benefiting from the lineage shrines was narrower than the local community having a single Rainmaker and one Defender, but as noted previously, extended beyond the confines of the lineage itself. Both members of the lineage and the offspring of female members could be affected by the anger of lineage shrine assemblages, anger aroused by not having received ritual attentions from someone falling under its influence. Lineage shrine assemblages seem not to have been concerned, in the Taita view, with the rights and wrongs that were the concern of Creator,

the ancestral shades, the hearts of living persons, and the Defender
medicine. They claimed only ritual attention, giving the good things of
life without regard to moral worth. They were sometimes called medicine
of wealth (*ßuganga gwa mali*) and wealth, to Taita, was productive of
moral ambiguities.

At least some lineage shrine centres were supposed to contain an
especially powerful complex of components known as *Chago*, the name
given also to its principal component, a human arm bone. *Chago* was a
matter of great secrecy and Taita discussed it with great reluctance and
visible signs of discomfort.[16] On the surface, use of a human arm bone
in a shrine might seem of no more doubtful morality than the exhumation and installation of ancestral skulls. There were grounds for
discomfort, however, in the fact that a human arm bone, decorated with
beads, was considered one of the most powerful instruments of sorcery,
a point discussed at greater length elsewhere (see below, pp. 39, 164).
Although in at least one instance the social identity of the arm bone in
Chago was known (it was supposed to come from the lineage founder's
daughter), the bone did not enshrine an ancestor; it was a medicine,
albeit a component of a shrine used to benefit the lineage. However
morally ambiguous the use of the arm bone might have seemed, the fact
remains that the whole of a lineage shrine assemblage, including *Chago*,
was treated as a legitimate source of lineage well-being. The anger of
Mlimu or one of its component shrines could appear in divination as
responsible for an individual's misfortunes; the shrines were there to
receive tendance and to bring benefits in return.

Lineage shrine centres contained three shrines that were duplicated and
owned by individual men. These were, in order of acquisition as well as
power and prestige, Bag (*Mfuko*), Stool (*Kifumbi*), and Bell (*Mmanga*).
The Bag, Stool and Bell in the lineage centres received tendance from
and on behalf of men who had not yet risen in the age-status system.
A man advancing toward elderhood expected that one day a diviner's
diagnosis would name Bag as wishing to 'have a fire kindled for it'.
That meant that to effect a cure of whatever misfortune had sent the
man to a diviner, a Bag must be made. It must be consecrated and put
into possession of the man who would then count as one of his lineage's
elders, albeit not one of the highest ranking.[17] After that, the Bag's anger
at insufficient tendance or at transgression of its taboos entered the roster
of possible diagnoses whenever its owner visited a diviner. Bag consisted
of a soft woven basket or sack filled with small gourds containing for the
most part charred herbal materials mixed with sheep fat. (One Bag we
saw included a container of chalk said to be a bit of the snows of
Kilimanjaro.) Illness among the human dependents or livestock of a

Bag owner could be diagnosed as requiring tendance of the shrine. But diviners also sometimes told the parents of a sick infant or small child to have it treated by a man of Bag (*mundu wa Mfuko*) with medicines from his Bag. The contents of individual gourds were not a shrine, but medicine. As a permanent, albeit constantly renewed *assemblage* of medicines, Bag itself was a shrine, *ngoma*. As a shrine, Bag concerned its owner as head of a thriving household, a man of some means with human and animal dependents. Its proper tendance helped to assure continuing prosperity, for it was one of the shrines 'of people and of wealth'. As an assemblage of medicines, each with a virtue of its own, a Bag served an indeterminate number of people in the local community. These were heads of younger households with infants and small children in need of ritual medication. Bag's curing rites were centred on the household and, in particular, on the relationship between a small child and its mother (see Chapter 3, pp. 52–6).

After some years as a holder of a Bag shrine, a man whose affairs continued to prosper learned from a diviner that *Kifumbi*, Stool, demanded to have a fire kindled for it. With a group of neighbourhood elders assembled, a small, three-legged wooden stool was carved with a hole drilled in the centre to take the medicines placed there at its consecration. Following the latter, Stool could demand tendance by sending illness or other misfortune to its owner by way of his own illness or injury or that of his human or animal dependents. Acquisition of Bell, *Mmanga*, again at a diviner's behest, marked a man's acceptance by the most prestigious elders of his community as one of themselves. Bell, made of iron, resembled bells tied round the necks of cattle. It was associated with prosperous herding and with that wide range of social relationships both requiring wealth in livestock and serving to increase it. As with the other major personal shrines, the requirements of tendance were made known by divinatory diagnosis of misfortune.

At the opposite end of the scale of power and prestige, minor personal shrines belonged to members of young households. Rather than being shrines of people and wealth, they affected the prosperity of agricultural enterprises. The most important of them was *Lufu*, Knife. By the time a man or woman acquired Knife during the early years of marriage, he or she should have been given *Saru* divining seeds as a shrine putting the owner in touch with the diviner's own *Saru* (see Chapter 3, pp. 51–2). Acquisition of the major shrines accompanied not advancing age by itself, but the realization of hopes for a thriving household in a later phase of the developmental cycle. Prosperity was never its own guarantee. Though acquisition of a shrine marked achievement, translating success into ritual possessions and knowledge, misfortune remained a possibility, indeed an expected one. The anger of shrines was identified as causing misfortune, while their tendance provided one of the ritual means of returning humans and animals to health and prosperity. When a shrine owner died, his shrines were 'thrown down', deconsecrated by placing them on the ground. Their material components might or might not later be acquired by a son of the deceased. However that might work out, every man had to advance through the sequence of shrine acquisitions on his own. Shrine-holding, bound as it was to the age-status system related to household development, formed part of a series of rites of passage. The rest of the series was composed of performances which the Taita did not reckon to be religious at all: the festivals (*ndima*) of infant cliterodectomy, circumcision, initiation and marriage.

Taita said that 'all Bags are one; all Stools are one; all Bells are one'. The phrasing announced that all shrines of one variety were alike in constitution, none was reckoned to be more powerful than any other of the same variety, and none of the men owning a shrine of a given variety knew more about that medicine than his fellows. Whether Taita also implied that a single non-corporeal agent stood in relation to diverse material enshrinings I cannot guarantee in the absence of evidence. What is certain is that the existence of a sentient, volitional, person-like agent did not come into being at the physical construction of a shrine. Addresses to a new shrine spoke of it as having announced its desire for consecration by sending misfortune to a particular man. So far as I am aware, Taita did not attempt to spell out the nature of the relationship between a 'pre-existent' shrine entity and the material creation and consecration of the shrine. The proneness to anger of shrines and the consequent need to placate them, together with their responsiveness to human speech and action, made shrines similar to Creator. However, in religious utterances Taita spoke to a shrine more directly in urgent supplications and addressed it as 'you'. In this respect a shrine was more like ancestral shades and the hearts of living humans, a point to which I return further on.

To facilitate further comparison of mystical agents, I move on to discussion of 'medicines' by way of a summary roster of the entities that were the concern of religious ritual:

    I. Creator (*Mlungu*)
   II. *milungu*
       A. the hearts of living humans and domestic animals
       B. ancestral shades
  III. shrines
       A. shrines that were not medicines
          1. ancestral skulls
          2. *Saru* divining seeds

B. medicine shrines
    1. Great Medicine shrines
       a. of defense (*Figi*)
       b. of people and livestock
          i. lineage shrine assemblages (*Mlimu*)
          ii. personal shrines: Bag, Stool, Bell
    2. minor medicine shrine: Knife
IV. Great (non-shrine) Medicine (rain medicine)

In *βutasi* Taita attempted to rid themselves of misfortune in its moral dimension by getting rid of the anger of mystical agents. Those agents, their action diagnosed by diviners, intervened in the everyday affairs of human beings. Apart from Creator and the mystical agents based in humans and domestic animals, a variety of artefacts associated with mystical action entered religious action. As can be seen from the above roster, a complex relationship held between 'shrines' and 'medicines' necessitating discussion of the latter category.

The religious use of medicines fell within a wider domain of ritual, and, furthermore, the term 'medicine' (*βuganga*) cut across ritual and non-ritual action. 'Medicine' was far from being an undifferentiated category for Taita.[18] On the contrary a fundamental distinction separated the medicines of ritual from the non-ritual medicines I call 'curings', many of which were known to every Taita. Most curings consisted of vegetable materials gathered and prepared as needed from roots, bark, stems, leaves, seeds and seed pods, etc. The category included wild spinach, also a food (*vindo*), considered useful for the prevention of constipation. Infusions induced vomiting or purging or lowered the temperature of a fevered patient. Poultices relieved the pain of sore and injured limbs. Some people especially knowledgeable about curings bore the title of doctor or physician (*mganga*, pl. *βaganga*), the same title being used for European medical doctors. Specialist physicians applied massage, set and manipulated bones, pulled teeth and seared with hot irons to cure persistent headaches. Traditional physicians relied for their success on the properties of the curings they used, the character of the bodies they treated and the courses they believed illnesses to follow. Most of their medicines did not physically resemble the many ritual medicines that consisted of charred, powdered materials mixed with fat. More critical from the Taita point of view and for this discussion, the use of curings involved no use of speech other than the description of symptoms by the patient and the issuing of advice by the physician.

In all other uses of medicines, speech was a necessary part of the performance, for the medicine's efficacy depended on it. That was as true of *βutasi* as of juridical rites and of non-religious rituals apart from festivals.

Juridical rites ('religion but not primary religion') included the use of oaths and ordeals to discover and punish sorcerers, thieves and perjurers; the swearing of blood pacts; the pronouncement of conditional curses to protect crops and other property; the performance of conditional curses against any sorcerers who might be affecting the outcome of a religious ritual; the cancellation of oaths and curses; and the unconditional cursing of public enemies by the Executioners' Society. Although *kutasa* was done in conjunction with some juridical rites, its performance was not the main point. And though animals might be killed, they were not offered to a mystical agent. Instead, presiding elders used the intestines for divination or the blood for making up the medicine (see Chapter 6).[19]

Three medicines were at the centre of juridical ritual: *mwalola*, *mugule*, and *mtero*. The name of the first, an herbal potion, is related to the verb *kulola*, to look for or search out. In former times, reportedly through early Colonial days, mass drinking of *mwalola* took place in neighbourhoods thought to be objects of Creator's wrath for their failure to root out sorcerers. Its drinking caused sorcerers to confess their evil deeds. Confessed sorcerers could be dealt with in various ways, including requiring them to drink *mugule*, the medicine that killed them if they were indeed guilty of what they confessed. *Mtero* forged bonds of blood pact partnership between formerly quarrelling individuals or groups or between men who wanted to extend the range of their social relationships; *mtero* killed those who broke its regulations.

In rituals using *mwalola*, *mugule*, and *mtero*, performers submitted themselves in action and speech to the power of the medicines to 'seize' wrong-doers. As he prepared to drink *mwalola*, the accused person swore that, if he were really guilty, the medicine should search him out. One undergoing ordeal by *mugule* swore, 'If I am indeed a sorcerer (or thief or perjurer), may I die before the next crops ripen'. *Mtero* required each pact partner to say, 'If I do not do [thus-and-so] may this *mtero* kill me as well as my entire small lineage'. Conditional curses linked juridical rituals using medicines to the other rites included in the category. By means of conditional curses, men protected property against unknown thieves. Similarly, routine anti-sorcery (added to occasions of *βutasi*) used such conditional curses as, 'If there is any sorcerer ensorcelling here, may he die'. Removal of curse-bans and cancellation of oaths belonged to juridical ritual as a matter of properly reversing what had been properly done and later regretted or no longer considered necessary.

Mugule, the ordeal medicine for punishing sorcerers, thieves and perjurers, was under the supervision of elders who kept supplies of the basic ingredients together with certain other paraphernalia required for the ritual. Stocks of *mwalola* also had their keepers, but the medicine of blood pact partnership (*mtero*) was made up on the spot by the presiding elder. It was unclear to me whether there had ever been a time when every neighbourhood had kept its own supply of the ordeal medicines as some Taita thought proper. Certainly at the time of our field study that was not the case. Whatever the distribution of ordeal medicines might once have been, their control and use remained under the direction of elders. The latter, in the late Colonial days, operated with the consent and to some extent under the jurisdiction of Government chiefs and their courts. Since the results of some of the rituals brought death to individuals, their use had to be properly authorized and public. Ultimately they were supposed to benefit a community. Unlike *βutasi* in the primary sense, juridical rituals did not restore well-being by casting out mystically dangerous anger. They dealt with past or potential *actions*, to the end that good relations be restored or established and offenders punished. In anthropological terms, they were rituals intentionally used for social control. Submission of one's self and/or others to judgement and action of medicines is the common feature. Anyone would be affected by *mwalola* or *mugule* who drank the medicine and swore the ordeal oath.[20] Similarly, any two men, whether kinsmen, neighbours or members of communities remote from one another, could submit themselves to *mtero* as blood pact partners. In practice, the use of these medicines in juridical rites followed the lines of political divisions and of the links between pact-making elders who crossed the divisions.

The most heinous crime (and sin) dealt with in juridical rites was sorcery. Its malevolent secrecy was the opposite of *βutasi*. Taita attributed to sorcerers (*βasaβi*; sing. *msaβi*) some of the features bestowed elsewhere on 'witches'. But they did not hold that anyone could *intentionally* harm others without the use of medicines and/or malevolent gestures and speech.[21] A sorcerer, also called *mlogi* or *mlogi mundu*, one who ensorcels someone, was thought motivated chiefly by greed and envy turning to angry malevolence. He was thought to use herbal preparations, hiding them in his victim's food, roof-thatch, path or field. Or he might strike his waylaid victim at night with a human arm bone decorated with beads and wire; bury dead cats in farms; scatter blood around a homestead while dancing naked by moonlight. Any of these acts required *magemi*, curses, in order to succeed in causing victims' illness, bereavement, poverty or death. A sorcerer also could act without medicines, for example by wading naked into a stream (again at night), striking the surface of the water with the palms of the hands and pronouncing a curse. But medicines or actions without speech were held inefficacious in sorcery as in juridical rites and religion proper. As one Taita said, 'The sorcerer *must say something*, or his work has gone for nothing' (see below, pp. 169–70). Sorcery was credited with the power to damage those very good things which religion guarded and restored. The fertility of fields, the life, well-being, and reproduction of humans and livestock were thought to be continually threatened by the evil workings of greedy, envious, and spiteful individuals lacking in normal controls over their behaviour (see pp. 148–9). In addition, as has been noted, the proliferation of sorcerers within a neighbourhood caused the anger of Creator. Hence the battle between the virtuous performing rites openly and in the light of day and the sorcerers working at night in secrecy.

Overlapping with the juridical rites that were 'a sort of religion' was the ritual of which it was said, 'It is a sort of sorcery, but not sorcery proper' (*ni βusaβi, ela si βusaβi tiki*). It was the means of protecting the public good by destroying its enemies through the use of *mbaro* medicine. This medicine of execution was controlled by *βandu βa wabasi*, the Executioners' Society operating in each neighbourhood. The critical feature by Taita standards was the administration of *mbaro* medicine with an unconditional curse to persons whose guilt or dangerousness was considered established without a doubt. They included recidivist sorcerers and thieves as well as persons reckoned criminally insane.[22] The Executioners did not form a secret society, for their membership was widely known. *Wabasi* was euphemistically called a *kilabu*, 'club', when Taita pointed out that members wined and dined each other and had special burials. The similarity between alleged sorcery practices and the use of *mbaro* lay in the unconditional use of destructive ritual aimed at a particular known individual. Also, the execution curse was not revocable like the curses sometimes put on a person by his parent or mother's brother angered by disobedience.[23] It was therefore quite different from the conditional curses of the main body of juridical rites, including those of routine anti-sorcery as directed against 'any sorcerer ensorcelling here'. The dissimilarity of the execution rite from sorcery lay in its legality as a means of exercising powers delegated by the community for its own good. The use of execution medicine presupposed that the legally chosen victim was not redeemable, that his heart would lead him over and over again to steal or commit sorcery, or that his madness would drive him to harm others physically. Those who administered execution medicine were supposed to be acting for the public good and not out of malice, whereas sorcerers were assumed to be malevolent. But members of the Executioners' Society, being killers, were in theory excluded from the main activities of the lineage shrine centres. However, such exclusion was in fact impossible since some of them were among the most influential elders.

Like the main juridical rites and also like alleged sorcery, execution ritual made use of medicine that was not a shrine. Outside the categories discussed so far was a variety of ritual performances for which Taita used no group label, but all employing medicines. I refer to them as ritual using miscellaneous medicines. Each of the latter had its own name or was called after the disease, condition or situation for which it was suited. There was in principle no limit to the number and variety of miscellaneous medicines that might be discovered, invented or taken over from other peoples.

Lineages claimed to have special medicines for the fertility of land, livestock and people. Unlike the lineage shrines that were Great Medicines, miscellaneous medicines that were not shrines were supposed not to duplicate one another. They could be transmitted to members of other lineages by special arrangements, claims having been made about their superiority to other medicines. That happened especially with medicines acting against specific diseases or blights. Personal specialities much like lineage specialities could be transmitted to others and their use and manufacture taught for a fee. Love and beauty medicines were in the control of old women who sold them mostly to lovelorn youths and maidens to enhance their attractions and to cause a favourable response from the beloved. Finally, some elders were, as individuals, supposed to have medicines wherewith to cause rain to fall over their own fields, to set mortars to pounding in pestles, to cause lions to appear, and so on. Stories related the adventures of famous practitioners and their contests, when days and nights were made noisy and mysterious by the action of such wonder-workers.

Love medicines and wonder-workings, in conversations of an abstract sort, could be treated as amusing and trivial. But discussion of cases made it clear that the alleged use of these medicines might be either approved or disapproved. There was room to argue about whether or not particular performances were acts of sorcery. A young girl's use of beauty medicine to make the youths notice her charms was one thing. Causing a particular youth to be wildly distracted in spite of her ugliness was another. Duelling with another wonder-worker to make pestles pound might be funny; causing leopards to circle another man's livestock corral on the plains was not so amusing. No one complained if someone shut the wind up in a calabash to calm a storm, but getting all the rainfall for one's own fields was selfish and bad. (Taita did not, so far as we know, see private rain-making as an unusual personal access to what was supposed to be *Mlungu*'s benefits to mankind. But since the potential issue did not arise in discussions, it is impossible to say any more about it.) Not uncommonly, users of miscellaneous medicines found themselves charged with sorcery. Someone seen out alone picking plants might be accused, when someone experienced a misfortune, of having picked and used sorcery medicines.

Even some custodians and owners of shrines were accused of misusing their medicines or of hiding sorcery medicines in among the others. Hence the practice of taking witnesses along on plant-gathering trips and of having a trusted friend come to witness the performances employing medicines.

The use of miscellaneous medicines aimed at securing many of the same good things of life guarded and restored by religion and threatened by sorcery. Yet the use of miscellaneous medicines was more narrowly instrumental than religious performances, which sought personal and group health, fertility and prosperity. Users of miscellaneous medicines sought not only the same benefits as were available to all through religion, but they hoped also to score gains over others. The treatment of miscellaneous medicines as property to be bought and sold and otherwise guarded jealously from others contributed to that impression. Between the components of lineage shrine assemblages and lineage-owned miscellaneous medicines lay the difference between a mystery guarded from unsuitable viewers (strangers, women and uninitiated males other than small boys) and a secret profitable to insiders. A secret benefiting one could damage others, in Taita thought, and so miscellaneous medicines had perforce an ambiguous moral status.

The main juridical rites, the ritual use of execution medicine, sorcery and the employment of lineage and personal specialities shared certain features. All consisted of highly formalized actions making use of objects and materials called medicines supposed to have intrinsic properties or virtues. Crucially, all of the performances mentioned required speech in order to be complete and efficacious. In both respects these performances differed from the use of curings; the former were *rituals* and the latter were *technical* acts. Contrasting ritual with technical performances employing medicines reveals the characteristics of the wider ritual domain of which βutasi was the dominant part. Performances of βutasi did not all use things or substances called medicines, but they all required the use of formalized actions and speech. The former might be reduced to a minimum but, whether elaborated or not, always would remain incomplete and inefficacious unless performers accompanied their actions with appropriate utterances. The requirement of speech accompanying action or gesture points to a central fact about Taita religious and other ritual. In ritual Taita did not only act upon the world. They interacted with a variety of agents seen as in some measure capable of volition and as responding to human intentions and volitions embodied in speech. In that respect βutasi and the rest of Taita ritual were distinguished from what I call ceremonial or etiquette and also from ceremonies. The latter consisted of formalized action and speech; it involved interaction among humans in their non-mystical aspects but not interaction between mystically-endowed humans and other agents. Taita ceremonies consisted of *ndima*, festivals of passage (see pp. 57, 59 and 64) which, unlike shrine acquisition rites and funerals, were not religious. The performances of *ndima* were usually preceded by acts of *kutasa*, but were themselves not part of *βutasi* as specified by Taita. Figure 2 sets out the relations among religious ritual, other ritual, and ceremony, as 'symbolic' acts.

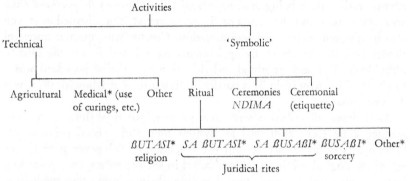

Caps = categories recognized in Taita speech
l.c. = analyst's categories
* = some variety of 'medicines' employed

Figure 2. Religion in relation to other domains

In their capacity to respond to and interact with living human beings, the mystical agents attended to in *βutasi* and the medicines used in other rituals displayed various combinations of person-like attributes. One point on which agents may be compared is that of concern with morality. The hearts of living humans (and domestic animals) were angered by transgressions of their rights or by actions that seemed to slight their worth, and ancestral shades sent misfortunes when their descendants transgressed the norms of kinship; Creator visited drought and plague on morally degenerate communities. Among these morally concerned agents a complex relationship obtained. Creator, having both personal and non-personal aspects, as discussed earlier in the chapter (see pp. 29–30), qualified for the label *supra-personal*. Ancestors were, so to speak, divinized human persons wielding power over their surviving descendants. And within each living human, capable of surviving death as the non-corporeal aspect of domestic animals could not, lay the heart as a mystical entity requiring ritual action. To the *personal* agents, ancestors, and the hearts of living humans, some Taita attributed a special connection with Creator that attended to shared concern with morality.

The shrines (other than ancestral skulls) were either Great Medicines of people and wealth or minor shrines for lesser goods. Bound up with material well-being and authority, interaction with shrines took place within the framework of approved acquisitive activities (see Chapter 3, pp. 66–7). The action and responses of shrines were not concerned with the morality of their owners except very indirectly. In that respect they lacked a crucial dimension of human personhood even though personification was registered in addressing them as 'you'. They were *personified* agents, rather than being *supra-personal* (like Creator) or *personal* (like ancestral shades and the hearts of living humans). The distinction is seen also in different degrees of individuation. Creator was unique; ancestral shades and the hearts of living humans were based in unique human individuals. But such minimal individuation as a shrine possessed was a function of its ownership by a particular living man at whose death it was deconsecrated.

As I have described above (see p. 36), when shrines were consecrated they were addressed as though they had existed prior to the human acts of manufacture and ritual tendance. Whatever potential or actual theological subtleties are embodied in such speeches, they point to a feature distinguishing medicines that were shrines from other medicines. Taita treated the former as capable of taking the initiative, demanding of a particular man that he have Bag, Stool or Bell consecrated for him. Nothing of the sort was implied of non-shrine medicines, which also lacked moral awareness. Plant parts, animal substances and minerals possessed virtues intrinsic to them of which men could avail themselves. But medicines made out of them came into being in the course of manufacture and ritual. Once brought into being they responded to humans engaged in ritual, but they were not capable of taking the initiative and demanding to be manufactured. Non-shrine medicines thus displayed minimally the attributes of persons; they were *quasi-personified* agents. Great *Figi* medicines in some respects straddled the divide between *personified* shrine-medicines and *quasi-personified* medicines that were not shrines. Like other defensive medicines and like all non-shrine medicines, each Great *Figi* was manufactured out of various substances possessed of intrinsic virtues. Great *Figi* had to be renewed periodically lest they lose their effectiveness. Yet they had qualities of permanence and externality, being beyond the control of individuals, that made them resemble the 'pre-existent' shrines. In that light it is understandable that some Taita should be willing to call Great *Figi ngoma* while withholding that title from the Great Medicines made and used by Rainmakers as 'accessory' medicines of religion.

Supra-personal, personal, personified and quasi-personified mystical agents displayed a number of concomitantly differentiating features. Although *personified* agents (shrine medicines) did not attend to the moral (and/or jural) derelictions of those they affected, they shared with *supra-personal* and *personal* agents freedom from constraint. That is, *supra-personal*, *personal* and *personified* agents intervened in human affairs, making demands; demands were not made on them. *Quasi-personified* agents were subject to human use. Differentiated among themselves in part according to their uses, they affected humans in terms of the latter. Failure to meet the demands of *supra-personal*, *personal* and *personified* agents would be read into later misfortunes, requiring humans sooner or later to meet the demands of these mystical agents. That was not the case with *quasi-personified* agents.

Non-shrine medicines operated when their action was set in motion by *speaking* human beings acting within the framework of various aims: to affect rainfall (as part of Rainmakers' ritual); to punish known or unknown wrong-doers without harming the innocent; to establish or strengthen social bonds; to acquire and protect the good things of life; and, in sorcery, deliberately to work harm against other persons. Set in motion, medicines worked according to their own powers. For sorcery medicines the latter included the likelihood of turning upon a possessor who did not use them.[24]

The forms of speech used in interaction with and action upon various mystical agents varied in accord with differences among them. Ritual speech always included performative utterances: utterances achieving an action in, not by means of, the saying. However, interaction with *supra-personal*, *personal* and *personified* agents required *malombi*, 'prayers', while action upon *quasi-personified* agents did not. The *malombi* of religious actions concerned directly with Creator included *wishings*; *personal* and *personified* agents were addressed in *malombi* that included *blessings, offerings, urgings*, and *supplications*. All *malombi* contained explicit or implicit acts of *rejecting anger* from the heart of the actor in addition to the explicit actions mentioned. With the *quasi-personal* medicines of the main juridical rites, Taita spoke *conditional curses*, as they did also in the routine acts of anti-sorcery appended to the prayers of *βutasi* proper. In those juridical rites, human persons submitted themselves to the action of the medicine of blood pact partnership, the medicine for searching out sorcerers and other criminals, or the medicine for conditionally cursing persons whose criminality had already been suggested. In the use of the rain medicines of *βutasi* and in rites using miscellaneous medicines, the characteristic utterances were *commands* mobilizing the virtues of the medicines and wishings for their effectiveness. In execution rituals humans acted upon the medicines in uttering commands that took the form of *unconditional curses* mobilizing the harmful properties of the medicines. The utterances therefore registered the range of variation from *supra-personal to quasi-personified* agents differing in their orientation to morality, their individuation, their degrees of autonomy and other related features. Outside ritual, ceremonial utterances *exhorted* novices, *confirmed* their new statuses, and *proclaimed* the achievement of fuller social person-hood.

Various aspects of *kutasa* as the central and defining act of Taita religion now emerge more clearly. In *kutasa*, utterances directed towards turning away the anger of a *personal* or *personified* mystical agent were at some point matched by declarations signifying and effecting the end of anger in the performer. But Taita held that for the entire ritual to be efficacious, it was necessary for the celebrant to be 'sincere': he must not have inner reservations. Although the performance of *kutasa* was correctly achieved in gesture and word, these had to be matched by the person's inner state.

In juridical rites (*sa βutasi*), public submission to the *conditional curses* carried its own assurance: an accused sorcerer might be certain of his own innocence, but for that very reason feel it perfectly safe to pronounce the *conditional curse* on himself and drink the *mugule*. Someone knowing himself guilty placed himself in jeopardy from which escape was possible only by finding someone willing to give him an antidote secretly. How-ever, *sa βutasi* included a counterpart to the *βutasi* performer's sincerity. For example, when *mugule* oath medicine was administered to an accused sorcerer, thief or perjurer, each man witnessing the ritual removed his knife from his belt and placed it on the ground with the tip pointing towards the accused who was in this way made to stand within a ring of pointing knives. It signified that the witnesses added their 'agreement' to the oath, i.e. they held no reservations. That not only committed them publicly to refusing the accused an antidote, but strengthened the efficacy of the oath itself.

Outside *βutasi* and *sa βutasi*, mobilizing the powers of medicines by commands required no assurance of a correct inner state. It could be assumed that no one would command what he did not wish to occur, whether he be aiming to shut up the wind in a calabash, to cure gardens of destructive worms or to harm a neighbour by sorcery. Members of the Executioners' Society would not set *mbaro* medicine in action with a curse directed at a specific malefactor unless they intended his destruction. In non-religious ritual, then, motives and intentions were assumed as the ground for action; they did not enter into the requirements for efficacy. The correct inner state as intrinsic to the efficacy of ritual performance therefore was a distinguishing feature of *βutasi*.

It is easy to see now why routine anti-sorcery was almost always used as an adjunct of religious rituals. An insincere participant could perform *kutasa*. But not only would his performance lack efficacy; his retention of 'words hidden in the heart' might be leading him to perform sorcery that would produce effects counter to those sought by the religious ritual.

Linkage with the social order was also built into the requirements of religious ritual, both for its validity and its efficacy. All participants performed *kutasa*. But on any occasion one performance of *kutasa* was more essential than others; I call this *primary kutasa*. For example, no performance of rainmaking ritual was complete, valid or efficacious without *kutasa* done by the locality's Rainmaker: his was the *primary kutasa*. Rituals focussed on an ancestral shade required *primary kutasa* by the senior male surviving lineal descendant of that ancestor. Similarly, *primary kutasa* must be done by a person whose angry heart was injuring a close kinsman; by the keeper of the lineage shrines when someone made offerings at the shrine centre; by a shrine owner whose misfortune had been attributed to his shrine, and so on. Through *primary kutasa* especially, participants in religious ritual were required to act in accord with social roles and relationships. *βutasi* was therefore bound to the social order and to the legitimacy of its forms. That was true of juridical ritual (*sa βutasi*) only by way of its attachment to political organization, roles and aims. Keepers of juridical medicines were reckoned to have official standing in the public interest.

Outside *βutasi* and *sa βutasi*, linkage with the social order was not built into validity and efficacy. That is not to say that there were no connections with the social order; ownership of miscellaneous special medicines by lineages and individuals was legitimate and socially patterned. But social factors were not intrinsic to the completeness and efficacy of a ritual employing such medicines. For sorcery the same was true. Although Taita asserted that in practice sorcerers confined their activities to their own local communities, acts of sorcery could be performed by anyone against anyone else, whatever their relationship. The social aspect important for sorcery was its criminality. The medicine of execution, *mbaro*, was similarly believed effective whomever the user and whomever the victim. Its dangerous qualities (there was supposed to be no antidote) required its control. The relationship of morally ambiguous *mbaro* execution to the legitimate social order which it was supposed to uphold was perhaps most clearly shown by the special form of mortuary ceremony for members of the 'club'.

It was consonant with the distinguishing features of *βutasi* that the major act accompanying the central one of *kutasa* should have been offering and food sharing. They fit the Taita pattern in which all relationships with expectations of long-term involvement and mutual concern were marked by gifts and commensality.

The central acts of *βutasi*: *kutasa* as a combination of speech and bodily movement, offering (*kizongona*), and commensality are discussed at greater length in the last chapter, after various bodies of religious ritual have been described and discussed. In this chapter, discussion of the mystical agents with which Taita interacted or upon which they acted has helped to delineate Taita religion as a domain of action in relation to other ritual, ceremony and technical activities. It has to be remembered that beliefs and practices were not laid out for Taita by pedagogues or theologians. What I have described in this chapter and in the previous one was experienced by Taita over their lifetimes, in greatly varying contexts. Interaction with mystical agencies was embedded in the experience of misfortune as interpreted after the fact by diviners. Misfortunes themselves, as well as interpretations of them, changed as individuals moved through the life cycle, into and out of the society of the living. Religious truths and necessities were therefore unfolded as individuals experienced changes of social personhood. Religious experience as a dimension of the moral career is the subject of the following chapter.

3

RITUAL AND THE MORAL CAREER

In a phrase recurring in religious ritual, Taita hoped that the subject of a rite would 'not be divined-for again', that is, that he would remain free from misfortune requiring divination. In fact everyone required being divined-for repeatedly. In diviners' interpretations of misfortune, the characteristics of mystical agents and their anger were realized in relation to the nature of human persons. Personhood depended in the first instance on life, then on continued growth and maturation of the body and its capacities. Full personhood resulted from social growth, in the course of which changes were wrought by ceremony and ritual. The experience of misfortune changed as various religious means were called upon to transform happenings amoral in themselves into moral events within a moral career.

Taita conceptualized the human person as an entity made up of various components and capacities, some of them surviving death, and connected with bodily parts and processes. The head (*chongo*) was associated with the total person. It was seen as the locus of consciousness, speech, memory, and knowledge: with those capacities conceptualized elsewhere as aspects of the 'mind'. A serious disturbance of those faculties was classed as 'illness of the head' (*βuƙongo gwa chongo*) or 'madness' (*isu*). The person defined as mad 'mixed up his words' (*wagaluƙa malago gaƙe*); he was incapable of ordinary discourse, liable to behave in strange and unpredictable ways. Since Taita associated true madness with violence, those labelled mad were subject to drastic treatment and on this account Taita were cautious about using the term.[1] They left scope for a variety of eccentric forms of behaviour (including temporary abberations, drunkenness, etc.), commonly asserting that 'everyone has his own way'. Various individuals were considered to speak more skillfully than others or to show greater acumen; others were judged clumsy of speech and slow-witted. But, except for rare occasions, such judgements were spoken privately. Public pronouncements were shaped by the egalitarian principle that everyone could aspire to the good things of life appropriate to a mature man or woman, irrespective of social affiliation and individual peculiarities. The liver (*idima*), seat of the will, was related to strength and activity. But for *βutasi* the organ of greatest importance was the heart, *ngolo*. The heart as a mysical agent attended to in religious rituals has been mentioned and receives fuller attention elsewhere (see Chapter 4), but some comments are called for in the present context.

The word *ngolo* referred to the heart of any living human or animal; its operation could be felt most clearly at the pulse beside the breast bone. Of someone who had just died, Taita said, 'the heart is finished' (*ngolo yameria*). But as has been indicated, in humans and domestic animals the heart as a bodily organ was associated with sentiments and with the mystical capacity to affect others through those sentiments. For humans, the heart in the mystical senses did not cease to function at death and because of that a human being could become a *mrumu*, one of the shades of the dead. A related usage of *ngolo* distinguished individual temperaments or dispositions, people being spoken of as having different kinds of hearts. Someone easily angered had a fierce or 'hot' (*modo*) heart. A mild and kindly person had a cool, clean or 'pure' (*ielie*) heart. One lacking compassion was 'stone-hearted' (*ngolo igo*). Tastes and inclinations such as greediness, covetousness and selfishness were located in the heart. Further, certain recognized disturbances of the emotions qualified as 'illness of the heart' (*βuҟongo gwa ngolo*): such were *lwafuo*, a sort of kleptomania, and *saҟa*, the affliction of women possessed by foreign spirits.[2] Head and heart were not the same in men and women, according to many Taita men, who asserted that women were less wise than men by nature and more given to disturbances of the heart requiring their governance by men.[3]

Some Taita believed in inborn dispositions of the heart. However they, with others, emphasized the effects of parental influence in the rearing of children to be cool, clean or pure of heart. Stress on the desirability of good-heartedness, far from being of hypothetical interest alone, carried importance in everyday life. It was important for an individual to find out how the hearts of others were disposed towards him so that conflict might be mitigated and mystically dangerous anger not allowed to fester. In the effort to learn the state of hearts four aspects were important. First of all, human hearts were inscrutable: a proverb said that 'no one can sojourn in the house of the heart', that is, no one can know the innermost feelings of another person. Second, human hearts, even those of persons of good disposition, were prone to anger. Third, the arousal of anger was directly related to a person's jural status through the rights which he would jealously guard against others, for no one was expected to see his rights trampled on without taking umbrage. Fourth, the consequences of anger were different for persons of different disposition, in different circumstances and in different stages of the life cycle.

The belief in inscrutability did not prevent speculation about feelings. On the contrary, people observed details of posture, facial expression and tone of voice in attempting to assess others' responses.[4] As for the second point, since proneness to anger was seen as a natural human characteristic even for people of good temperament, no moral blame attached to anger as such. With respect to the third, although one should avoid being silently resentful by 'hiding words in the heart', it was up to other people to avoid that disrespect for others' rights which aroused anger. Finally, though anger as such was not morally blameworthy, some of its possible consequences were. Anger could issue in the physical violence of which Taita so strongly disapproved and which was severely controlled, or in the sinful crime of sorcery.

The ceremonies and rituals of birth, infancy and early childhood showed the potential person as one whose survival was sought by its parents and grandparents. A woman gave birth to her first child at her own parents' homestead, cared for by her mother, mother's sisters, and sisters. Aside from seven days' seclusion and the naming of the infant by its mother, the birth was celebrated after a month at a feast given by the father for his parents and parents-in-law. The child was anointed with goat's blood by its paternal grandfather, who performed the first *kutasa* for it, praying for its health, long life and general well-being. This first performance of *primary kutasa* showed well the status of the infant as 'someone's child' – an asset of its father who was himself still someone's child because his own father was still alive. On this occasion the performance of *kutasa* did not wait upon divination: the critical nature of infancy was sufficient to require it.

Three aspects of infancy appeared in ritual. First, though not a full social person, an infant was a potential person before whom lay the manifold possibilities of being divined-for. As such he needed his own divining seeds. Secondly, the infant was closely identified with its mother. Failure to thrive could result in the prescription of curing rites emphasizing the mother–child bond. Thirdly, the child was an asset of its parents, particularly of its father; its illness, considered a misfortune directed at one of them, might require ritual in which the parent or parents were the focus of attention. That the three aspects were weighted about equally seems to be indicated by the absence of a set order for the associated rituals in actual practice as against ideal sequence. Their performance took place after a diviner interpreted an infant's illness, failure to grow properly or persistent fretfulness.

Following prescription of 'the apportionment of divining seeds' (*kuβaga Saru*), the child's father took beer and a goat to the diviner. Both performed *kutasa* and then divined from the intestines of the goat to see whether any mystical agent would impede the efficacy of the ensuing ritual. The diviner presented, in a gourd, the divining seeds originally furnished by the father: seven 'apportioned' seeds for a boy and six for a girl. Anointed with fat and having had *kutasa* performed over it, the gourd of seeds now constituted an *ngoma*, shrine. It was the first shrine acquired, the only one available before marriage, and one of only two shrines owned by females. It hung on a peg in the dwelling. In later life when its owner was divined-for, diagnosis and prescription might require him or her to anoint the gourd with fat and to perform *kutasa* to it.

The apportionment of divining seeds was sometimes cited as the first ritual for a child that should occur after the initial anointing and blessing by the paternal grandfather. In fact its prescription might occur in early adulthood rather than in infancy. It was sometimes said that apportionment put someone in touch with the divining apparatus of diviners, making it possible for him to be divined-for. That it could be delayed for so long was a sign of the prolonged dependency of Taita sons and daughters, whose illnesses could be interpreted for many years as misfortunes visited upon their parents.

Rituals employing the medicines of Bag (*Mfuko*) emphasized the mother–child bond while requiring also the participation of the father. Mother's brother was welcome to take part in accord with the proverb saying that 'every person has three parents: mother, father and mother's brother'. *Kindo cha kugu*, 'leg-thing', prescribed for a sickly small child, exemplifies the Bag rites aiming at prospering (*kudenda*, causing to thrive) the subject.

Parents, with perhaps the mother's brother of the ailing child, waited alone for the Bag man and his assistant. At their arrival, the child's father spread an ox hide in the doorway of the house with its outer side facing upwards. The mother sat on the hide with the child on her right thigh while the father led the goat of offering into the house, tethering it behind the mother's right shoulder. The Bag man, removing the calabashes of medicines from the Bag, selected the seven most important and powerful for this ritual. These he set in a row on the hide in front of the mother and child as he squatted before them. He then took up the calabashes two by two, knocking each pair together seven times to the right and seven times to the left. Meanwhile he exhorted the child to grow up without further illnesses, that it might not be divined-for again. Then the goat was led around to the front so that the mother could bump the child's head against that of the beast.

The Bag man used a small knife to make four tiny cuts on either side of the child's breastbone and four on either side of the upper spine. He poured into his left hand a little of the charred and powdered herbs from each of the seven calabashes, mixing them together with saliva. While rubbing the medicine into the cuts he blessed the child, saying:

We say, may this illness leave you. Get well. Be very well, and may no illness ever seize you again.

After the goat was strangled and butchered, its intestines were examined to see whether the ritual would be efficacious, whether parents and child would have an auspicious future and also to be sure that no other mystical agent required tendance. A protective device was made from the Bag medicines tied up in a bit of banana leaf. This, the 'leg-thing',[5] was tied around the child's right ankle for a few moments, then removed. That night the mother tied it on again, loosely, so that the child turning in its sleep would cast it off, after which it was thrown away into the bush.

Kioro, 'that which is spread or sprinkled', was made from the goat's stomach contents and blood, red ochre (always carried in Bag), and the medicines from the seven calabashes. Washing the child's head with this mixture, the Bag man said:

We say, may you get well. Grow up. Be prosperous. Become a person.

The calabash containing *kioro* was set inside the house to the right of the doorway so that the mother could wash the child's head with it at each of seven movements of the sun.

While the scraps and internal organs of the goat were roasting on skewers, *kutasa* was performed with beer and cane juice given by the child's father and prepared by the mother. The Bag man and his assistant did one *kutasa* together at the doorway, followed by the parents (and mother's brother if he was present). Both performances were required for different reasons. In that *kindo cha kugu* was a ritual of Bag, the latter's owner must perform *primary kutasa* to the shrine on behalf of the child. As a ritual of the domestic family, it required *kutasa* by the parents, who had to reject anger from their hearts.

The parental performance of *kutasa* was one of blessing and wishing for the child's recovery. The Bag owner addressed the shrine:

You, leave this child alone that he may be healthy, that he may thrive, that he may be well, that he may beget his own lineage and gain much wealth.

For a girl child the last two requests would be omitted. 'People and wealth', the good things of life brought by good relations with the shrines, were the province of males, who were expected to achieve fuller social personhood than females. The roasted pieces of meat were eaten by participants; the men finished whatever beer remained.

The main part of the ritual ended after the mother had washed the child with *kioro* for the last time. The father poured the mixture out on waste ground near the house early in the morning. Later in the day the second and final phase began with the arrival of the Bag man. This time the ox hide laid in the doorway had its inner side facing upward, marked by seven stripes made with a mixture of red ochre and sheep's fat. The child, seated on the hide near the stripes, had its head, arms and legs anointed with the same mixture. If the child was still unweaned the mother's breasts were anointed as well. The Bag man blessed the child in relation to the shrine, doing *kutasa*:

We say, may this Bag leave you alone, may it never cause you to be divined-for again. Get well, thrive.

He also blessed the mother:

Do not make worms to hurt this child. May your milk be sweet, may it not cause illness. Bear the herder [boy] and the herded [girl], the elephant [female] and the rhinoceros [male].

More medicines were mixed with a little beer, the men together using the mixture to do *kutasa* twice silently. Then the mother wrapped the child in the ox skin with the inner, marked side facing out. The men performed *kutasa* a third time, speaking aloud and spitting the mixture on the child's outstretched legs:

You, we say indeed, may you recover, may you be left in peace by this Bag. Thrive, fatten, be as fertile as the melons that grow on old dwelling sites.

The same actions were gone through a second time using water which was then poured out under the eaves of the house as the mother passed the child through it seven times; any water remaining was poured over the child's head.

The mother, carrying the child, ran seven times to the fence or stile at the homestead's entrance, each time coming back to the others. Each time everyone went through the usual greetings as though she had returned to find ordinary visitors seated in her courtyard. Then she and the Bag man pretended to remove thorns and chiggers from each others feet. After the last repetition the mother carried the child into the house. She brought out a dish of 'stiff food' (*kimanga*) made with beans or lentils. Each adult, taking a bit, threw some towards the house and then away from the house, blessing the child and exhorting it to have numerous offspring of both sexes. Finally, the child's father performed *kutasa*, praying that the child would never again be divined-for on account of Bag. After that, the Bag man's small fee was handed over and, when the remaining beer was drunk up, he and his assistant returned home.

Numerous features linked *kindo cha kugu* with other rituals, religious and non-religious. Like most rites of *βutasi*, it was performed following divination undertaken out of concern for misfortune, in this case an infant's repeated illness or failure to thrive. As always, when an infant or small child was involved, parents, and more particularly the father, had the responsibility of going to the diviner. *Kutasa* was the central act, the spraying out of beer, cane juice and water being accompanied by a variety of utterances which, while varying among themselves, were all *malombi*, prayers. Some exhorted the child to be well and thrive; others called down blessings on the child and/or its mother; others were directed to the responsible mystical agent, the Bag shrine.

The requirement of *kizongona*, offering, did not necessarily include the explicit presentation of the animal to a mystical agent. In this case, as in many others, an implicit element of offering lay in the examination of the animal's intestines to see whether the responsible agent would cease to be angry (and whether any other agent might impede the ritual's success).

The requirement of religious commensalism was met by sharing out the roasted scraps and internal organs of the animal, leaving most of the meat to be distributed for domestic consumption.

Bag as a shrine was a *personified* mystical agent intervening in human affairs and responsive to human action and utterance. The individual medicines making it up exhibited the ordering imposed on the non-human world by Taita thought and practice, for the various vegetable medicines had their specific beneficent power or virtue (see Chapter 6). Sheep's fat and red ochre had an association with life and prosperity. The stomach contents of an offered animal formed the main component of *kioro*, spread, sprinkled or used for anointing in numerous religious rituals; it was associated with continuing life processes (see p. 165). Taita killed in bloodless fashion any animal used as *kizongona*. Later, before the animal was dismembered, the blood might be collected for use as life-enhancing medicine as well as for cooking. Numbers and spatial relations were also ordered ritually: three and seven were auspicious numbers, matching right as against left. The virtues of medicines acted through their application to the proper parts of the body (see p. 169). Treatment of the mother's nurturant breasts had obvious significance in a ritual concerned with the well-being of an unweaned infant.

Social relationships, as intrinsic to religious rituals, appeared crucially in the various performances of *kutasa*, but their significance was exhibited in other ways as well. Seating mother and child on the ox hide both joined them together and segregated them from others as the subjects of ritual, after the fashion of many Taita rites. Placing the ox hide in the doorway of the dwelling marked *kindo cha kugu* as one of many rituals concerned with persons as members of a domestic group. The representation of friendship when the mother and Bag man pretended to remove thorns and chiggers from each other's feet dramatized a central feature of the ritual: persons as members of a domestic group were brought into relationship with a mystical agency having its focus in wider relationships. The Bag man was, of necessity, an elder; the child's father would (probably) be a non-elder; the mother was dependent on male-dominated ritual. The child was dependent on both parents, and only through them could he be brought into relationship with social and religious fields wider than the domestic family.

Important similarities connect 'leg-thing' with the juridical rite of establishing blood pact partnership. In the latter, the two men establishing a blood pact partnership sat on an ox hide placed at the threshold of one partner's dwelling. Each fed the other tiny bits of meat spread with blood taken from a small incision cut next to the giver's breastbone. While the presiding elder clashed two swords together above their heads, each partner swore the oath, giving himself, his wife and children and the entire small lineage founded by him as hostage to this faithfulness. The performance concluded with commensalism preceded by the partners pretending to remove thorns and chiggers from each other's feet. In both 'leg-thing' and 'eating *mtero*', persons as members of a domestic group were brought into contact with a mystical power of non-domestic nature. The oath medicine of pact partnership affected the domestic dependents and small lineage of a man who himself had entered the arena of political relations. As I have noted, the first *kutasa* by a neonate's paternal grandfather showed the infant as a dependent of a dependent. 'Leg-thing' encapsulated the infant or small child in the politically focussed system of shrine medicines as child of a non-elder who held no major shrines of his own.

In every respect, infants and children entered religious life as accessories of others, as non-persons contributing to the personhood of their parents and grandparents. However, maturational processes laid the foundation both for changes within the framework of dependency and for future autonomy. About the age of three a child reached the age of 'sense' (*akili*), judged by its ability to perform certain actions competently. For example, taking a brand from the hearth and carrying it to the father (for lighting his pipe) without falling into the fire demonstrated sense. Especially for a girl the teaching of proprieties had begun and the child played at imitating adult activities. Cognitive capacities and the ability to behave appropriately were also accompanied, Taita asserted, by development of the heart as the organ of sentiments. Before the age of sense a child could feel bodily pain but could not judge right or wrong. One who had reached the age of sense could make such judgements. He could assess the actions of his parents towards him, knowing whether, for example, they were admin-

istering punishment justly or being over-severe. That amounted to knowing when his rights were being infringed; that, in turn, made it possible
for the child to 'hold anger in his heart' after the manner of adults.
At this stage the child had been incorporated into the circle of close
kinship relations to which the mystical danger of angry hearts was largely
confined. The following chapter treats this aspect of Taita religion at
length, but one point is important here. Although the small child continued to experience religious life largely as a passive participant defined
as 'some people's child', his more active role was foreshadowed. In possessing a heart capable of responding to wrongs done him with mystically
dangerous anger, the child was at least minimally a person.

The many years of social dependency were punctuated by ceremonials
advancing and differentiating the social personhood of the sexes, and leading to greater social and religious participation. Female infants underwent
cliterodectomy at the hands of skilled elderly female kin. Circumcision of
boys took place when they were between eight and eleven or twelve, preferably before puberty and sometimes as early as the sixth year. As times
of crisis and danger, both ceremonies were framed by performances of
kutasa but were themselves *ndima*, festivals. Before initiation, girls and
boys were alike *mwana*, child. Following initiation at puberty, a girl
became *mwai*, maiden; a boy became *mdaβana*, youth or bachelor. Performance of the elaborate sequence of *mwari* initiation rites advanced girls to
maidenhood. Boys had only to take part in the final 'showing of wonders'
(*ngasu*) ending *mwari*, to be initiates.
　Initiation opened a complicated transitional period for both sexes. Much
concerned with matters of courtship and marriage, adolescent girls tended
to band together in giggling groups.[6] But they were also earnest cultivators, not only labouring in their mothers' fields but forming work clubs
to cultivate and weed in return for payment. They accompanied their
mothers and other female kin and neighbours to the public phases of
rituals and festivals, helping with the tasks of cooking and serving food.
Adolescent boys were much less integrated into the work life of men,
although they were expected to help their fathers. Some joined with girls
in the formation of joint cultivating clubs celebrating the end of a season
with a feast supplied from the fees earned. They too were concerned with
courtship and marriage, but at a later age than girls. When they did
undertake serious courtship, the accumulation of resources for paying
bridewealth claimed their attention. Their association with ritual performances changed strikingly. Before initiation, a boy, frequenting the
company of a grandfather, often watched the central and most esoteric
parts of the rituals carried out by elders. Old men tolerated the antics of

small boys, only occasionally hushing them or trying (fruitlessly) to per-
suade them to sit still. Once initiated, a youth, far from being welcomed at
ritual performances, was excluded. It was brought home to him over and
over again that in all ritual matters he was 'just a child' who knew
nothing. On serious occasions, including rituals, youths were conspicuously
awkward, less at ease than maidens, acting as though conscious of their
exclusion from adult life. That very exclusion, however, derived from the
expectation that in later years they would become truly knowledgeable in
religious affairs as active participants, while their sisters and wives would
play accessory roles for the most part.

During the Colonial period other factors, while affecting both sexes,
bore especially on male careers. More boys than girls were in school where,
so it was hoped, they would acquire the skills of literacy enabling them
to get good employment. In actuality most boys of 16 or so entered employment without enough schooling to qualify them for more than un-
skilled or semi-skilled jobs. For a few whose more extensive schooling
headed them for careers in teaching or in Government posts, adherence to
one of the Christian churches played an equally large part in cutting them
off from the traditional religious life as carried out by the elders. In the
long run, that might even separate them to an extent from their own
brothers. In many of those Taita families affected by the missions, one son,
usually the eldest, moved ultimately into traditional elderhood, the only
non-Christian in an otherwise (perhaps only nominally) Christian sibling
group.

Whatever the combination of purposeful exclusion and the effects
of schooling, employment and mission influence, youths (and, for that
matter, young married men) were on the fringe of active religious life.
Although they might claim to be much more knowledgeable than their
fathers in the ways of the modern world, and though they might be earning money to buy their bridewealth livestock, youths remained social and
religious dependents. Exhibiting a certain wistfulness at their exclusion
from ritual action, they often expressed intense curiosity about what elders
were doing. Divination still named them as dependents and accessories, as
illustrated in a prayer to ancestors on behalf of the father of sons at work
in Mombasa:

Listen, you father and his fellows: eat this meat and drink this beer. Leave this man
in peace, he and his village, and may his people be healthy. If it is you who are
sending leopards to kill his goats, we say, may you leave off doing so. May his
children come home from afar. May they come home and sit down and cleave to their
father. And we who are here, may our bodies be well. Here is the goat and the beer
which we give you. May your hearts be cooled. Part this man from his illness forever.
Indeed thus we say.

Here the sons employed in the city counted, along with the goats threatened by leopards, among the assets of the father, whose health and general well-being were sought. They were included among 'his village' and 'his people'. More active experience of religion waited upon marriage and its consequences.

As one occasion for public celebration, a Christian wedding surpassed the traditional form when the latter became attenuated during the Colonial period. Since Christian Taita were all either Anglicans or Roman Catholics, marriage for them was a sacrament, while for *βatasi* a wedding counted as a festival. A church wedding required a licence and so had more clear-cut legal consequences, calling for some rearrangement of traditional bridewealth practices. People married in church were wedded once and for all. Marriages among *βatasi* were confirmed gradually over many years. For them the establishment of co-residence was the critical event even though it was not sufficient to turn the couple finally into an indubitably married pair.[7] Still, there had formerly been some spectacle. A bride might be carried off in mock abduction, or there was a mock battle between her kin and kin of the groom who came to her parents' house to take her away. In pre-Independence days girls were often persuaded to elope, leaving a dance or their work in the fields – indeed, elopement was very common at mid-century. Many other brides were taken away at night by a few friends of the groom and were attended by female friends and kin of their own. Like the other major ceremonies of passage, marriage entailed a period of seclusion followed by a 'coming out'. *βatasi* in Teri Valley, Sagala, retained their own special form of pre-wedding ordeal-seclusion for betrothed girls. Most *βatasi* had given up anointing the couple with red ochre at the end of seclusion. But Christians and *βatasi* shared two practices: privately, co-residence was marked by the bride's serving a meal to her husband and by her acceptance of food in her new home. A European-style dance (*danzi*) with more or less elaborate feasting constituted the main public observance of the coming-out.

All of the features described above matched the Taita emphasis on jural relations, those between members of a conjugal pair and those between spouses and their affines. These non-religious matters, as I discuss in Chapter 4, were religiously relevant. They were attended to particularly in the early years of marriage when observances of ceremony and etiquette called attention to the couple's relations with their natal families. For example, when the couple visited the wife's home they could not have sexual intercourse; they should not even share a bed in the house where she was still a daughter. To the husband's avoidance of his mother-in-law was added the requirement that he behave with courteous formality to his wife's sister, who had become 'like a sister' to him. In their first place of residence, with the husband's parents, the wife had to avoid her father-in-law and behave modestly before her husband's brothers. Both sets of parents were concerned with the reproductive capacities of the young couple. A young man's failure to beget children or a young woman's barrenness could be diagnosed by a diviner as requiring another Bag rite for which his or her parents assumed responsibility. For the wife, general failure to thrive in her conjugal home might require her parents to call the Bag man to perform 'Bag of the house' (*Mfuko gwa nyumba*) on her behalf. Once the young woman did become pregnant, the differing roles of the seniors were recognized. A couple's first child was usually born in the wife's natal homestead, where she and the infant, looked after by her mother and sisters, could enjoy the affectionate concern associated with links through women. Back in her conjugal home, however, the new mother had to defer to her affines. Her husband's mother and sisters, not she, could bath the baby out of doors where 'their child' could be seen by neighbours and passers-by; if she was arrogant enough to do that herself, her husband's female agnates could pelt her with dung and otherwise abuse her.

Their marriage consolidated by the birth of children, the young couple moved into a house of their own, built for them at the expense of the two sets of parents. By this time the wife, cultivating pieces of land given over to her by her mother-in-law, would be supplying food for the new domestic group while still contributing to the parental unit. She and her husband would have achieved a degree of independence, but even in their own dwelling they and their children would constitute a satellite household.[8] The degree of independence which they did enjoy was treated as a gift conferred on them. That was indicated in the proprieties observed when, after both mothers had set up a hearth in the new house, a storage shelf for foodstuffs was erected there under the supervision of the husband's mother. The young woman and her mother, should they set up the shelf, affronted the husband's mother and sisters. Such an act was taken as a deep discourtesy to the household from which the new satellite and its resources had been socially derived. On his part the young husband, if not employed for wages, continued to help with work in exchange for milk from the jointly herded animals managed by his father and utilized as the latter directed. If employed, the junior householder was expected to turn over at least some of his earnings to his parents. Together, the husband and wife of a satellite household entered into the neighbourhood network of land transactions, chiefly as debtors, in an effort to meet the demands of a growing family. While barred from competing openly for the accumulation of wealth in livestock, the husband had to respond to affinal demands for further bridewealth payments. The wife was also under pressure from her kin to encourage her husband to provide them with cash, labour and bridewealth installments. All in all, this was a period in which participation in a wider field of social relations made a variety of claims upon the resources of people moving towards social maturity.

In religious life, a satellite householder was still in a dependent, junior position similar to that in which his wife would remain all her life. He had not those claims over 'people and wealth' that could be transformed into political authority, prestige and ritual knowledge. However much information he had acquired about religious affairs, a junior would claim only acquaintance, not genuine knowledge. Since he could not hold the position of a formally instructed elder, he could not claim an elder's knowledge, no matter how well informed he might be. When misfortune befell a satellite householder, *Saru* and *βula* continued to speak in terms suitable to persons of limited independence. Within their circle of close kin and affines, husband or wife was presented as 'some people's child' who was also a parent. Illness or death of such an individual's children, then, were sometimes interpreted as resulting from mystical anger visited on the young parent for transgressing against the rights of someone in that circle. In this way he or she came to participate directly in the domestic anger-removal rites described in the next chapter.

Satellite households were the growing points of lineages and of kinship networks extended through lineage daughters. Their concern with human reproduction and with the successful rearing of children brought them under the guardianship of the great lineage shrines as Great Medicines of people and wealth. A diviner might find, when a child suffered illness, that it was because one or more of the shrines of the father's own lineage angrily demanded tendance; or a young married man's mother's lineage shrines might be named. If divination showed that one or more shrines required a beer offering, the suppliant took the *Mlimu* custodian a small pot of beer called, after the fashion of Taita ritual rules, Seven (*Mfungade*). Primary *ɫutasa* had first to be performed by the *Mlimu* keeper inside the shrine centre, using the aged beer called *nyarigi*, of which a stock had to be kept on hand. Alone with the shrines or, preferably with an assisting elder, the *Mlimu* man did *ɫutasa* to Bell and to whatever other shrine or shrines had been named. Outside, the custodian and the suppliant, if male, did *ɫutasa* again, using the beer of offering. A woman suppliant also brought unfermented cane juice for her own *ɫutasa*. Whatever beer remained belonged to the *Mlimu* man. Lineage shrines might be named as also demanding anointment with fat (*ɫushinga mavuda*). Again, the actual tendance would be done by the *Mlimu* man or by an assistant under his direction. A little sheep's fat mixed with red ochre was rubbed on the shrine or shrines named in divination. The offering of beer and performance of *ɫutasa* were still central and carried out as at other times. The same was true on those rare occasions when lineage shrines demanding a goat received small bits of meat as an offering, the rest being divided between the custodian and the suppliant.

In former days, satellite householders would have participated in the shrine centre rites, performed on behalf of the lineage as a whole (see Chapter 5), but those rites had lapsed in pre-Independence years. What remained were the ordinary rites, described above, focussed on the well-being of persons in their capacity as junior lineage men, daughters of the lineage or men who were offspring of the latter.

Training for the eventual custodianship of a lineage shrine centre was in the nature of things restricted to a very few junior men, mostly sons of custodians. Such training, foreshadowing elderhood, did not in itself enhance the position of the novice. He could not act during his father's lifetime unless the old man wanted to retire on account of poor health. The son had to present a gift in exchange for his training, as did anyone taught about rituals, medicines and divinations. All juniors, then, remained ritual dependents of the *Mlimu* custodian and his assisting elders. But as socially maturing persons on whom others in turn were dependent, they played a more active part than did children, youths or newly married people.

Everyone looked to the work of the Rainmaker and the Defender for the benefits of rainfall, crop-prospering and protection against enemies of the people. These values were realized within the local community. As members of a neighbourhood all householders formerly would have parti-cipated in the public parts of the appropriate rituals. In the late Colonial period some adherents of the Christian mission did not take part, but many Christians, and not only nominal ones, did attend, if only to avoid being blamed for failure of the rites attributed to dissension within the community. A junior householder was as much a neighbourhood member as anyone else, one of the *βeni mwana* or 'indigenes'. Since most marriages were neighbourhood endogamous, most married men and women were integrated into that network of agnatic, matrilateral and affinal ties summed up in the assertion that neighbours 'understood one another'. Cooperation in carrying out the many tasks entailed in community-oriented rites was assumed as an aspect of being one of the 'indigenes'. Further-more, satellite householders were much occupied in cultivating foodstuffs to support their domestic groups and to contribute also to the households of demanding senior kin and affines. Rain and crop furtherance rites touched on their pressing concern to nurture their families.

The legitimacy of that concern was shown in the acquisition by men and women of satellite households of *Lufu*, the Knife shrine. Apart from the personal divining shrine (*Saru*), Knife was, as I have noted, the only shrine a woman could own and the only one available to men whose fathers were still alive. Following on a diviner's diagnosis and instructions, Knife was manufactured under the direction of an elder. It actually consisted of two miniature knives consecrated by *kutasa* and anointing, following the offering of a chicken, lowliest of domestic livestock. From that time on, misfortunes suffered as a cultivator and supplier of food could be attributed to Knife's demand for tendance. The major shrines, 'Great Medicines of people and of wealth', were not available and a junior man would not be divined-for as one requiring Bag, Stool or Bell. A woman could never be so divined-for.

Taita held that when a man had a legitimate son of his own, he and his own father 'had become like brothers'. Being householders and fathers, they shared critical attributes of full social personhood. They also became more rivalrous, in the Taita view, for, it was said, a father believed that his son hoped for his death so as to come into his inheritance. The son on his part, so it was held, resented every reminder of his subordination, especially the requirement not to build up publicly his own wealth in livestock lest he be accused of trying to 'surpass' (*kuchumba*) his father.[9] A woman with children was reckoned to have become like her own mother. However, the slightness of persisting jural relations between mothers and daughters muted rivalry, a manifestation of which might be seen in the taboo on their being pregnant at the same time. A man or woman with a growing family was *mundu wa henga*, a 'person of consequence', a 'well-grown person' even though not jurally or religiously independent.

By the time someone had reached maturity his or her qualities of mind and disposition were well known to kin and neighbours. That is, the person was known also as an individual with idiosyncracies attended to in nicknames and perhaps in the songs composed and sung to mock the nonconformist. Features of the mature but not yet complete social personhood were deployed in more standard ways in ritual and ceremony. On various occasions male heads of satellite households found themselves playing supporting roles in relation to the main performers. As sister's son or son-in-law a man might carry required ritual paraphernalia from a presiding elder's house to the site of the performance; skin and butcher animals for offering, handing out the portions to designated participants; tend to the roasting of internal organs and scraps over the fire which he had built and tended; serve out the beer to male participants; and do any other jobs suitably delegated to a junior. He showed the effects of the economic and political clientship that usually coincided with another social tie. Junior householders, by having entered the network of neighbourhood land and bridewealth transactions, had also become part of the web of political relationships as followers and supporters of elders who lent or pawned land to each other's sons. In public discussions supporters would speak for the policies favoured by their patrons, who often remained largely silent in public. So in ritual and ceremony, they would be the highly visible bustlers-about except during the central actions when they were usually subsidiary participants and witnesses. Also in their role as citizens of a neighbourhood, junior householders turned out for the juridical rites over which elders officiated: most of the knives encircling a person swearing the *mugule* oath (see p. 172) would belong to junior householders witnessing and therefore giving public support to the action.

Wives of junior householders had a subsidiary role on most ritual and ceremonial occasions. They might have contributed beer of their own brewing for use by the men but would themselves use unfermented cane juice when performing *kutasa*. They cooked vegetable food when that was required, serving out the portions to the main groups of participants seated according to sex and age-status. These statements apply particularly to most of the rituals focussed on the shrine centres or on individually owned shrines. As already indicated, women as mothers of infants and small children were central to some of the curing rites of Bag and, as is shown later, women as wives had to take part in shrine acquisition rites. The success of rainmaking and crop-prospering rites required the participation of women as mistresses of households, cultivators and citizens of the local community. In order for the ritual establishing a blood pact to take place, the wives of the prospective partners had to give their consent, since their well-being and that of their children was placed at risk by the oath's conditional curse. That requirement calls attention to the basic difference between the religious lives of men and women. Their differing participation and, therefore, their different modes of experiencing religion related to the confinement of women to the domestic domain. When domestic and political met, as must occur in a society where a man's political position was founded on (but not restricted to) household headship, women as wives, mothers and daughters were involved. Their actions were in a sense subsidiary to the main ones but vital to success. Also, when rituals focussed on the common values of successful crops, fertile herds, human reproduction, health and peace, women as female members of the community, its mothers, cultivators and housekeepers, had to take part; the cooperation of the sexes was essential. The festivals of cliterodectomy, circumcision, initiation and marriage, as well as mortuary and funeral observances, saw women in important and occasionally (as in some phases of girls' initiation) supervisory roles. In the body of anger-removal rites centred on relations within the family and circle of close kin, both women and men were found in central roles. But as will appear in detailed discussion (in Chapter 4) those rites, involving men and women for different reasons, were influenced by the relations between the familial and the jural, between domestic life and the political domain. Training to be a *Mlimu* custodian, Rainmaker or diviner was closed to women, who were barred also from becoming keepers of juridical medicines. A very few women became Seers.

As a mature person, a junior householder or the wife of one had a large network of relations with kin, affines and neighbours. Among the seniors, some of whom would be prominent elders, were father and other senior agnates and senior matrikin (especially mother's brother) who mediated between a junior person and his or her ancestors. They were political, economic and ritual superiors under whose authority a mature junior might chafe. Others were contemporaries and members of the same genealogical generation. The latter included, for males, the other men with whom relations were especially vital: brothers and brothers-in-law. The enjoined amity of brothers, in the Taita view, was inevitably accompanied by rivalry. Wife's brother or sister's husband, on the other hand, became increasingly a friend and helper on ritual as on other occasions. For women, the balancing of kinship and affinal ties continued to be important. In addition to relations with seniors and contemporaries, a mature person would have become parent of a growing family of children on behalf of whom economic and, increasingly, ritual and ceremonial responsibilities had to be assumed. All this meant that despite the subordinate status of satellite households, their religious activities, like all their affairs, were enormously complex. They brought the person into relationship with all the mystical agents, in the company and under the supervision of many other persons acting together in various social constellations. The social personhood of a mature woman was nearer completion than that of a man, who could aspire to elderhood. But in either case, the individual had acquired a multiplicity of roles in relationships stretching across the generations. In some of these relationships conflict was certain to occur. If angry hearts in the circle of close kin were named, the circumstances of conflict would be explored in the course of calling for and carrying out anger-removal. If, as rarely happened, anger issued in physical violence, the result was a protracted court case preferably settled at the local non-statutory tribunal, and perhaps a juridical peacemaking. Sorcery suspicions and accusations were a more common consequence. Junior male household heads could find themselves accused by seniors[10] of trying to gain by evil guile what they could not have legitimately. The political aspects were recognized by some of the junior members who held that, although it was possible to poison people, the belief in evil spells and medicines was the deliberate creation of elders who kept juniors in line by the threat of sorcery accusations. Mistresses of satellite households were accusers and also accused in some sorcery cases. However, vulnerability to sorcery accusations was far from being limited to non-elders and their wives. The move into elderhood was not without its disadvantages.

After the father's death a man and his brothers came into their inheritance of rights in land and livestock. They might continue to herd jointly for a time, but each man was now free to compete for wealth in herds and to be primarily concerned with the well-being of his own wife and children. He might now consider marrying a second wife unless the bridewealth needs of his own sons strained resources. As an independent householder he had a more active role in affairs of his great lineage for he was now head of a potential segment. In the neighbourhood context a man might now become a source of land lent and pawned to juniors, especially daughters' husbands. And he might also find it useful to establish special relationships, including livestock keeping, mutual-aid partnerships and blood pacts with men of his own and other neighbourhoods. People knew whether he was honest and cool of heart; whether he was persuasive in public speaking; whether he was forceful in the face-to-face consultations that laid the groundwork for all apparently spontaneous public discussions. The deployment of these qualities in public life was now possible because, freed of paternal control, the man himself controlled human and animal dependents. It was necessary, too, because a senior man's ramifying social ties increasingly involved him in disputes and other matters requiring public decisions. All this was absent from the career of a woman except insofar as she wielded informal influence.

A senior man, unlike a senior woman, could be divined-for in terms of the Great Medicine shrines because of his control over those good things which the shrines affected. It might seem strange that the shrines were supposed to do good to humans and animals, considering that not only was a shrine acquired after a misfortune was laid to its 'desire' for consecration, but its angry demand for tendance could cause further trouble to people and herds. But medicine shrines, whatever else they might be, focussed the expanded personhood of the man who had acquired dependents and wealth in the proper way. The shrines further enhanced that personhood, turning their owner after his instruction into a knowledgeable, qualified elder. Many men acquired Bag, some went on to acquire Stool; in any neighbourhood only a few elders became owners of Bell.

Two features of the Taita shrine system would seem anomalous were one to think primarily in terms of lineage shrines. One is that, although the eldest of a man's sons had prior claim to the father's own shrine or shrines, they had to be consecrated anew for him after misfortune caused him to be divined-for. All sons could ultimately acquire their own shrines. Acquisition of shrines was therefore not a matter of succeeding to the father's position. The second superficially anomalous feature is that when a man did acquire a shrine, the elder supervising the consecration did not have to be a member of the new elder's lineage, let alone a *Mlimu* custodian. He could be a member of one of the other lineages in the neighbourhood chosen because of a close matrilateral, affinal or friendship tie with the recipient. What explains both features is the context of the personal shrine rites: elderhood as a politico-ritual role rooted in successful headship of a senior household within the neighbourhood.

The acquisition ritual for Bag emphasized the personal relationship between the recipient and the elder who 'gave' him the medicine shrine. Much knowledge had to be imparted concerning the gathering, preparation and use of the various medicines. As the new Bag owner acquired this knowledge, he was introduced to the greatest part of the lore of good medicines, for the same ones were used in connection with the other shrines. He who imparted knowledge of them set the new elder on the path to prominence in his ritual life.

On the first day, called 'plucking medicines' (*kurura βuganga*), the supervising elder and his helpers took the neophyte out to gather the ingredients for the medicines that would go into his Bag. On this occasion juniors could not be called upon to help since they were not allowed to learn about medicines officially. However, they could be called upon for services at other phases of shrine acquisition. They gathered plants growing near cultivations and dwellings as well as plants found in wild and uninhabited places, plants of the uplands and those of the plains. After their reward, a beer drink, the supervisor with one or more elders assisting him prepared the medicines. In this long and painstaking job, the various plant parts were charred and pounded, then put into thin tubes made of maize husks to await the day of putting them in their gourds. On one of the days of preparation a goat called 'needle' (*lugumba*) was supposed to be slaughtered and its skin prepared for sewing into the actual bag for the medicine gourds. In actuality, that could be passed by. A hemp sack or plaited straw bag could be used instead; this called attention to the fact that the bag or sack was not itself the shrine, the latter consisting of the assemblage of medicines.

The major celebration followed putting the medicines into their gourds. The filled gourds received the blessings of the supervising elder and his assistants who performed *kutasa* over them, praying for the prosperity, health and fecundity of the new owner, his herds and his people. If they had not already been given gifts, each one who helped in the gathering and preparation of medicines received a 'thank-offering' (*minga*) of two shillings and an 'apportionment' of fifty cents. Beer, cooked vegetable food and roasted bits of goat meat were served out to all who helped bless the new Bag owner or who publicly bore witness to his receiving the shrine in the proper way. Portions of uncooked goat meat went to the chief supervisor and his assistants. After acquiring Bag the new owner undertook a course of lessons from the supervising elder in the use of the medicines in their various Bag rituals. On completing the course he gave his instructor a gift of his own choosing.

In a more detailed description of a Stool acquisition one can see features linking it to Bag consecration on the one hand and to acquisition of Bell on the other. When a man already owning Bag had been divined-for and declared in need of Stool, he had to arrange for the ritual with a *Mlimu* man who need not be the custodian of his own lineage shrine centre. The day fixed, the recipient undertook to furnish a sheep and three pots of beer. One pot went to the elders who jointly consecrated the shrine and conferred it on its owner; one was for junior witnesses; the third was drunk by all the men present, juniors and elders sharing together. The beer would actually have been brewed by the neophyte's wife and women assisting her, who also provided a pot of unfermented cane juice for use by female participants. There was supposed to be a fair sample of men from the recipient's neighbourhood, members of his own and other lineages.

Like the other shrine acquisition rituals, that for Stool took place at the homestead of the recipient. To it the presiding elder brought a small stool roughly made from either one of two suitable woods (*mkoroβo* or *mwangola*). When all the men had gone into the herd enclosure, the *garo*, an ox hide was spread out. On it the master of ceremonies squatted while he drilled or chipped out a hole in the stool's centre for the reception of medicines. Shavings and chips were gathered and saved.

Initially, *kutasa* was done by all the men present, led by the supervisor. Women then and later did *kutasa* by themselves at their place outside the *garo* from where they could watch proceedings by looking over the top of the fence. They could not enter the *garo* unless called in by the men. At one Stool consecration the first person to perform *kutasa* alone was the recipient's wife, who was called in. She said:

Ai! I say, you Stool, you have a fire kindled for you today [i.e. you are consecrated]. Allow the stock and the people to be well. Let the herds multiply like grains of sand; may they fatten and may every person here grow healthy. If there is a sorcerer here among our herds, may he surely die, and the man of peace, may he surely thrive!

Similar recitations were made by the presiding elder, echoed by the chorus of everyone present.

The supervisor and an assisting elder made a little altar (*kilili*) from the branches and twigs of medicinal plants, some of the same ones used in providing Bag medicines. The sheep was then strangled and, as it died, its urine was collected in a leaf cup. Some of the urine was then put into the hole in the centre of the Stool together with a bit of the dung of hyrax, goat and cow. Some of the sheep's stomach contents was added together with medicines from the presiding elder's Bag. The elders did *kutasa* again (theirs must be reckoned one *primary kutasa*), this time spraying the beer over the stool and saying:

You Stool, let your wrath cool; leave this man alone. His possessions do not prosper and his claims come to nothing. May his illness, we say, be at an end, and may there be peace and health for herds and herder alike. If a sorcerer is at work, may he die in a single day; if he is bitten by a snake may he get no antidote, may he not find a doctor to cure him, may he not get up again – indeed, thus we say. You – cool, and cure this man and his possessions and his people also.

βula was read from the sheep's intestines in order to see whether the offering was acceptable and whether anyone's secret anger was threatening the effectiveness of the shrine. On this occasion the signs showed anger in the heart of the recipient's aged mother, who was involved in arguments between her sons concerning bridewealth still owed from their inheritance for the mother's marriage. She was called into the livestock enclosure to do *kutasa*, casting out anger, blessing her son and addressing Stool:

You, Stool, today you are consecrated, and may the anger seen in *βula* be ended altogether. May this man get along peacefully with his brother, may they be like one thing, may they not hold themselves aloof from one another as they do now. I perform this act sincerely,[11] asking health for humans and animals and all things, indeed thus I say. If there is a sorcerer harming this man, may he surely die; even if it is the herds which he is harming with his medicines, may he surely die, may he find no doctor to lift him up.

The Stool together with three containers of medicines and the lump of red earth to be used in tending the shrine were laid on the altar. On a fire lit beneath the altar burned pieces of three selected 'strong' woods. Then a thong was cut from the sheep's skin and tied around the right wrist of the recipient. Over the thong, called 'the thing of preference' (*kikundi*; *kukunda* = to love, like, prefer), the elders did *kutasa*.

Next, cooked cowpeas were brought from the dwelling by one of the women assistants, one pot for the elders, one for the junior men and one for the women. The new Stool man and his wife now 'initiated' (*kutamana* = to originate the use of, to initiate) the food by taking the first mouthfuls. Together they walked about the herd enclosure, tossing the cowpeas about them, blessing the herds and people and appealing to the Stool:

We say, may the herds bear plentifully like cowpeas, and we too, may we do so.
May there be so much livestock as to defy herding, and so many children as to defy
overseeing. You Stool, cause the herds to bear, and may you never be angry again.

The children requested were not necessarily supposed to be those of
the Stool man and his wife, who might be past the age of childbearing.
Sons whose children would continue the husband's line counted among
the human increase sought. There remained the possibility that the Stool
man himself, as a prosperous elder, might take one or two junior wives
who would add to his progeny.

Male assistants brought out 'beer of the altar' (*chofi ya kilili*) in two
portions, one for the elders and one for juniors. They also built two fires
for roasting the scraps and internal organs of the sheep. From the elders'
portion seven small pieces of meat were initiated by the new Stool owner,
who thereby became one of the senior elders. Further performances of
kutasa followed and a general beer drink ended the day's proceedings.

At each of six succeeding movements of the sun the new Stool man
kindled a fire under the altar, assisted by the presiding elder. They put
herbs into the fire along with the shavings left from drilling the hole in
the Stool. Each time this was done the recipient's livestock, or at least
some of it, was medicated by being made to walk through the smoke of
the fire. The man himself, forbidden to bathe in the river, continued to
wear the sheepskin thong on his wrist.

On the eighth day or at the eighth movement of the sun the master of
ceremonies and his assistant(s) ritually dismantled the altar (*kudua kilili*),
sharing afterwards in a pot of beer to which honey was added. Supervising
elder and new Stool owner planted lablab beans, some close to the house
and others in the livestock enclosure in the holes left by the posts of the
altar. The posts themselves were wrapped in bark cloth and stored with
the new shrine. (Any beans that grew from those planted in the kitchen
garden were to be eaten by humans, the ones from the altar site being
fed to the livestock.) The crosspieces of the altar, the leaves and twigs
laid on them and the other bits of debris were scattered about the waste-
land near the homestead. A final *kutasa* by the presiding elder, his assis-
tant(s) and the Stool owner ended the ritual of acquisition. Following it
the new senior elder removed the thong from his wrist and bathed in the
river. Should he be divined-for again on account of Stool, he would now
make an offering of beer to the shrine, offer an animal to it or anoint it
with fat. He could also assist the custodians of lineage shrines, especially
the custodian of his own lineage's *Mlimu*.

The ritual by means of which Bell was acquired followed the general
lines of the Stool consecration. The performance took place in the livestock enclosure, with *kutasa* and animal offering as the central acts. Com-

mensality in the form of drinking beer and sharing bits of roasted meat and cooked vegetable food followed the lines of sex divisions and age-status groupings. The new owner's wife played a part like the one she had in Stool acquisition. Bell was consecrated on an altar that had to be ritually dismantled, and the altar smoke was again supposed to be used to medicate the new owner's livestock. The owner himself was not given a thong to wear. Instead, he was anointed with fat and red ochre similar to the way in which an infant was anointed at the conclusion of a Bag treatment. Restrictions lasting for seven movements of the sun intervened between the main acts and the final ones.

The man acquiring Bell had to supply an ox to offer, an expenditure marking a major ritual. Otherwise, one feature stood out. That was the use of a chant, appearing in only one other rite, the Ox of *milungu*. Called simply *Mraru*, chant, its performance required the presiding elder to call out a series of statements and questions to which the other elders chorused their agreement. The leader called out:

Haya-haya! We give our brother his shrine. May all possessions cleave unto him. If I say this, is it well?

The others chanted a formula of assent, whereupon the leader shouted again:

Now then, if I say that today we make our brother a man of the shrine, a man of Bell, is it well?

After another chanted agreement the leader finally asked:

This beer we drink today, do we not drink it for the sake of the Bell of our brother? If I say this, is it well?

They all respond again, with the leader joining in,

It is *mraru, mkengera, mrasimbo, mriaŋombe.*

Elders denied knowing the meaning of all the words. *Mraru* was simply 'chant', *mkengera* was a medicine plant reckoned to have powers of blessing. No one offered a meaning for *mrasimbo*, and only one man suggested that the last word was an archaic form of *mrijaŋombe*, 'eater of cattle'. Whether or not the words separately had 'meanings', the significance of the chant was clear: it pronounced the new Bell owner one of the most senior elders by consent of those who, in his neighbourhood, already occupied that position. Importantly, *Mraru* was chanted by the elders as they danced together on an ox hide laid in the livestock enclosure and, for the last chorus, the new Bell owner was made to dance there with them.[12] As with the lesser shrines, the owner could now be divined-for on account of Bell's demand for tendance, when he would have to offer an animal, offer beer or anoint it with fat mixed with red ochre.

The shrine acquisition rites displayed a large number of features

characteristic of other ritual. The shrines appeared as personified agents
with which human beings *had to interact*. Acquisition and also tendance
made use of many accessory medicines. Some were of vegetable origin,
both domestic (cowpeas) and wild (plant parts gathered from uplands and
plains); others were from domestic animals (ox urine) or wild animals
(hyrax dung); red ochre was the chief mineral substance used. A variety
of actions conveyed the virtues of medicines to livestock, humans and
shrines: anointing, aspersing and fumigating were employed. *Kutasa* was
of course the central act, with the performance of *primary kutasa* by
specified persons making social relations intrinsic to the efficacy of the ritual.
The utterances accompanying the spraying out of liquid included blessings, supplicatings and urgings of the mystical agents and castings-out of
anger from the hearts of participants. To such *malombi*, prayers, were added
magemi, curses, pronounced conditionally against unknown sorcerers.
Shrine acquisitions required animal offerings, while tendance of existing
shrines included anointing and also offering of either beer alone or with
an animal offering. All of these features were found in other religious
rituals.

At the same time, the acquisition rites formed a specialized set of rites
within *βutasi*, with the sequential relations among shrines shown in a
number of ways. *Saru* and *Knife* were both minor shrines. The first was
the only one that could be acquired by a child and that meant that responsibility for the ritual had to be assumed by the child's parents, particularly
by the father. It presaged the lifelong process of being divined-for in times
of misfortune, with the particularities of diagnosis and prescription shaping
and being shaped by the course of the moral career. Knife was the only
shrine that could be owned by a woman or by a junior male householder.
Its association with cultivating bespoke the arrival of individuals at the
stage of 'well-grown' but not completed social person. Only Knife required
the offering of a mere chicken. The Great Medicine shrines called for a
goat (Bag), a sheep (Stool) and an ox (Bell), the order of relative values
matching the order of the shrines from least great to greatest. The acquisition rite for Bag emphasized the teaching of medicines that even a
beginning elder should know about and which would be used as accessory
medicines in a host of other rites. Stool's acquisition, by including the use
of a wrist thong, resembled adoption ceremonies and marked this rite as
incorporating the shrine owner into the ranks of senior elders. The chanting of *Mraru* in the Bell acquisition, together with the dancing of old and
new elders on the ox hide, made the new owner one of the 'brothers' who
were the local community's supreme elders.

In terms of changes in social personhood, it is useful to compare the
Bell acquisition rite with the 'leg-thing' rite for infants and small children.

In the latter, the ox hide uniting the subjects of the ritual and isolating them from other participants was placed in the doorway of the house. As I have noted, the emphasis in this rite was on the relationship of mother and child in the domestic family, but the performance brought the domestic unit into contact with a mystical agent having a non-domestic focus. As the subject of religious action the small child was the passive, dependent recipient of adult care. The acquisition rite for Bell, as for the other Great Medicine shrines, took place in the livestock enclosure. The latter was part of the homestead, but that part associated with men for whom livestock were both resources for the support of the domestic unit and property entering into political standing. Centred on the entitlements available only to males, the ritual required female participants to remain outside unless they were called into the enclosure to perform *kutasa*. In 'leg-thing' the child sat on the thigh of the mother, whose nurturant breast might be treated. The major shrine rites presented an ageing man as one with human and animal dependents. In the example of Bell acquisition, the mother appeared as a woman dependent on her sons for completion of her bridewealth.

Nonetheless, it is highly significant that the mother's anger remained effective and had to be dealt with in order for the entitlement of elders to be effective. This calls attention to the fact that in the growth and elaboration of personhood, later developments did not simply *replace* early formations but *incorporated* them and built out from them. Here religious ritual provided recognition of a psychological truth. Officially, publicly, an elder was someone who had ceased to be 'some people's child' even though his mother remained alive. But he could never cease to be the son of a particular mother and father; indeed, as a human being he could never cease to be someone's child, even though he had become someone's father, perhaps someone's grandfather, mother's brother and so on. The elaborated personhood of the supreme elder, created and displayed in religious ritual, did not exclude the mode of the dependent child. It might even be argued that the ritual situation of women, for whom the persistence of early family formations was not elaborately disguised by the trappings of politico-ritual office, was truer to the psychological facts of Taita life.

The persisting centrality of close kinship relations, as set in a wider social and religious context, could be seen in a ritual held when a man or woman reached advanced age, with well-grown grandchildren. The *Ox of milungu (ŋombe ya milungu)* was sometimes said to placate *all* mystical agents, *Mlungu*, the Great Medicine shrines, the ancestral shades, the hearts of living kin, and even the hearts of domestic animals, all of whom had become angry. In fact utterances were directed chiefly or even exclusively to the shades and to living hearts. On this account a detailed description properly belongs in the next chapter, whereas my concern here is with the place of *Ox of milungu* in the moral career. When an elderly person was critically or persistently ill, he or she was divined-for, first by *Saru* divination and then by *βula* haruspication. Should there be many bad signs in *βula*, including an inauspicious sign for the subject's own path or future, the interpreters were likely to say that all the *milungu* were angry and required an ox. Offering of the most valuable of domestic animals marked the seriousness of the occasion, as did very wide participation. As many kin and neighbours were supposed to attend as possible and to perform *ƙutasa* on behalf of the subject. The performance itself was highly structured to incorporate, as intrinsic to its efficacy, the different kinds of social ties obtaining between the subject and various participants. For a male subject the rite included the chanting of *Mraru*, as in the Bell acquisition; a woman's *Ox of milungu* omitted it. In old age, then, a person had to take account publicly of the facts of a long life during which he had affected and had been affected by many other persons. He had to attend to the likelihood that his own actions had aroused anger in the hearts of those close to him, including the dead as well as the living, from whose influence he could not escape. The chanting of *Mraru* noted that the persistent importance of kinship in a man's moral career was supplemented but not supplanted by his political role. *Mraru* was omitted from an elderly woman's *Ox of milungu*, since a political role, associated with shrine ownership, was absent from her career. The actual performance, with its attention to the details of social relations, structured this religious experience of old age, presenting the completed living person in his inter-dependence with the senior dead, with still living equals who were both friends and rivals and with juniors in subordinate positions. Their relations with each other were also presented, providing the schema of the wider society within which the moral career had its being. In a real sense, *Ox of milungu* was a retirement ritual. It completed the unfolding of religious experience this side of death. After it there was, religiously, nothing left for the person to do but join the ancestors.

Not all persons who survived to old age had the respect of others. Some were heartily disliked for their individual qualities of character, some loved and admired. Some had considerate children, grandchildren, children's spouses and sisters' children, others were treated with discourtesy. Those who found themselves impoverished in old age might suffer neglect – that was true especially of old widows without sons or whose sons had died or gone to the towns. Ideally, old women were the repositories of valued lore and skills: as midwives, performers of cliterodectomy, instructresses in girls' initiation, tellers of folktales, purveyors of love medicines. Above all, old women were admired quite realistically for their thorough knowledge of food crops in all their varieties. A few old men, besides having acquired personal shrines, assumed other ritual positions: as custodians of lineage shrine centres, Rainmakers, Defenders or keepers and administrators of juridical medicines. Usually such men would have succeeded their fathers, but individual qualities would have insured their acceptance by lineage and neighbourhood members. In each case the ritual official would have undergone a period of training at the completion of which he would have given a gift to his father, who could not simply give away elders' knowledge. Someone who became a *Saru* diviner also had to be trained by a practising diviner who need not have been father or other kinsman. A fee had to be paid for that training, in addition to which a man had to feel assured that his ancestors, willing that he practise as a diviner, provided him with inspiration.[13] All men were supposed to learn *βula*. Since haruspication was done in public, juniors could pick up the details. And some elderly men were laughed at for their clumsy attempts at interpretation while others were listened to respectfully. Seers did not have to be prominent elders, for their inspiration by the 'people of long ago' enabled them to direct that the great public rites be held without requiring them to know how to carry them out.

One elderly man in central Dabida owned Bag, Stool and Bell; he was custodian of his lineage *Mlimu*, neighbourhood Rainmaker and a prominent diviner. He had realized the most elaborated social personhood possible in traditional Taita society.[14] A man like that, together with his fellow elders, dominated the *ad hoc* councils in which lineage and neighbourhood decisions were adumbrated. In any one neighbourhood, there were no more than a dozen such men in whose control lay all community affairs of moment; in some neighbourhoods a tight group of only four or five elders really settled everything. They regulated both the ritual and the non-ritual affairs of their local group, insisted on the ritual settlement of disputes, the retraction of curses, the cursing of sorcerers and thieves and so on. They were the acknowledged authorities on *βula* divining and, through it, influenced the course of sorcery accusations. When they fell out among themselves, the local community experienced a major crisis.

No 'big man', *munda mbaha*, was autonomous. Big men, through the system of shrine acquisitions, operated as a self-recruiting body of authorities who kept watch on each other. In addition, public opinion limited the independence of individual elders through the notions about sorcery. A man who looked to be extraordinarily successful could arouse the suspicion that his wealth had not all been gained legitimately. The threat of being accused of sorcery made elders go carefully. They had to avoid performing rituals alone. Shrine owners, *Mlimu* custodians, Defenders and Rainmakers always called on other elders to assist them, to bear witness to the correctness of their performance and to share responsibility for it. Sister's husband or wife's brother most often functioned in that capacity. Especially when they went out to gather plant materials for making medicines, elders took along assistants and witnesses who would testify that they had not gathered sorcery medicines. It was said that a man knowing a great deal about medicines must know as much about the harmful ones as about the good ones. In short, the men who 'knew medicines', who really knew 'the Taita way', were thought of as having potentially dangerous powers requiring the vigilance of their neighbours and kin. It did happen in fact that some elders were accused of sorcery. Of others it was said at their death that sorcery medicines in their possession had turned against them after remaining unused for some time. The result of being divined-for could signal an ignominious end to a moral career. Conviction of sorcery barred a person from installation as an ancestor. It set up a barrier between the dead person and his or her descendants whose tendance should have insured the influence of personhood from beyond the grave.

In pre-Independence days the position of 'modern' men held different ambiguities. Wealth that had not received ritual recognition, remaining untransformed into traditional religious participation, could not be the basis of legitimate authority. Therefore young men who accumulated money from wages or from the sale of cash crops were anomalies. So were Government-appointed chiefs and headmen, most of whom were Christian and therefore could not be shrine owners or ritual officials. The younger of them, not having gone through the boys' part of initiation, were not socially adult. No matter how much money or livestock they accumulated, no matter how many powers Government conferred on them, they could not become big men. Many readily acknowledged themselves to be 'little children who [did] not know the Taita way'.

Every religion includes an image of personhood. Every religion in practice helps to create personhood, by ritually conferring its elements upon the individual, and by transforming happenings in the life cycle into moral events. Religious conversion must inevitably entail acceptance of a new concept of the self if it is to be more than a nominal change in 'religious affiliation'. The difficulties felt by white Christian missionaries working among the Taita undoubtedly resulted in part from conflict between different concepts of the person. Some Roman Catholic missionaries to the Taita had fewer difficulties. Their views of natural religion seemed to encourage investigation of *βutasi* along lines closed to low church Anglicans. It was asserted by some of the Holy Ghost Fathers that traditional Taita religion included rituals corresponding to the seven sacraments of the Roman Catholic Church, a view that was put to use in writing a Taita catechism. They also seemed to recognize the organic bonds between what Taita were and did religiously and what they were and did in other aspects of their lives, without condemning all aspects of the traditional culture and society. Anglican missionaries varied considerably among themselves, but on the whole took a much more sombre, disapproving view of the Taita way. It therefore does not appear strange that some Taita influenced by the Anglican missions felt the attractions of the puritanical revivalist sects moving through parts of East Africa. One would occasionally meet a member of a revivalist sect wearing a large wooden cross around the neck. He (or she) would ask whether one had a 'Christian name', which simply meant a Biblical name. There would follow a vociferous confessional sermon that told how the individual had given up various sinful practices and that advised the listener to do the same. But what was troubling to many Taita, both βatasi and Christians, and to some missionaries as well, was the way in which sectarians rejected their non-sectarian neighbours and kin. They judged all who did not join them to be sinners with whom it was wrong to associate. Some went so far as to refuse to eat together with members of their own domestic families, and might declare that the white missionaries were too steeped in sin to be considered true Christians.[15] Whatever else was happening in the lives of the sectarians, they were, I believe, attempting a radical redefinition of their personhood, one that would not allow of being rooted in the traditional social order. In accord with this, one church elder, inclined to favour the sectarians, preached a sermon in which he denounced all concern with the kichuku, with everything to do with kinship and lineage. For such Taita, to put off the old man and put on the new required them to reject all the old attributes of personhood insofar as these were bound to the old social order.

In every religion part of the image of the person is provided by the meaning attached to death. For those Christian Taita who were Anglicans, there were of course no masses for the dead and no cult of the saints. Therefore there was nothing that *ritually* replaced the tendance of ancestors. To eternal life in Christ, they were taught, participation in any of the rites of βutasi was a stumbling block. Roman Catholic Taita had the cult of saints and masses for the dead. On the other hand, they found it difficult to accept the celibacy of priests and nuns who, in their view, were wasting valuable reproductive resources and depriving themselves of ancestorhood. For βatasi and Christians alike death did not put an end to the person. But for βatasi, the relations between close kin were important both before and after death. Someone who had been divined-for could therefore be required throughout his moral career to perform the anger-removal rites, to which I now turn.

4

THE HEARTS OF KIN:
ANGER-REMOVAL RITES

Being divined-for in terms of angry hearts was an experience shared by all adult *ßatasi* whatever their stage of the life cycle, whatever their sex, age, lineage membership, wealth or political advancement. Divination for anyone might identify misfortune as the result of incurring the anger of a living person or one of the dead. Formulations concerning the mystical danger of angry hearts comprised (among other things) an idiom in which Taita treated of the sources of conflict and its consequences. That idiom made sentiments or emotions the very stuff of relations among the living and between the living and the dead. Overt conflict was dealt with partly by non-ritual means, partly through juridical rites and partly through sorcery accusations that did not always lead to a juridical rite. Mystically dangerous sentiments arising out of conflict within the family were the theme of anger-removal and placation rites. Those rites aimed at alleviating misfortune by restoring good feelings. An individual's well-being was made dependent on restoring good relations with others. That peace, health and general well-being could all be referred to as *sere*, the same word used for a 'cool' or 'clean' heart purged of anger, shows the connection between individual welfare and the sentiments aroused in interaction.[1]

Divination matched results – misfortune, with likely causes of anger. Knowledge of the subject's affairs played an important part. Here the particulars of social personhood were attended to since the nature of the persons' social involvement differed. Diviners also drew upon their knowledge of individual lives. Although everyone was divined-for in terms of hearts, sources of conflict and reasons for anger could differ widely. Divinatory interpretations were circumscribed by the conviction that the dangerous anger of hearts arose only in certain social relationships and for certain reasons.

Taita stated it as an ideal that anyone from among the People of the Hills deserved courtesy and hospitality. Yet it was said that in the past people unprotected by a blood pact partnership had preferred not to go into distant communities. During pre-Independence years, strange

Taita entering a neighbourhood unannounced were often received coldly and suspiciously and not infrequently with rudeness. In practice only kin and neighbours were treated as having a right to good treatment while strangers received it, if at all, as a sign of special good will. A stranger who was treated rudely, refused food and lodging, or mocked by the local children might well become angry. But his anger could not bring misfortune automatically on the inhospitable indigenes. Diviners never named strangers as the source of mystically dangerous anger. Strangers might be held to have put the evil eye on a rude child, but their angry hearts could not operate directly.

A neighbourhood was comprised of people who were said to have come to 'understand one another'. But a neighbourhood was the arena for innumerable disputes over livestock and land. A series of misfortunes suffered by a party to a dispute could lead to covert or open accusations of sorcery. Also, children were generally discouraged from accepting food, which might conceal sorcery medicines, in neighbourhood homesteads other than those of close kin and affines. But except under very restricted circumstances, neighbours who were not close kin or affines could not harm one another by means of their hearts. They were not named in divination as the source of damaging mystical anger.

For people who were close kin or affines, divinatory interpretations worked on the principle that when two people stood in a particular relationship certain kinds of action on the part of one would be likely to cause ill-feeling on the part of the other, whose anger might bring misfortune upon the first or, in certain cases, upon himself. Actions arousing this dangerous power transgressed the rights of another who was expected to feel angry or resentful. The doctrine of hearts operated, then, as a folk theory of social psychology encompassed within and contributing to the larger view of misfortune, its nature and its causes. Misfortunes caused by angry hearts included the bodily and 'mental' illness of the subject of divination. Where the subject had human and livestock dependents, misfortune also included bereavement and impoverishment. The latter misfortunes, which I call 'indirect', as against the 'direct' affliction of illness, complicated the picture of mystical responsibility, as will be shown.

I state some general principles here, leaving the details of social patterns for a later section. When someone other than a child was divined-for on account of a serious or persisting illness, his misfortune could be attributed to the anger of someone among his close consanguineous kin, either living or dead. The anger of someone other than a consanguineous kinsman or kinswoman was not named in such cases, with one partial exception. A husband's anger at his wife was considered potentially dangerous – but to himself, not to her.[2] When the illness or death of a child occasioned divination, the cause could lie in the mystical anger of a person, living or dead, who was a close consanguineous kin to the child. But since a child was treated socially and religiously as an extension of the parents' social personhood, particularly as an asset of its father, the latter might be under 'indirect' attack from the anger of either consanguineous kin or affines, who were kin to the child itself. A child's anger at its parents was also effective, but acted by turning against the child. Impoverishment through the illness or death of livestock could be treated in the same way: as an 'indirect' attack upon the livestock's owner by his consanguineous kin, living or dead.

The words 'could' and 'might' appear above in relation to possible diagnoses because, as previous chapters have shown, the human heart was only one among a number of mystical agents whose anger might cause misfortune. That is not to say that all kinds of divinatory interpretations were equally likely in all circumstances. For example, with independent householders striving for wealth in livestock as well as for thriving children and grandchildren, diagnosis in terms of personal shrines competed with that in terms of hearts. Young married people, on the other hand, were focussed on the birth and nurturing of children, and their interest in livestock was in large part limited to the problems of paying bridewealth. For such persons, the possible need for Bag curing rites or offerings to lineage shrines competed with interpretations requiring anger-removal and placation rites.

To treat misfortune caused by a living person's anger required understanding how the anger had been aroused. It was not enough for the sufferer to acknowledge his actions. The first step was rather for the angry person to acknowledge his anger. Sometimes that required 'looking within the heart' (*kuzigana ngolonyi*) to uncover the reason for anger of which the person might have been unaware, or which he had forgotten. In an emergency, as when someone was desperately ill, people sometimes recalled being offended by the sufferer. They then proceeded to cast out their anger ritually without first consulting a diviner. Divination was soon performed to be sure of a diagnosis both correct and complete: more than one mystical agent was sometimes involved in the same misfortune, in which case a variety of ritual actions resulted.

As in all rituals of *βutasi*, *kutasa* was central, with *primary kutasa* performed by the angry person. In anger-removal rites, the utterances accompanying the gestures of *kutasa* declared the anger to be 'finished'. Performance of *kutasa* in that way, together with sharing beer, cane juice and perhaps food, constituted the whole of many rituals. The person casting anger out of his heart was said to be 'cutting the curses' (*-dumbua magemi*) even though outwardly he had pronounced no words and intended no harm. Refusal to cast out anger amounted to cursing the person and in some relationships it would be considered sorcery. In fact I never heard of anyone refusing to do *kutasa* when named by divination at a time of crisis. (There were, however, parents who refused to 'cut' actual curses pronounced, justifiably, in the Taita view, on recalcitrant offspring.) Not only did the responsible person cast out anger, but he or she called down blessings on the sufferer, demonstrating positive good will. It was impossible in a crisis to wait for the sufferer, whose own actions had aroused anger, to make amends. Neither could anger-removal wait on ideal ritual arrangements. If no beer or cane juice was available, water had to be used or saliva alone, if necessary.

More elaborate procedures were followed when an ill person ordered the slaughter of a 'goat of aid' (*mburi etesia*) for haruspication. If *βula* showed a kinsman's anger responsible, a pot of beer was sent to him with a message asking for *kutasa*. First of all the angry person squatted outside his house near the right side as one faced the dwelling. He performed *kutasa*, declaring that the curses were cut and expressing the wish that his kinsman should recover. Then he went to the house of the ailing person where there was more beer as well as porridge prepared with a relish of chicken. Again the angry person did *kutasa*. If the two people had had an open quarrel recently or if both had been angry, they did *kutasa* alternately, declaring their anger at an end. Each blessed the other to have health, prosperity and peace with his fellows. Then they shared the food and drink, joined by any kin or neighbours who might be present. If the misfortune was illness of a child the same performance took place, and so also for sick livestock.[3]

The simple anger-removal rites described carried the implication that the suffering transgressor would cease his offence, whether of omission or commission. Should he not set things right he could expect to be divined-for again for the same reasons. Taita did not always rush to do what was expected of them but sometimes they were pressed to do so. Someone might announce that his heart had been injured. Adult son or adult daughter were the ones named as having behaved so badly that the wronged parent required placation (*kuvoya*) by means of a gift, in order to cool his heart. Persistent refusal of *kuvoya* was dangerous, for to the original anger was added anger at having been refused what had been demanded. Should the offender suffer misfortune, a diviner, pointing to failure to *kuvoya*, would direct that the placation gift be offered. Beer or a small gift of money or purchased goods were the usual placation gifts. In other situations no open demand for *kuvoya* was made. But seed divining or haruspication showed that the sufferer had failed to give or do something very much desired by one close to him. Adult children and husband could be named. A parent might be angrily dissatisfied with a son's failure to supply a desired blanket, or a wife might be angry because her husband had refused to give her money for a new headscarf or to help her with the heaviest farming tasks. The offender then had to make amends with a small placation gift as well as by doing or giving what he formerly had refused. The gift had to be proffered before witnesses, with the pronouncement that it was given to cool the heart of the angry person. The latter did *primary kutasa*, declaring an end to anger and calling down blessings on the offender, who also might do *kutasa*.

Some rituals focussed on the dead were more complex than those concerned with the hearts of the living only. As with the living, anger, dissatisfaction or resentment of a dead kinsman could bring 'direct' or 'indirect' misfortune, according to the general principles stated above. Anger had to be removed that well-being might be restored and further misfortune averted.

The dead retained their personal identity and communicated with the living by visiting misfortunes on them or threatening them by means of evil omens. Death was figured as the crossing of a bridge or road lying between the world of the living and the world of the dead, *βarumunyi*, 'where the dead are'. Tales were told of people who, fainting or suffering from a nearly fatal illness, had crossed part of the way and spoken with some of the shades whom they recognized. In pre-Independence days some of the more interesting of the stories dealt with the relations of *βatasi* and Christians in the world of the dead.[4] Some stories mentioned unquiet dead who returned to the world of the living as ravenously hungry ghosts. While ghost sighting had little importance in Taita life, the conceptualization of ghosts as hungry fits the oral emphasis of Taita ritual discussed in Chapter 6.

βarumu were supposed to take an interest in the affairs of the living and particularly to oversee the maintenance of the norms of kinship. They were angered by quarrelling among their descendants, visiting mystical rebukes upon those who took advantage of their fellows when estates were divided or loans recalled. Diviners and haruspicators named individual angry dead, seldom farther back than great-grandfather and more usually parents and grandparents. They also cited reasons for anger. The rituals placating the dead then had to call upon those individuals, announcing the offerings and repeatedly supplicating for an end to anger. *βarumu* were also treated as taking up each others' grievances and combining their anger to produce a single misfortune or series of misfortunes. With few exceptions the effective dead were the forbears of the living persons who offered them tendance. That is, the dead were for the most part tended as ancestors, but not everyone who died became an ancestor.

Transition to ancestorhood began with the mortuary observances, which lasted a full week for a married person with children. A month later came the funeral, called 'Hair', *maridia*. *Maridia* effected the end of mourning when the hair was cut that had grown since the chief mourners had shaved their heads at the death. During the last part of the mourning period most of the problems of the estate were supposed to be settled, together with the future of the widow(s) and children. The cause of death should have been ascertained through *βula* divination. Although disputes might proceed behind scenes, the funeral had to be a public occasion of solemn peace, when in a series of seven orations elders told how they came to learn of the dead person's final illness, how they visited him and how the death had surprised and shocked them.

The main attention by a man's sons and heirs was the offering of the *Ox of settling the earth* (*Nombe esiria ndoe*). In theory, it was supposed to be done as part of the funeral, but that seldom happened. Disagreements among the heirs might prevent its being carried out quickly, in which case they risked arousing the dead father's anger on two counts, their dilatoriness and their quarrelling. If sons were children or unmarried youths, they would not take possession of their inheritance but would be in the care of their father's brother or other close agnate. Then the offering would wait until they were in a position to divide the estate among themselves. The usual Taita inclination to delay ritual attentions also operated. The animal to be offered had to come from among those left by the deceased. Its slaughter required the heirs to give up part of what they received from him. If the estate did not include an ox, then they might have to go through long and tedious transactions to acquire one, given the fact that the purchase of animals by 'money in the hand for cattle on the hoof' lay outside the customary exchange system. The *Ox of settling the earth* was also offered to a mother. That attention was delayed until after the father died if she had pre-deceased him, for it was the duty of her sons, not her husband.

Ultimately, every person who left adult children and who was not disqualified by conviction as a thief or sorcerer was supposed to be installed as an ancestor by having his or her skull placed in a lineage *Ngomenyi*, place of the (skull) shrines.

Inside the small grove or thicket concealing a lineage skull repository might be a tiny cave or rocky cleft in which the skulls lay; elsewhere slabs of rock had been placed in the ground as shelves. Strictly speaking, the skulls were supposed to be kept upright, set on their bases,[5] and placed in rows according to the principles cited below. Actually wind, falling branches and the incursions of browsing goats disturbed the arrangement. With or without a natural rock shelter, rainwater softened the earth and skulls sank into it. In one grove some seventy skulls were counted which were wholly or almost wholly visible, standing on rock slabs placed in the slope of a little wooded hill. Parts of unascertainable numbers projected from the muddy ground into which they had sunk. In this way the physical stratification of the skulls paralleled the structural position of the dead; those whose skulls had sunk far into the earth had ceased to receive tendance as individuals.

The chaotic appearance of skull repositories signified no lack of concern. The only attentions to the dead requiring people to visit the skull places occurred when someone was installed as an ancestor by placing his skull in *Ngomenyi* and when, if necessary, a skull was replaced after being knocked out from the midst of the others by an invading goat. At other times it was dangerous to touch a skull. No lineages were completely Christianized or secularized in late Colonial times, and so everywhere there were living persons who cared about what happened to the skulls. They made offerings to the dead at the side of the paths leading towards the repository and also at the homesteads.[6]

In theory, a man's skull should be set in front of that of his own father so that the most recent dead were in the front row (as well as vertically topmost) seen from the bottom of the slope or from the opening of the cave or cleft. Women's skulls belonged to the left of their husbands', in order of marriage – except that a barren wife could not be installed.[7] Whatever the actual arrangement of skulls, installation, which Taita characterized as occurring 'one year or perhaps two' after death, never took place immediately after death. If a man left young unmarried sons, his skull would not be exhumed for many years. If the sons were grown and married, exhumation waited on an appropriate divinatory diagnosis. When it was determined that misfortune had been visited upon a son because the dead father wished to have his skull placed in *Ngomenyi*, installation took place. A woman pre-deceasing her husband would not have her skull installed until after his had been placed.

Most people were buried at the edge of their homestead clearings, if possible under a tree. The actual exhumation was done with digging sticks by a son (usually the eldest), accompanied then and later by an elder of his lineage. The latter had to come along to give instructions, to bear witness to the propriety of the actions, and to 'help with the work'. He did not have to be a close agnate.

After the skull was cleaned and wrapped in banana leaves, a sheep supplied by the son was killed and its stomach contents collected in a wooden basin. The basin, a small pot of beer and the wrapped skull were then taken to *Ngomenyi*. Having smeared the skull with the stomach contents, the son placed it according to the elder's directions.

1. *Yale* peak, source of rain medicines

2. Mid-day at a homestead

3. Elder addressing a council of neighbours

4. Young women dancing home after a day of farm work

5. Divining from entrails (*Bula*): reading the signs at a Bell acquisition

6. Divining from entrails (*Bula*): examining the flap and the veins

7. Ancestral skulls in a lineage repository

8. Calabashes of medicines belonging to a Bag shrine

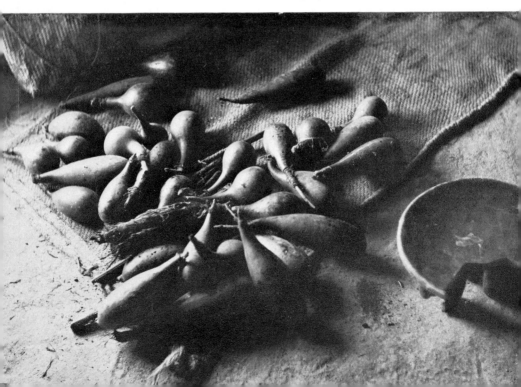

9. Chipping out the hole for medication in a new Stool shrine

10. Medicating a new Stool shrine

11. A new Stool shrine on its altar for fumigation

12. A new Bell shrine on its altar for fumigation

13. Keeper of the oath medicine (*mugule*) administering the potion to another elder

14. Elder orating at a funeral

15. 'Someone's child' astride his mother's back while she pounds maize cobs

16. Father and son await the Bag man

His was the *primary kutasa*. He told the father that on that day he was being taken to *Ngomenyi* as he wished, that the beer was offered to him and spat for him, that he should accept it, and that his heart should be cool towards his descendants. The men asperged the vicinity of *Ngomenyi* with the stomach contents using, as was required, twigs of the *mvumu* tree as an aspergillum. Finally the men purified themselves by washing their hands with the stomach contents. Returning to the village they read the sheep's entrails to see whether the dead man would be cool or whether the son and his fellows were endangered by the father's anger or by that of some other mystical agent.

We knew of only one person installed as an ancestor whose skull had not been put in *Ngomenyi*. The father of a living elder was said to have announced to his wife and sons on his deathbed, 'I am human and must dwell forever among humans'. His directions were followed by placing his skull on the storage shelf of the house still occupied by his widow and youngest son.

Although convicted thieves and sorcerers could not have their skulls enshrined, they did cause people to be divined-for. They joined the ranks of those who had died a violent death by murder, suicide or execution, whose death or burial sites became places of *Seso*, the curse of violence. Such places were marked either with a stone or by planting an *isai* tree, said to be especially long-lived. A person divined-for on account of *Seso* had to slaughter a chicken unless the deceased had ordered greater offerings before going to his or her death. That was the case with a woman supposed to have hanged herself because men of the village killed and ate a calf given her by her father. She said that all of her descendants would have to offer a sheep when divined-for on account of *Seso*, Cursing.

A *Seso* ritual required visiting the accursed place in order to asperge it with *kioro* made from the stomach contents of the animal to which had been added some of the blood and the crushed leaves of 'cool' and 'peaceful' plants. As usual, a twig of *mvumu* served as an aspergillum. *Kutasa* was performed at the site with beer and also with small pieces of meat, asking the shade to be cool. Since the animal was usually a chicken, there could not be a reading of the entrails. But if a sheep had been killed, haruspication would reveal whether the offering was acceptable or whether more danger threatened. The ritual of *Seso* thus resembled that of skull placement, but did not install the deceased as ancestor. Violent death worked a curse that installed the deceased as a shade requiring tendance, one visiting misfortune on the living irrespective of their conduct. The sufferer did not in every case have to be a descendant of the deceased. A person could be affected by any *Seso* of his own great lineage or of his mother's great lineage except when the deceased had specified those of whom tendance would be required. Violent death apart from execution as a criminal did not officially bar someone from regular installation as an ancestor. I am not certain how often it happened in practice that a murder victim or suicide was actually installed. The woman who hanged herself guaranteed that she would receive the attentions of her own descendants whether or not she was installed in *Ngomenyi*. Furthermore, she insured that offerings to her would be more rather than less onerous than the ordinary ancestral ones which required either goats (less valuable than sheep) or chickens, the lowliest of domestic livestock.

The barring of criminals from *Ngomenyi* was thought to work a hardship on their descendants. For that reason descendants, notably grandsons, tried to have the deceased rehabilitated. Sometimes, as happened during our stay in Taita, they were successful. Their plea that they suffered an unfair disability, being unable to offer normal tendance, could be met sympathetically when events of the past no longer echoed in bad relations among the living. The curse of a violent death kept alive the memory of the deceased. But only a properly installed ancestor was thought to exercise a benign influence whatever misfortune he might visit upon his descendants.

When someone was divined-for on account of ancestral anger, either beer was offered alone or with an animal, according to the seriousness of the misfortune and the nature of the signs. Who participated and who performed *primary kutasa* varied somewhat. Usually, however, *primary kutasa* was done by the senior-most male descendant of the shade, with the closest and most senior male collaterals joining with their own *kutasa*. Commonly an elder closely related to the subject acted as master of ceremonies, supervising the proceedings, aided by other kin in carrying out the various tasks.

When beer was offered, two men, one carrying a small calabash of beer and the other a calabash fragment containing a small quantity of beer, left the subject's village by way of a path leading toward the *Ngomenyi* of the shade's great lineage. Not far from the village they stopped and the man carrying the calabash fragment placed it on the ground in the vegetation at the side of the path. Then, with the calabash of beer, they crossed to the other side of the path where, facing in the direction of *Ngomenyi*, they did *kutasa*. Though varying with the circumstances, the prayers were all much like the following examples:

We give you your Seven [ritual beer]. If it is you who are ruining this man's body, let him live in peace, you and your fellows.

Your Seven is here. Drink it, So-and-so [addressing the shade by his personal name as X son of Y], you and your fellows. Let this man recover. Let him get well and prosper.

After *ḳutasa* the men returned to the homestead without looking over their shoulders. On the plaza in front of the subject's house, the master of ceremonies led another *ḳutasa*, for which a common container passed around the circle of male participants. Each man took a little beer in his mouth and, waiting until the bowl had gone around, all spat out together and gave their chorused assent to the prayer of the supervisor.

If the shade had demanded a goat, the animal was then led to the plaza. The master of ceremonies seized it and rubbed its nose with the leaves of the *mḳengera* tree, forcing some of the leaves into the animal's mouth.[8] While doing so, he urged the shade to accept the goat as an offering. Assistants throttled the goat, then butchered it and put some of the scraps and inner parts to roast and other bits to boil in a pot together with some of the goat's blood. Seven small pieces of cooked meat, each taken from a different part of the animal (including the liver) were placed on one banana leaf as an offering to the dead, while seven similar pieces were put out for *ḳutasa*. The two portions were taken to the path in the same way as the beer. The men accompanied the spitting out of meat fragments with similar prayers:

All you shades, you our grandfather and his fellows, let this man be in peace. Tomorrow and the day after and the day after that, may he ask for porridge [i.e. may he be well enough to have a good appetite].

When the men returned to the village all participants joined in *ḳutasa*. The roasted bits of meat and any remaining beer and cane juice were shared after reading the entrails. If *βula* showed some lingering ancestral anger but the subject's future or 'path' was all right, no further steps had to be taken at the time. But the next time an animal was slaughtered in the homestead for whatever reason seven small pieces of meat would be placed at the pathside. It was supposed to be inauspicious if pathside offerings were left completely untouched. On the other hand, some Taita held it to be virtually impossible for offerings to remain untouched, for even if no other creature partook, a small insect like a fruit fly, the *chiβiriri*, would do so.

A person, especially a man of advanced years, might be required to offer the sacrifice of *Ox of milungu*. Coming towards the end of his life, it was almost a retirement rite: after its completion there was nothing new left for the subject to do religiously. *βutasi* had unfolded within his own lifetime which, as it drew to a close, should have been leading towards his own installation as an ancestor. Therein lay the ritual's special importance. A series of inauspicious *βula* readings or one showing an unusually bad combination of signs was the immediate occasion. More especially, a number of bad signs combined with one indicating that the subject's own 'path' or future was 'dead' called for *Ox of milungu*. Significantly, the 'path' signs for such a man were interpreted not only in terms of his own possibly failing health, and his own possible death, but also emphasized his livestock and, more especially, his offspring and their relations with him. The need to offer *Ox of milungu* arose, so Taita said, from the anger of all the *milungu* and of *Mlungu*. Although 'all the *milungu*' was taken by some to mean all the shrines as well as all the hearts of the living and the dead, in practice the ritual consisted of offering to the dead and anger-removal from the hearts of the living; *Mlungu* was not specifically called upon. Elaborations surrounding the features shared with other anger-removal and placation rites required the participation of many people in various capacities.

The supervisor, an elder, was assisted in certain crucial tasks by the subject's son-in-law and by the subject himself, who on this occasion was required to perform tasks normally assigned to subordinates. The ritual began with the slaughter of the ox by the son-in-law aided by contemporaries and supervised by the presiding elder. As in the other offerings described here, the animal had to be rendered unconscious bloodlessly. Then its throat was cut. For *Ox of milungu* the beast was struck on the head with a small battering log. As it fell its mouth was held shut, for its bellowing (indicating that it was still conscious) would be a bad omen.

While the animal remained whole all those present, men and women, did *kutasa* over the fallen beast's head, calling down blessings on the subject and praying to the shades to leave him in peace, allow him to recover and his people to thrive. (One offering of *Ox of milungu* in 1951 called attention repeatedly to the fact that the subject and his sons were not on good terms. Prayers reiterated the hope that sons gone to work in the cities would return and cleave to their father, that he and his children should live together in peace, that the sons should come back and help their father by herding his livestock.) Men other than elders took in and spat out ordinary beer while elders used aged beer (*nyarigi*) from the lineage shrine centre; most women used unfermented cane juice but some past childbearing used beer. Among those doing *kutasa* with ordinary beer, the men who killed the ox made use of the 'beer of the battering log' (*chofi ya kiringo*); it was ordinary beer, but supplied by the subject himself, who also served it to them himself in individual calabashes or tins rather than delegating the task to a junior. (Of course if the subject of the rite were very feeble, someone else would have to perform this and other tasks. But I think it likely that this retirement rite was ideally carried out before someone was devastated by illness or infirmity.) The other non-elders got their beer from a common pot in which beer contributed by the subject was mixed with beer requested of kinsmen and brought by the latters' unmarried daughters.

While some assistants butchered the ox, others built two fires. On the men's fire built near the livestock enclosure, the usual bits of meat and internal organs were roasted and blood was cooked in a pot. Near the house, the women's fire was used to boil soup made with water and scraps of meat. Male elders and junior men had to receive separate portions of meat and blood, with elders laying claim to the internal organs, especially the liver. Women ate their own portions of meat and blood. While the meat and blood were still cooking, however, a reading of the ox's entrails would show whether someone held anger in the heart that threatened the subject's future, or whether sorcerers were at work. Actually, it was unlikely that those close kin whose hearts could individually affect the subject would still be alive for his *Ox of milungu*. Injury suffered by *all* of his living and dead kin and neighbours was the theme and, as usual, the possibility of sorcery had to be considered. It was important that people search their hearts, cast out anger found there, and pronounce blessings on the subject.

In this 'all hearts' ritual, tendance was given separately by women and men, to male and female shades. Women did *kutasa* and offered at their hearth near the house. After putting out the fire once the cooking was done, old women, led by one of their number, spat beer over the hearth-stones. Junior women spat cane juice. Their prayers on one occasion included the following:

We say, you shades, eat your goat. Leave this man in peace, him and his homestead, that he may live in peace with his children. And your beer which is here, drink it.

Then they poured out a cane juice offering on the three stones of the hearth and followed it with an offering of soup, similarly poured out.

Near the men's hearth, the usual seven pieces of meat, this time mixed with cooked blood, were set aside for the shades, and similar portions were for the men assigned to perform pathside *kutasa*. Two or three went to the path leading in the direction of the *Ngomenyi* of the subject's own great lineage. If his mother came from a different great lineage, a separate group of men had to make pathside offerings in the direction of that group's skull repository. While close agnates offered on his behalf to his lineage ancestors and close matrikin offered to the shades of his mother's lineage forbears, the subject himself remained in the homestead. He divided the ox's carcass so that every participant could take home a separate portion of uncooked meat.

Upon the return of the men from the pathside, another *kutasa* was done, followed by commensal eating and drinking according to groups determined by sex and age-status. It was considered most important that for the men's beer drinking there should be no unmerged pots of contributed beer but rather that drinking vessels must be filled from the one common pot and then circulated within a group of men.

Some time after the bear drinking had been in progress, the elders sang *Mraru*. They did not dance on an ox hide as when a Bell shrine was conferred nor did the presiding elder offer a formula for aggregating the subject to a new status. He called down blessings on the subject and the other elders joined by chanting *Mraru*. In this way they completed the most elaborate of the anger-removal and placation rites. Placation, anger-removal and blessings offered by men and by women, by the subject's agnates, by his matrikinsmen, and by his affines and neighbours were rounded out with blessings pronounced by fellow elders. *Mraru* was not chanted at the *Ox of milungu* offered by an old woman, as I have noted, but otherwise the ritual was the same.

For both men and women, this offering, which perhaps is better called a 'completion ritual' rather than a retirement rite, set the subject's relations with those closest to him or her in the context of a wider social network. At the centre of that network the most critical relations remained those between parents and children and between spouses. To explicate anger-removal and placation rites, it is necessary to turn to the nuclear family, its roles and relationships as they were presented in *βutasi*.

A general view of the effects of angry hearts within the nuclear family reveals differences among relationships respecting mystical anger. Unmarried sons and daughters were subject to ordinary parental discipline. They were not divined-for on account of mystical anger aroused by their own wrong doing. After marriage, both men and women could suffer from the anger of living parents on account of refusal to meet specific obligations, through disobedience or disrespect, or by failure to show affection. Living father and mother could both visit 'direct' or 'indirect' misfortune. It seems to have been the case that in practice the mother's *hidden* anger was more often cited than that of the father when an adult child suffered, but the father was more likely to demand a placation gift (*ķuvoya*). A daughter who eloped without there having been any courtship proceedings, who encouraged her husband to neglect her parents' demands for gifts, or who neglected her duty to visit her mother to help with the farming courted parental anger. So did the son who, working in town, neglected to send money to his parents or who, living nearby, shirked his portion of the herding work; who disposed of animals without his father's consent, had married against their wishes or had moved out of the parental homestead without their permission.

Such wrong doing was sometimes shown through divination to have been dealt with inadequately during the parent's life, the grievance festering on after death. A dead parent might also cause trouble over failure to offer the *Ox of settling the earth* or in order to make known the wish to be installed in *Ngomenyi*. Dead parents were also much interested in proper division of property among their children and would angrily visit misfortune on sons who quarrelled over their inheritance or tried to cheat one another. A dead mother was dangerous to sons who delayed finishing off the bridewealth payments for her marriage. Besides, dead parents had a claim to tendance and from time to time might demand an offering of beer or the slaughter of a goat. Offspring were not reciprocally dangerous to parents no matter how bitter their feelings. I know of only one case in which a 'father' was divined-for on account of an adult 'son's' anger and then, as the punctuation shows, the two men were not true father and son.

A non-adult child above the age of sense could be effectively angry at its parents, especially on account of overly severe punishment. But the child's anger could not cause a parent's illness; it could not visit direct misfortune upon a mother or father. Neither could a child of any age bring its parent indirect misfortune by causing herd animals to fall sick or die. A child's anger turned back upon himself, causing his illness or even his death. This self-threatening anger of a child added to the load of mystical threats hanging over its precarious life. Even a child's or infant's own mother could be cited as the source of its sickness or death, although her anger was not directed at the child itself but at her husband (see below). Dead children threatened no one.

Living siblings, when children, presented no danger to one another through the anger of hearts. As adults, matters varied according to the nature of the sibling pair. Very rarely, diviners cited a living brother's anger as the cause of a man's illness, but never (to my knowledge) as the cause of his indirect misfortune. Brothers were far more likely to harm each other reciprocally through their quarrelling over property, or else one of them felt the effects of their mutual anger but both were assigned responsibility in a diviner's diagnosis. Living sisters could affect each other directly. Very occasionally, a woman's physical distress, as in one case of difficult childbirth, was attributed partly to her living sister's anger over a transgression of propriety (see below, p. 119). I know of no case in which a dead sister visited misfortune on a woman. It was the brother–sister relationship in which mystically dangerous anger developed, because of the special position of mother's brother.

The relationship of spouses also showed asymmetry, but there the greater mystical danger came from the female partner. Although a husband might, with justification, put a curse on his wife and remove it only after she had made amends, her transgressions did not arouse anger that threatened her mystically with illness or death ('direct' misfortune) or with illness and death among their children ('indirect' misfortune). A husband's anger turned back on himself, making him ill. Furthermore, it operated through the food that the wife cooked for and served to him: he could not safely eat it while very angry at her. On the other hand, the wife's anger was mystically very powerful. Though it was unlikely to cause the husband's own illness, let alone his death, it could harm the herd animals belonging to him and also threaten him indirectly by causing illness and death among their children. Her anger did not rebound upon herself. All this pertains, of course, to living spouses. I know of no case in which someone's misfortune was attributed to the anger of a dead husband or wife.

A few points stand out from the general survey of angry hearts in the nuclear family. First of all, that infants and children were common victims of angry hearts, as they were also victims of other angry mystical agents, accords with two facts. One is the social fact that, as I have stressed repeatedly, children were the assets of their parents, the greatest good. Sons grown to maturity were among the chief guarantors of their father's progress through the age-status system and the sole guarantors of both parents' ancestorhood. Another is the demographic fact of the exceedingly high infant mortality in Taita as in other tropical countries. The high infant mortality coupled with the high value set on children no doubt helped to shape the belief that the death of an infant or child was to be seen as a mystical attack on the parent.

A second point is that if the wife's anger at her husband is set aside, the operation of angry hearts followed the lines of authority in the nuclear family (and otherwise) in Taita society. By and large, members of the senior generation affected members of the junior generation. Excluding the self-damaging anger of a child, there was no reciprocal threat from the angry hearts of juniors.

The third point is related to that near coincidence of the line of authority and the effectiveness of angry hearts. Whether the source of mystically dangerous anger was identified by seed divining, by haruspication or by 'searching the heart', diagnosis brought the reasons for anger out into the open. Conflict had to be acknowledged and dealt with, however fragile settlement might turn out to be in the long run. The power of the ancestors as glorified parents contributed much to the airing of disputes among their descendants. For some persons, the threat of further misfortunes provided an incentive for settlement. Certainly the ritual event occasioned the intervention of other interested parties with advice and persuasion.

All three points are useful and must be given a place in an analysis of anger-removal and placation rites. But they are too general and take too little account of apparent anomalies in the pattern. Furthermore, they do not leave room for developmental aspects of nuclear family relationships as these were presented in *βutasi*. How can the effectiveness of the wife's anger be understood without using one explanation to deal with persons weak in authority and another for those well equipped with it? When dealing with the relative effectiveness of angry hearts among siblings, how is one to understand the differences between the brother–brother pair, sister–sister pair and brother–sister pair as these changed ritually over time? Perhaps above all, how is one to understand how it was possible that a Taita mother could be named as the source of anger killing her beloved child? To answer such questions requires turning first to the nature of the Taita nuclear family in its domestic and developmental aspects, to selected cases, and then to an explanatory model that utilizes critical features of each relationship within the family.

Taita domestic groups were not large and complex formations. The nuclear family, composed of married parents and their children dominated its structure at all stages of the developmental cycle. A new nuclear family began its existence within the household of the husband's parents when a son and his wife established co-residence and so were recognized as a married pair.[9] When the young couple had a child or two surviving early infancy – when they were properly parents – they looked towards moving into a dwelling of their own as satellite householders (discussed in Chapter 3). Just when they did so, however, depended on whether or not the next younger son in the husband's natal family was ready to marry, assuming that the husband was not an only or youngest son who must remain at home. In any event, there were never two married sons resident at the same time. The household grew as more children were born to the head and his wife and it grew further when the eldest son's wife took up residence and began to bear children. It lost members both at the marriage out of daughters and when sons, ideally according to birth order, moved out to become satellite householders. After all departing offspring had gone out, the household could still be large – the youngest son and his wife might have many children, but structurally it would be relatively simple. Somewhat more complex households were headed by the relatively few polygynists, whose wives' sons and daughters followed the usual patterns. The death of the founding spouses brought the household to an end. If he wanted to do so, the youngest son could remain on the old dwelling site with his wife and children. But if he did so, his would be a newly independent household, not a continuation of the old parental one.

Given the large proportion of intra-neighbourhood marriages and the absence of lineage exogamy (by rule and practice), most married daughters remained within the same local community as their parents and brothers. Married sons headed households variously distributed according to the ideals relating to birth order (see pp. 114–15). Their scatter might be measured by the hundreds of yards, especially in areas of concentrated settlement, or they might be spread out over a series of sites on neighbour-ing small ridges where each was closer to other kin than to a brother.[10] As time passed and the parents died, brothers as independent householders could and did change their place of residence, though almost always remaining within the same neighbourhood. Dispersal might increase, but there was often partial or complete reassembling of brothers. In particular, there was a tendency to concentrate again in later life when elderly brothers settled down side by side on adjacent parcels of inherited land. Rights in those parcels had come to them at their father's death, by way of the use-rights of their mother who had transferred use-rights to their wives after the earliest years of their marriages.

To review: the movement out of sons was connected with endowing each one in succession with a nucleus of property rights in land. Residential separation of sons from their parents and from each other was accom-panied by growing jural and economic separation regarding land rights and land use. Matters were somewhat different with livestock, for what-ever the sons' ideal claims over their sisters' bridewealth, in practice the father's control over all livestock extended to determining the disposition of all beasts used in all transactions. Paternal authority in this respect, as also in matters relating to land not assigned to sons through their wives was mitigated by the rights of a man's wife and eldest son. They had to be consulted before any property was disposed of.

Once the father died, brothers, after managing their livestock jointly for a time, held a formal division overseen by senior agnates and mother's brother (the latter as the 'third parent' interested only in seeing justice done). Loans made between them on their own authority or, earlier, by the father in their names, were left for their own sons to collect. For example one man, knowing that his brother's son was planning to marry, would offer an animal or two 'for the sake of my child'. (No bridewealth went to a man at the marriage of his brother's daughter.) If the offer was accepted, it was said that one man had 'given' an animal for the marriage of his brother's son. However, in the next generation the giver's son would claim repayment from his father's brother's son as part of the final settle-ment of their grandfather's estate. A gift between brothers became a debt between patrilineal first cousins, members of an *ifwa*, inheritance group. Members of an *ifwa* also finally settled matters connected with land that had been lent for cultivation to their fathers' sisters, recovering such land from fathers' sisters' sons.

When brothers reassembled late in life, then, they were independent householders who helped or had helped each other with what were major concerns of men's middle and later years. They were still bound together by the rule that there could be no debts between them. At the same time, each looked after the prosperity of his own household and herd. As for religious ritual, by that time they should have offered the *Ox of settling the earth* for both parents and perhaps one or two had seen to the installation of the parents' skulls. Anger-removal rites could still bring them together in tendance of the dead mother or father. They (and their half-brothers by the same father if the latter had been a polygynist) formed a single 'house', *nyumba*, within the three-generation *kinyumba* founded by their father's father. Their own patrilineal first cousins made up the other houses within the small house. In relation to those cousins, who with them made up a single inheritance group, they might by that time also have settled the grandfather's estate. Such men often had close ties of affection and friendship with their agnatic cousins in adjacent houses within the inheritance group and with agnates at the next remove within the small lineage founded by their great-grandfather. Ties of matrikinship, affinity and friendship bound them to other cousins of the same or different great lineages. In particular brothers-in-law and classificatory mothers' brothers' sons made trustworthy friends and helpers. But much as they might look outward to other persons, brothers remained very special persons to one another.

In sum: besides the loving concern enjoined by morality, jural and economic ties demanded that members of a nuclear family maintain life-long involvement in affairs of each other's households long after they had separated from one another. Husband and wife, parents and children, brothers and sisters, first shared the intimacy of domestic family life in a household that never became the large and structurally complex formation found in many other parts of Africa. Residential separation, accompanied by the growing independence of sons and brothers did not end their close association, nor did the incorporation of daughters and sisters in their own conjugal homes. This peculiar combination of familial domestic intimacy and lifelong involvement in jural and economic matters found a place among the truths and necessities of *ßutasi*. Three cases, seen in this light, contribute to an understanding of anger-removal and placation rites.

1. A man, the head of an independent household, was divined-for on account of the blindness of a cow, the animal's trouble having failed to respond to several applications of curing medicine. Seed divination showed the wife's anger to be responsible. Responding to questions put by the diviner, the man revealed that he had refused his wife's repeated requests to buy her a new cloth. The diviner said that the wife would have to perform *kutasa*, casting out anger in her

heart, if the cow was to recover. The husband had better let her buy the cloth and in the meantime should placate her (do *ƙuvoya*) with an additional small gift of money.

2. Persistent but not acute troubles with his digestion sent a man to the diviner. The signs in seed divination were ambiguous and the diviner was not able to elicit any helpful information from the client. The man's wife then suggested that it might be his own anger, directed at her, which was making him ill. She pointed out that he had been critical of the way she did her household tasks and suggested that his anger made it impossible for him to eat her food without falling ill. He answered that that was impossible, that he had not been sufficiently angry for him to harm himself that way. There was nothing to do but wait a little, then try another divining session.

3. In 1952 a man of central Dabida had a goat killed so that a reading of its entrails might reveal why, after three of his children had already died, a fourth was seriously ill. *βula* showed that the wife's anger at the husband had killed the other three children and was now threatening the fourth. Since the couple had not been getting along well for some years, the wife had no difficulty in bringing up many grievances against her husband. She said that he neglected her and that she did not think he loved her. She said that she had felt that 'there was no use in bearing all these children' if all she was to get was ill treatment or indifference.

At the direction of the presiding elder, a senior agnate of the husband, the couple squatted just outside their doorway, facing each other. The husband, using beer which the wife had brewed for him, did *ƙutasa* first, saying that 'The curse of her anger upon the children should be finished'. His wife, he said, had been making a lot of fuss. She ought to realize that it was *he* who married *her* – he had given bridewealth for her.[11] He was therefore master of the house and she should realize that she had no right to make so many complaints. The wife then did *ƙutasa* with cane juice. She said that it was true that her heart had been injured and she was sure that her anger had caused the death of the three children and the illness of the fourth. Now she was casting away her anger forever, so that the remaining children would be well. The curse of her anger would be 'completely cut'.

Some of the witnesses to this anger-removal rite told us privately that they did not think it was the end of the affair. They considered the husband harsh and the couple unlikely to be at peace with one another. 'We'll find them doing it all over again another time', one man remarked.

At their most general level, the three cases exhibit the difference between the occasions for seed divination and some of those requiring haruspication. The blindness of one cow or the persistence of mild digestive troubles, though serious enough to send someone to a diviner, were still 'little matters' or 'affairs of the house'. A child's serious illness following on the deaths of three of its siblings called for killing an animal to read *ßula*, and getting the opinion of several elders as to the meaning of the signs. The asymmetry of husband and wife in the doctrine of hearts also appears. Case 1 shows the wife's anger causing illness among the livestock, and Case 3 the illness and deaths of children she herself has borne. The speculations offered by the parties in Case 2 illustrate the notion that a man as husband harms only himself when his anger is directed at his wife. The partner with the least authority is shown as most dangerous mystically. All three cases show how divinatory diagnosis, in requiring exploration of possible sources of anger, brought disagreement and conflict into the open. Husband and wife had to talk about their actions and feelings in the presence of at least one other person. When the presence of dangerous anger was confirmed, the person who was its source *had to do ḳutasa*, no matter how justifiable the anger might be. The person arousing the anger was liable to reproof when, as in Case 1, the diviner instructed him to offer a placation gift even when none had been demanded by the angry person.

The actions identified in the first two cases as arousing anger would not in themselves have been grounds for formal complaints to kin or affines. A woman might well grumble to her mother and sisters about her husband's stinginess; only real deprivation would make her father and brothers bring pressure on the husband to treat her more generously. Similarly, although a man would make no secret of his wife's shortcomings as a housekeeper, he would not formally complain to his affines (her father or brothers) unless she had persistently refused to cook for him or otherwise defaulted on a large scale. For either spouse to go further, taking public action that verged on litigation, signalled the breakup of the marriage. Therefore in one aspect, the anger-removal and placation rites aired marital conflicts for which no forum was provided outside *ßutasi*. Case 3 concerned a couple engaged in chronic conflict, whose marriage might well end in divorce. Witnesses certainly did not take the view that repeated anger-removal rites would purge feelings and so solve marital troubles. On the contrary, they expected the quarrels between such spouses to continue, bringing anger and misfortunes, and requiring more acts of *ḳutasa*.

The facts of this malfunctioning marriage, as referred to by the parties themselves, point up those critical features of the family appearing in *ßutasi*. The wife complains of neglect and ill treatment, expressing doubt that her husband loves her. His bad treatment of and indifference towards her have made her wonder 'whether there was any use in bearing all these children': she thus speaks of child bearing in terms of an expectation respecting the quality of her husband's behaviour towards her. The husband, on the other hand, reminds the wife and the witnesses that he is to be respected as the jurally super-ordinate partner (it was *he* who *married her*). Since he, not she, is the master of the house, she should stop complaining. He tells her, in effect, that she has no right to be angry. Talking at cross-purposes, the wife speaks about love and indifference, the husband of duty and default. One refers to the spirit of the marriage, the other to the letter. Together they show what could happen when letter and spirit were not joined, according to the doctrine of angry hearts.

All bounded and persisting social groupings exhibit two aspects which I call the *jural* and the *consociational*. The term *jural* refers to the aspect manifested in specific rights and obligations that are defended either by legal sanctions or by their functional equivalents.[12] When a party to a relationship defaults respecting a *jural* obligation, the issues raised for him and for others (both inside and outside the social grouping) concern the nature of publicly recognized rules defining and governing the relationship. Typically, *jural* rights and obligations concern property, services and the exercise of authority. In the *jural* aspect of their relationships, members of a social grouping stand as persons having specific expectations of one another. Judgements, whether made by members or non-members, announce that a party has or has not satisfied expectations by carrying out particular obligations. Concern with real or alleged feelings enters not at all, for the issues are those of conformity or non-conformity to rules. In the jural dimension members of a social grouping cannot escape from the fact that they are also members of a wider society whose rules and practices govern the way they act towards one another. They must look outwards to society at large, to its political structure and institutions and to the instruments with which public authority enforces the conformity of 'private' persons.

In the consociational dimension of their relationships, members of a social grouping look inwards to the fact of their long-term involvement with each other in ways that set them apart from other like groupings. Their expectations of one another are diffuse rather than specific, covering the many different social contexts in which they interact. As persons engaged in interaction (though not necessarily face to face) members focus on the nature of their relationship in general, over time, rather than on mere conformity to the rules. Indeed, rule-governed action becomes reinterpreted. The fact of continued observance of *jural* obligations is treated as based in interaction itself, and the latter is seen as founded on and requiring appropriate sentiments and attitudes.[13] Defaulting from jural obligations is assimilated to failure to meet diffuse expectations. Both are interpreted as demonstrating a deficiency in the allegedly necessary feelings. Judgements are therefore made in terms of the presence or absence of feelings and attitudes. Members attend to the quality of their relationship, to the spirit rather than to the letter. Depending on the nature of the grouping, the required sentiment may be phrased in terms of patriotism, loyalty to comrades, collegiality, civic pride – or familial love.

It may well be that the more extensively relationships are regulated by legal and quasi-legal sanctions, i.e. the more elaborated the *jural* aspect, the less elaborated is the *consociational* aspect and the less they are phrased in terms of sentiment. Yet the importance of both aspects is attested by what happens when obligations are not met. To take some examples from American society: the man who evades being drafted into the nation's army is not only said to break the law, but to be lacking in patriotism. The union or faculty member, who defaults on either specific or diffuse obligations is 'disloyal', 'a bad colleague'. The neighbour who will not clean up his yard has no 'civic pride' and 'doesn't care how the neighbourhood looks'. And the spouse, parent, child or sibling who defaults is said to lack 'love'. Typically, such failures are met in two ways: by withdrawing what are considered demonstrations of positive feelings from the defaulter and by visiting (or wishing to have visited) upon him the full force of jural sanctions, where that is feasible.

Important features of the jural aspect of various Taita relationships have been described in previous chapters. Taita attended to the details of jural rights and obligations, being very ready to discuss relationships in those terms. They also employed formulations that summed up the consociational aspect of social groupings, formulations in which alleged sentiments and attitudes were given a large part. The distinction between a proper member of humanity and one who fell short of general humane expectations appeared in assertions about who did and who did not have proper feelings. A decent human being was said to 'love people' (*wakunde βandu*). Someone thought not to love people might in fact observe the letter of his jural obligations. But he would never go the extra mile, for he lacked the spirit.[14] A true Taita was one who, whatever his origins or those of his forbears, had 'become Taita' and stood with Taita against outsiders. At the level of the local community, the concept of 'understanding' came into play. Here the long-term involvement of neighbours was seen as founded in sentiment: people of a neighbourhood inter-married 'because they have come to understand one another'. That mutual understanding entailed loyal attachment and not merely knowledge of local custom. It therefore contrasted with the disloyalty of the traitor, called 'an eater in two places' (*mja ƙuβi*), i.e. a person who only seemed to give and take the good will demonstrated by the mutual hospitality of neighbours. Above all, it was in the family that love and lack of love were seen by Taita themselves to be crucial.

The *jural* aspect of relationships in the Taita nuclear family was governed by a number of inter-related bodies of rules and institutions. Concerning these, individual persons had little or no choice, being bound by the laws of the society at large. First of all, the rule of descent made the sons and daughters of a married couple members of the husband–father's patrilineage; the husband–father in the nuclear family was therefore closest senior *agnate* to his children, who were also agnates of each other. Secondly, valid marriage was established by the transmission of bridewealth, on behalf of the husband, from his father or himself, to the father and mother's brother of the wife. This passage of bridewealth shaped one side of the husband–wife relationship as *affines*. It also made the mother–child relationship, in one aspect, a relationship between sons and daughters on the one hand and their father's closest affine on the other. Thirdly, marriage rules prevented unions between first cousins. Therefore even couples who belonged to the same great patrilineage had to come from different 'inheritance groups' and most commonly were members of different small lineages within the same great lineage, or of different great lineages within a neighbourhood. Though in the wider scheme of relationships a mother could be agnate to her children, within the nuclear family she was, effectively, their closest *non-agnate*. She linked them with their matrikin and, especially, with their closest senior male matrikinsman, the mother's brother. Fourthly, the rules governing the ownership and transmission of rights in land and livestock as property and resources made mens' rights dominant but not exclusive with respect to the rights of women as wives, mothers and daughters. Fifthly, *jural* rules structured domestic organization by (a) designating the proper residence of spouses as 'patri-virilocal': that is, a woman went on marriage to live with her husband, initially in his own father's homestead; (b) designating the husband–father as head of the family: he held ultimate control over land and livestock as property and claimed specified services from the wife and children, especially the sons; he exercised final authority over all members of the nuclear family so long as they resided under his roof, and over wife and sons so long as he lived. The superior rights of the husband–father were, however, only part of a set of reciprocal rights and obligations.

Insofar as members of a Taita family were close agnates, close non-agnates, and close affines to one another, they looked outward to the wider scheme of patrilineal organization, the bilateral kinship network and the overlap of these in the long-term affinal relationship binding lineages of a single neighbourhood. But the family was also in important respects a closed system. As a residential unit in one phase of its existence, the family formed the basic unit in the land use system and the fundamental unit in production and consumption. It was also the group within which children were produced, trained, and reared to adulthood.[15] Participating as they did in this inwardly focussed system, members of a family were more to each other than the *jural* labels indicate. Their relationships also had a *consociational* aspect which for convenience I simply call the *familial*.[16]

An explanatory model making use of the distinction between *jural* and *familial* (*consociational*) aspects of relationships in the nuclear family can account for the pattern of diagnoses and their corresponding rituals. It must be phrased in *as if* terms. The explanation says that, in the area of anger-removal and placation rites, there is a pattern of diagnosis such that an observer's predictions can coincide with actors' choices by positing that the actors act *as if* they were using certain principles.

My explanatory model makes use of the distinction between *jural* and *familial* (*consociational*) aspects of relationships within the nuclear family. Since Taita themselves did not use the categories *jural* and *familial*, but rather talked about rules and feelings, the explanation is not one that they themselves would offer. It is based on what Taita actually said and did. But it places their words and deeds in the context of more general social processes having a wider occurrence.

I have said above (see p. 98) that in bounded, persisting social groupings, jurally based actions are reinterpreted, being seen as founded in and requiring appropriate sentiments and attitudes. Defaulting from *jural* obligations and failing to meet diffuse, *consociational* expectations both come to be treated similarly in certain contexts. Either can be looked on as signalling a breakdown in the relationship *as a composite one*, having both letter and spirit, with the spirit seen as somehow more truly fundamental to maintenance of the relationship. It is as though a failure to observe either kind of obligation leaves the relationship stripped down to the barest *jural* requirements. The injured party, 'freed' from the moral demands of diffuse obligations, may take recourse to jurally based redress or its equivalent, which may be ritual in nature. Relationships in which this process occurs chronically are precarious ones, possibly on their way to dissolution. But all relationships of the kind I am referring to are subject to such disturbances from time to time.

In the case of the Taita nuclear family, we should expect to find that failures to observe either *jural* obligations or *familial* expectations had some similar results. That did in fact occur: while massive and persistent *jural* defaults ultimately brought jural consequences, occasional *jural* defaults and also failure to meet diffuse expectations mobilized mystical anger. It is *as if* the relevant family relationship had been reduced to its barest *jural* requirements, whereupon the injured party's mystical anger attacked by way of the transgressor's *jural* claims. *Jural* and *consociational* rights and obligations were distributed in a complex way within the family. We should therefore expect the diagnosis of mystical anger to display corresponding complexities requiring examination of each relationship within the nuclear family.

HUSBAND AND WIFE

Taita marriage, as a jural transaction, assigned obligations or duties to each spouse. The wife was required to provide sexual, reproductive, domestic and agricultural services for the husband. Through the marriage transaction, any children borne by the woman were affiliated to her husband's line. She went to the village of her husband, a non-agnate, to reside and cohabit with him; she tilled the soil of a non-agnate in order to feed him and the offspring who were jurally his. For his part, the husband had to take a non-agnate into his village and ultimately provide her with a house, acquiring thereby a 'friendly stranger' (*mugenyi wake*). Allotting fields for her use, a husband had to allow his wife the freedom to arrange her gardening tasks as she liked. He owned both land and herds as property, but he could not avoid recognizing her claim to lifelong use-rights in both; hence the requirement to consult her before disposing of any property.

Simply as affines, husband and wife shared interests in each other's well-being, in their progeny, and in the land and livestock available to them as property and resources. But their shared interests were the product of differentiated interests. The husband, to the wife, was the person to whom certain obligatory actions were owed. They were owed because the livestock paid by him or on his behalf were the source of the bridewealth claimed by her own kin for the transfer of rights in her services. Similarly the wife, to the husband, was the person to whom certain complementary actions were due. Above all, her reproductive capacities were the source of the children he claimed for agnatic affiliation. Sexual services, seen jurally, were simply the means by which children, the 'profit' of the marriage, were to be produced. Attention to the woman's claims as wife and as the mother of his children was required of a man. But, in the last analysis, he could point to the payment of bridewealth as underlying his super-ordination. He 'had married her'; she 'had been married' by him. He was head of the family in the very nature of things. Looked at this way, in the narrowest *jural* terms, there could be no necessary implication of personal, affective involvement in the relationship of spouses as affines. Of course in order for their differentiated interests to be realized, they had to be meshed in the running of the household economy and in the breeding and rearing of children. But, in strictly *jural* terms, no 'love' was called for: only duty.

Persistent, massive default by either party could occasion *jural* action by the other. In the extreme case (and only after numerous quarrels and reconciliations) a man could send his wife back to her parental home with the *Ox of escorting*. Or she might on her own initiative leave her husband, refusing her kinfolk's urgings to return. Thus whatever the ultimate outcome, either spouse could set in motion *jural* proceedings leading to the dissolution of the marriage. A very large proportion of Taita men and women did enter first marriages that ended in divorce, after which they settled down in lasting unions. However, that is not to say that those marriages that lasted were all happy or free of occasional troubles. Even if *jural* duties were met, spouses might default on *familial* (*consociational*) obligations.

The *consociational* aspect of the Taita nuclear family, to which I shall henceforth refer simply as the *familial* aspect, was founded on the fact that the members of a family lived or had lived together intimately, sharing the most ordinary of daily activities. Husband and wife were drawn together by their common interest in maintaining their *household* as a residential and economic unit while the children were unmarried. They were also jointly concerned to maintain the family as a grouping whose activities satisfied individual needs for food, shelter, sexual satisfaction, reproduction and a variety of psychological satisfactions. In its *familial* aspect, the husband–wife relationship was one obtaining between a man and woman as fellow householders and mates, with a common interest in producing and rearing their children. Economic and other tasks, seen in this aspect, were apportioned between husband and wife in a complementary fashion, for the maintenance of a physical and social environment and for nurturing and training their offspring in that environment.

Anecdotally, the point I am making can be seen in a brief account of a visit to a homestead where the family was awaiting the arrival of a local Bag man. There were two children, a boy of about four years and another son of about eight months for whose ailments the shrine treatment was sought on the word of a diviner. The husband, very much a junior householder, sat in the shade of the thatch with the baby on his knee, talking to his wife's brother and the visiting anthropologists. The wife, busying herself with household tasks, became aware that the older boy was too hungry to wait for the cooked meal and so gave him a piece of cassava and a knife with which to peel it. The child sat down on a log where, kindly admonished by his father to take care with the knife, he found all adult eyes watching him. Both of the parents then proceeded to display the child's cleverness, laughing at his 'cute' replies to questions. When a butterfly alighted near him and the child answered a visitor's question by correctly calling it *kifurute* in a rather precious way, both parents chuckled and beamed with delight. In this small scene, in nature like others beyond number, there was no question of *jural* niceties such as patrifiliation. Husband and wife were a conjugal pair taking pride in *their* son.

Given the *familial* aspect of the husband–wife relationship, obligations laid down jurally could in part be reinterpreted. For *her family*, not merely for the man who 'married her', a woman carried out her tasks of supplying the bulk of the garden produce, keeping the house tidy, collecting firewood, drawing water, caring for the children and so on. These were jobs which had to be done if family life were to be maintained. In the same way, the carrying out by the husband of his tasks of heavy gardening, herding, building, wage earning, and so on, contributed to family life and so were not isolated *jural* observances.

Moreover, between members of a Taita family there was the expectation, continuing after the family had ceased to be a residential group, that members display a generalized, diffuse willingness to meet requests, to acquiesce in each other's wishes, to give help and material assistance when called upon. Thus more than minimal performance of her tasks was expected of the wife. Her husband also expected loyalty to and affection for him, not as the man giving bridewealth for rights in her capacities, but as mate, co-resident and the co-parent of the children in whom their most important common interests centred. *General* consideration of his wishes and well-being was expected, making it possible to speak of diffuse, *familial* obligations. The wife similarly expected concern with her needs and deference to her wishes from the husband, whose total role consisted of a great deal more than his narrowly defined *jural* duties. The mutual expectations of spouses constituted a special case of the rule that previous demonstration of one party's concern for the other's well-being was taken to indicate willingness to remain concerned. The 'previous demonstration' consisted, as in all such cases, of the whole backlog of shared and complementary activities. For each party, renunciation of the limitations of the *jural* 'letter' for the *familial* 'spirit' maintained *their* family, and was identified by Taita as 'love'. Persistent and massive inattention to *familial* expectations showed, in Taita terms, a lack of love. Sporadic failures in duty or in love were expected to arouse anger.

In the first case outlined above, the illness of a cow was treated, as usual, as a misfortune visited on the man owning the cow. That misfortune was identified by a diviner as caused by anger on the part of the man's wife, the anger itself having been aroused by the husband's refusal to buy her the new cloth for which she had asked repeatedly. Now a man who left his wife in rags and tatters while investing in more and more livestock might well find his wife's parents or brother joining her complaint that he was failing to fulfill his *jural* obligation to clothe his wife properly. That seldom occurred. The case described was far more typical: it shows a wife asking for her husband's attention to her wish to have 'presentable' clothing, whether or not he 'owes' it to her. In fact, of course, the *jural* obligation to clothe the wife adequately did not lay down the requirements in detail – the vagueness of many *jural* duties, probably inevitable, undoubtedly obscured the differentiation between 'duty' and 'love'. But in a sense, that is irrelevant. Seen as a failure to fulfill the letter of an affinal obligation, a man's refusal to buy his wife a new cloth called attention to the differentiation of their interests *as affines*: particularly to aspects of her economic dependence on the man who 'married' her. But seen as the man's failure to fulfill the *familial* expectation of general, diffuse concern and deference to the other's wishes, it also registers that differentiation. In terms of the explanatory model, it is *as if* the relationship were stripped down to the barest *jural* requirements. Facing her husband across the gulf of differentiated *jural* duties, the wife attacked, through her mystical anger, the livestock which were *his property*.

The second case shows the workings of *jural* complexities in divinatory diagnosis of anger and its effects. The diviner could not give a clear diagnosis. But the wife's suggestion accorded with the assertion (by diviners and others) that a husband's anger at his wife would not harm her directly, but would rebound on himself through the medium of the food she served him. A wife's slovenliness, whether a matter of neglecting particular duties or of failing in diffuse wifely consideration, directed attention to the differentiated and potentially conflicting interests of husband and wife. So far this kind of situation, in which the husband's anger was supposed to have been aroused at the wife's transgressions, parallels that of the first case, in which the husband offended the wife. But the rebounding of the husband's anger on himself must be accounted for. It accords with the fact that for the Taita husband, *jural* and *familial* aspects were differently related to one another than they were for the wife. The major *jural* assets of the relationship always belonged to the husband, as the *jural* super-ordinate. The children of the marriage were always jurally 'his', and never jurally 'hers'. The wife herself was also his asset for as long as the marriage lasted, for he 'had married' her and was head of the family. Assuming that, according to the explanatory model, the wife's transgression would be treated as if it had reduced the relationship to the *jural* essentials, where would the husband's anger against his wife as affine be directed? If his anger caused her to be ill, he would only be harming himself, for he would be injuring a *jural* asset of his own. But if, as happened, his anger was thought to rebound on himself, then he would be attacking her indirectly by defining himself as the affine whom she was obliged to feed. The food that should have been given and eaten in the spirit of conjugal intimacy became the channel for dangerous affinal conflict.

In the third case, a wife's anger at her husband was identified as the cause of three children's deaths and the illness of the fourth. The case is a critical one even though rare in the extreme nature of the misfortune and its diagnosis. Taita men asserted that there were two types of women. A few, it was said, engaged in sex primarily 'for the sake of husbands', that is, for the sake of sexual pleasure. But most did so 'because they like children'. Men and women alike held that, once a woman had borne a child, it became the object of her greatest care and devotion. For a woman to be barren was a tragedy, to lose a child to death was a grievous blow, escaped by few. Yet this case presented a woman as capable of anger that mystically destroyed her own infants and children.

As indicated earlier, an unmarried individual appeared in Taita divination and ritual as 'some people's child', not as a person in his or her own right. That was especially true of infants and small children, whose social selfhood was merged with parental identity. The small child's or infant's physical self was closely identified with the mother and her nurturant function: the Bag shrine treatment that has been described registered the belief that a child could get worms from the mother's milk. However, the child as an asset was above all an extension of the father's personhood. In *jural* terms, the offspring of a marriage were 'his' and as such they were subject to the mystical danger of his wife's anger directed against him, not against them.

The third case therefore shows clearly the differentiation of *jural* and *familial* (*consociational*) elements in the family, specifically within the husband–wife relationship. I have pointed out that the case shows husband and wife talking at cross purposes. The husband reminded the wife of his jurally super-ordinate position relative to her, but the wife talked about his neglect and lack of love. In terms of the explanatory model, the husband concentrated on the *jural* aspect of the relationship while the wife emphasized the *familial, consociational* aspect – or, rather, the husband's withdrawal from that aspect. His own words seem to confirm the reduction of the relationship to its barest *jural* essentials. In the context of so impoverished a relationship, the wife could say that she felt 'there was no use in bearing all those children'. The children were not theirs but his, the assets of a man who was merely her affine. Her anger, corresponding to his withdrawal from the *familial* side of the relationship, attacked the children as his *jural* assets, not as her beloved offspring.

The capacity to destroy her own children through anger directed at her husband; the potential danger of her milk to her infant; and the danger of food cooked by her when eaten by an angry husband – these presented a Taita woman as mystically a formidable person. The three capacities were inter-related. Presenting the husband with cooked food was not only in itself a *jural* duty of the wife, but was also bound up in belief and custom with the sexual aspect of their relationship. Since for a man and woman to eat together indicated sexual intimacy, couples shared food only privately; providing cooked food was the duty of the woman who shared a man's bed.[17] Children resulted from sexual activity and, as I have indicated, Taita men showed some concern with the possibility that women might prefer sexual pleasure over the 'practical' consequences of intercourse. Both children and men had to be nurtured. *In toto*, a woman as wife and mother was seen as central to the satisfaction of the most intimate bodily needs of husband and children. While lacking jural control, a woman was expected to be diffusely and generally giving of nurturance and nurture-associated satisfaction. But such diffuse expectations could not really be controllable by jural means and, moreover, could be withdrawn in response to the offences of the husband. The absence of any jural power ultimately to compel good motherhood and loving wifehood may have contributed to the belief in the mystical potentialities of women. That in itself was related to the fact of women's place in the mother–child relationship, the paradigmatic kinship bond. Seen as the source of inescapable claims, that fundamental social bond shaped the view of women as endowed with vast powers for good and for ill.[18] The ease with which beneficent femininity could change into its threatening counterpart can be seen in the interpretations given by diviners of the shape of the caecum in *βula*. Full and rounded, the caecum was interpreted as 'breast', a promise of fertility and nurturance. Pointed, it was 'digging stick', a woman's agricultural implement and symbol, through its use in digging graves, of impending death.

PARENTS AND NON-ADULT CHILDREN

Taita held that a child's anger would not injure his parents directly by making them ill or indirectly by causing misfortune among the herds. During our stay we never heard of a diviner diagnosing such misfortunes in terms of a child's anger. On the other hand, a child could indirectly injure one or the other parent, but more especially the father, by means of anger aroused by over-severe punishment.

Each parent provided the Taita child with elements of his social position and social selfhood: the father by patrifiliation making the child a member of his agnatic lineage, the mother by providing the link with her own agnates, mother's brother's people to the child (his *βaβuye*; sing. *aβuye* = mother's brother). The child, for whose life, care and education the parents were responsible, was thought indebted to both mother and father. After he reached the 'age of sense', a child was expected to meet his filial obligations primarily by obedience, especially to the father as *jural* head of the family. Lapses brought punishment.

An unmarried child had only a limited participation in the social system outside family and domestic groups. His duties were few – that was certainly the case for uninitiated boys and girls, and the social consequences of his actions did not stretch very far. Primarily the *jural* asset of the father, a child was the evidence of the relationship between his parents and, through them, of their relationships with other kin. At the same time, parents had a common affectionate interest in the child (or at least they were supposed to) and the child in turn contributed to the maintenance of the family by performing such tasks as lay within his capacities. The child's function as object and source of affection, too, was part of the familial aspect of his role in relation to his parents. Here lies the significance of the child's claim against over-severe punishment.

To the father and mother, then, a child was obligated jurally. His *jural* obligations to parents were manifested in obedience. However, demonstrations of diffuse affection, respect and filial obedience were directed to mother and father, not only as closest senior agnate and closest senior non-agnate, but simply as *loving, caring parents*. Belief in the child's ability to injure himself on account of anger at the over-severe parent (father) registered this distinction. For over-severe punishment, according to the explanatory model, would have signified parental (paternal) withdrawal from the *familial* aspect of the relationship. Appropriately, the child's anger destroyed or threatened to destroy himself, for withdrawal of the father from the *familial* side of the parent–child relationship would throw the emphasis on the *jural* aspect according to which the child was only a *jural* asset. It was as an asset of his father that a child was attacked by his own anger, not as the loving and loved offspring whose very existence created a family where before was only a married couple.

1. *Parents and adult son*

The *jural* aspect of the father–son relationship in Taita was dominated by the facts of agnatic descent and the transfer of heritable rights in property from father to son. The body of *jural* rights and duties marking out the relationship had to be observed over the son's lifetime and beyond the lifetime of the father. A son's failure to observe filial duties subjected him to paternal discipline that might extend to a formal curse; and a father's anger reached out from beyond the grave.

For the mother, a son realized her primary affinal duty to bear the children continuing her husband's agnatic line. With advancing years she had the right to claim the honours due to the provider of an heir. From the son's point of view, his mother was closest non-agnate, the link with his maternal uncle's people. She had the right to his respect and obedience while she lived and to his ritual tendance afterwards. A vital feature of the mother–son relationship in its *jural* aspect was the son's duty to complete bridewealth payments for her marriage should any be outstanding at the father's death. Failure to observe his *jural* obligations subjected a son to her discipline; her curse was held especially potent, her post-mortem anger very dangerous.

The anger of a living father or mother could be named as responsible for an adult son's misfortune, calling for performance of *kutasa* and perhaps also for the offering of a placation gift in *kuvoya*. This ritual involvement of parents and adult son was connected with the developmental cycle of the family and domestic group. For over time, after the son married, had children born to him, and moved out into his own house, alterations in both *jural* and *familial* aspects provided numerous occasions for conflict, with its suggestion of affection withdrawn.

When the son had a son of his own born to him, his wife was supposed to name the baby after its paternal grandfather. The infant's father thereupon could say that he had 'begotten his father' (*wava ndee*). From the point of view of the older man, his own 'birth' in his grandson created his three-generation line within the four-generation small lineage founded by his own father; the continuation of his own segment was foretold. In the community at large his status was enhanced as a man with both an adult son and a grandson: advancement in shrine ownership could be expected. But the son's own special interests appeared as well. The birth of a child of either sex gave him his own family of procreation, enabling him to lay claim rightfully to greater independence from his father and mother. Also, the birth of a son began the emergence of his own sub-line within that of his father. Moreover, as a father, his own status was improved. By no means was he on an equal footing with his father, but the lessening of the gulf between them found expression in the saying that such a man had 'become like a brother to his father'.

The same circumstances gave rise to conflict. The father was advancing in years when his son's own fatherhood and householderhood portended the older man's decline. The son looked to the property under his father's control as a body of resources in which he needed to share for the support of his young family. But the father saw before him a future when his property must all pass to others because of his own death. Fathers whose own sons were increasingly independent sometimes accused them of wishing their father dead so as to inherit the property sooner. Sons complained that ageing fathers grew more and more difficult, denying them their rights to land and the produce of herds so as to cling to control as long as possible. Some young men went so far as to assert that the very notion of sorcery was an invention of old men who wished to use the threat of sorcery accusations as a means of keeping their sons in subjection.

A son's marriage was not without negative connotations for his mother also. Portions of the fields cultivated by her sooner or later had to be handed over to the son's wife for her own use. And some time after the youngest son married, the mother's role as guardian of her husband's estate (jointly with the eldest son) came to an end, for excepting the remnant due her, land and livestock would be divided among the sons. The marriage of any son called for some redistribution of family resources and so foretold the end of the mother's role in channelling resources even while that role was being activated.

After his marriage and establishment as a satellite householder, a son was expected to observe the diffuse *familial* obligations of concern with his parents' well-being expressed in consideration, help and acquiescence with their wishes. Nonetheless, the bonds inevitably loosened. As the son gave more and more of his time and attention to the affairs of his wife and children, his duties as son in one family constellation and husband–father in another came into conflict. Taita described the situation as a battle or war (*ßuda*) between a man's wife and his parents, and they expressly phrased it as a struggle for demonstrations of his affection and care, his 'love' or 'preferment' (*lukundo*).

The young man's father was supposed to have renounced the limitations of the *jural* (agnatic) aspect of their relationship: to have treated the son as dear offspring to be nurtured and educated, not merely as an agnatic asset and retainer who would come to rival him. The mother, similarly, had been supposed to have gone beyond the limitations of her *jural* obligations to her husband's heir and to have cared for her son as her own dear child.

While the father was *jurally* required to consult before disposing of property, his *familial* love was supposed to commit him to an effort to leave a substantial estate. The mother was *jurally* required to give up some of her use-rights in land to a son's wife; but her *familial*, motherly, care committed her to taking an active interest in her son's own dependents by helping her daughter-in-law with gardening and child care. The claim on a married son's affection and attention was the other side of the parental care that was supposed to have gone (and continued to go) beyond the *jural* letter. If, therefore, a married son in employment failed to give his parents a share of his wages, he was failing in love and not merely in duty; for had they not done for him what they could – and not only what they must? A diviner diagnosing a misfortune suffered by a married son might name a *jural* transgression (say refusal to perform his herding duties) as the cause of dangerous paternal anger or a gross discourtesy to his mother as the occasion of maternal wrath. But failure to accord the parents generalized deference and help could also be blamed. In the former case, ritual action called attention directly to the conflict generated by jurally differentiated interests. In the latter case, the same thing was achieved indirectly. It was as though, in refusing his *familial* obligations, a son was declared to be *only* junior agnate to his father and *only* closest junior non-agnate to his mother. But were the father through his anger to attack his own son, he would be harming himself, and I have already suggested that in the case of a man's anger at his wife that result was avoided. *βutasi* provided a way around this difficulty in the rite of *kuvoya*, placation by gift. A man whose adult son had wronged him could declare openly that he wanted to be soothed by means of *kuvoya*. For example, a man angry at his son's failure to do a proper share of the herding might announce that he was angry and that he would not give the son any more milk until *kuvoya* was done. Continued failure on the son's part, both to perform his duties and to offer *kuvoya* might result in the father's calling on elders to put pressure on the young man. In doing so, he risked being told (as was one man of our acquaintance) that he himself had been at fault as an unfair and overdemanding parent. Should the affair simmer on, it was likely to become the basis for a diviner's diagnosis in terms of the father's anger. The son would then be told to mend his behaviour and also perform *kuvoya*.

Both parents could demand *kuvoya* from an adult child of either sex and a diviner could name a man's wife as requiring *kuvoya* to soothe her anger over a particular slight. It was as though a way out was provided for members of the family in situations where conflict centred on highly specific defaults. If the latter were or became enmeshed in continuing disagreement – and failure to perform *kuvoya* would indicate that – then the festering anger would appear in divination. *Kuvoya* with the usual performance of *kutasa* was supposed to put an end to the unpleasantness.

At the opposite end of the scale, there was no way around the deepest anger of a mother except by her withdrawal of the explicit curse issuing from serious conflict with her adult child (usually a son). Such cursing, though rare, did occur. Then the mother's anger was not directed against her husband, harming their child as his offspring, but against the son himself. In effect she intentionally withdrew all maternal love and concern. Taita, who, like many other peoples, considered the maternal curse the most harmful of all mystical actions apart from sorcery, gave recognition to the human being's origin in complete dependence on the mother. Not surprisingly, a mother's curse was supposed to harm a person's reproductive capacities, as seen in the case of an accursed man of middle years, who, though married twice, had only two young daughters and no sons.

2. *Parents and adult daughter*

A daughter's position in the system of *jural* relations was quite different from that of a son. Since she could not inherit from her father, a daughter's role did not enter far into the body of property rights and obligations specific to agnates. The daughter's status as an asset of her parents, especially the father, lay in the fact that her reproductive, domestic and agricultural services were given up, Through giving them up her father acquired affines forever indebted to him. He also acquired additions to his herd, including the heifer calf which ought in maturity to bear the most important animal of the bridewealth given to obtain a wife for her brother. A young woman's mother also was viewed as a creditor by her daughter's affines ; she obtained a son-in-law who owed her deference and gifts. The interest of both parents centred on the well-being and stability of the daughter's marriage.

A woman's positions as daughter/sister in one family and wife/daughter-in-law in another depended on the exchange relationship linking her parents with her husband and his parents. Fulfillment of her affinal duties had to be balanced by fulfillment of duty to her parents. She failed in that duty when she eloped with a man of whom they disapproved, when she failed to encourage her husband to make further payments or when she otherwise interfered in the expected course of bridewealth arrangements. Thus in one case, a man's anger was supposed to have attacked his daughter when the latter told her father that he should not take all the bridewealth animals and she tried to bully him into giving her several goats: her attempt to overturn the *jural* rules and her deep discourtesy constituted failure in both aspects of the relationship.

As with a son, a daughter was expected to maintain the *familial* aspect of her relationship with the parents in special ways. Though she could no longer be her mother's companion and helper as a girl was before marriage, a married daughter was supposed to visit her parental home to help with the garden work; she should give her parents gifts of food and she should be hospitable to them. In her parents' homestead she was forever *mwai*, maiden, and daughter of the house; both the taboo on having intercourse with her husband under their roof and her return home to bear her first child there attested to the fact. Her mother visited her and helped with the agricultural work, and parents often took one or more of her children to stay with them, sometimes for months at a time.

There had to be some loosening of *familial* bonds in the same way as for a son. A married woman was obliged (and usually wished to) centre her concern on the family in which she was wife and mother rather than on that in which she was daughter and sister. Should she not do that, her affines would complain that members of her natal family were interfering in her conjugal affairs. As with the son, a 'war' ensued in the form of competition between the two sets of parents for the young woman's attentions. In that battle the affines had to win – at least up to a point. One sign of their victory was the eventual placing of a woman's skull in the *Ngomenyi* of her husband's great lineage, provided she had borne a son. Still, *vis-à-vis* her own parents, a daughter's gross failure in *familial* concern, as when she did not cook a proper meal for a visiting parent or when she neglected to visit an ill mother or father, could be blamed for her misfortune. She had marked herself out as a person rights in whom had been transferred to others, as one who therefore owed them no diffuse *familial* consideration. Their anger attacked her as one no longer their dear child. In accepting a gift in *kuvoya* or in otherwise doing *kutasa* to cast out their anger, parents agreed that after all she was more to them than an item whose value lay in giving her away.

SIBLINGS

1. Brothers

In the usual course of events, heart's anger could not harm a sibling. Instead, when a person's misfortunes were diagnosed as arising out of conflict with a sibling, diviners said that the cause was quarrelling *with one another* (*kurashana*). That is, they were mutually angry and either of them could be affected. Mutual anger, quarrelling, was an offence against the *parents*, either living or dead. An important exception occurred when a dead man's widow was taken over by his surviving brother: the deceased claimed a single placation offering for the invasion of 'his house'.

The necessity for good relations among brothers was the subject of many Taita homilies. Brothers, especially full brothers, were supposed to be very close and to depend on one another for help against outsiders. But their separate, differentiated interests in the heritable property of their father was seen as a potential, even inevitable, source of conflict. The brother–brother relationship, treated as one fraught with difficulties, was a good example of the well-known combination of the ideal of amity with the practice of conflict. For instance, it was said that while a brother makes a good companion, a man should not presume on his good will by joking too freely. The mock accusations of sorcery made between close friends were all too likely to be taken seriously and so should be avoided. For who would be the most likely victim of a man's sorcery, but the brother whose early death would leave more property for his murderer?

The Taita family manifested a division of labour, as it were, between the eldest and the youngest sons: the former carried (in conceptualization and action) more of the *jural* aspect of filio-parental relations, while for the youngest the *familial* aspect was stressed. In inheritance, slightly larger numbers of animals went to the seniormost son and the youngest took whatever milk cow was still held by the mother at the time of her death. An eldest brother to some extent took over the position of the father after the latter's death, wielding some measure of authority over brothers yet unmarried. However, inheriting more livestock meant also assuming more of the debts with which every estate was encumbered. Further, after division and distribution, some time after all brothers had been married, each brother was independent economically and in practice the eldest had no control over his juniors. Thus differences between brothers based on seniority were a function of relations to the parents. If an eldest brother had been attentive, he had learned more about the father's affairs during the old man's lifetime. Eldest brothers were also by rule the first to be married and so they were the first to assume the status of householders. Any discipline by the eldest was administered as father–surrogate, not by virtue of a distinctive role as educator and disciplinarian, nor according to a different position respecting property and filiation. No one owed his position in an agnatic group to a brother and no one was indebted to a brother for his *jural* rights in property.

The youngest child was 'finisher of the milk' (*kumeria mariβa*) and supposedly the mother's favourite. Among sons the youngest was supposed to be the most beloved of both parents – though in practice this was far from always being the case. But both belief and practice showed the combination and differentiation of *jural* and *familial* aspects. By the time the youngest son was ready to marry, the generational differences between parents and children had been stated, perhaps several times over. The

eldest son, whose marriage had begun the weakening of *familial* bonds
through the inevitable breakup of the family as a residential and economic
unit, was supposed to occupy a dwelling site removed from that of the
father. Middle sons had a wider choice. Since the youngest son remained
in the parental homestead after the others had left, he became identified
with the *familial* (*consociational*) aspect of relations in all its fullness.
Understandably, it was a great offence for him to refuse this special
position by moving out on his own quickly or by building his house at a
distance. Not uncommonly, a youngest son remained at the parental
homestead even after both parents' deaths. It is significant that one ancient
widower whose youngest son and daughter-in-law showed signs of wanting
to move out said to the young man, 'If you leave me I will die. I have
become used to your wife's cooking and if I am fed by someone else I
cannot live.' The son and his wife were being asked to nurture the old
parent as parents had nurtured them in complete *familial* love. They
stayed.[19]

All sons had a claim to the care and affectionate interest of the parents
despite the differences described above. They were all brought up together
in the same house and subjected to the same discipline, receiving care from
the same hands and milk from the same breasts. Full brothers were 'one
people' (*βandu βamweri*) and also 'people of one womb' (*βandu βa kifu
chimweri*). In both *jural* and *familial* aspects of their relationship with
one another, brothers were equals, but theirs was an equality in rivalry.
While they were still unmarried and while their parents were still alive,
brothers were rivals for their parents' interest, though that competition
was structured by attention to birth order. After the parents had died and
the inheritance was divided the rivalry of brothers was foremost.

Brothers, visitors in each other's dwellings, called each other's wives
mka wapo, my wife. If a man was at work in the town he expected a
brother to keep a friendly watch on his house, to help his wife if necessary
and to inform him if anything untoward happened. A brother's children
were *βana βapo*, 'my children', people in whose welfare a man should
interest himself. (Embedded in a complicated court case was the failure of
a man to go to a diviner during the illness of the child of an absent
brother.) On the other hand, a man had to go carefully in involving himself
in the affairs of his brother for fear of being accused of meddlesomeness.
Whereas for a variety of other kin it was permissible to cohabit occasionally with a man's wife, his own brother could not do so for fear that one of
the three parties would die. The basis for this and other beliefs was not
only the fact that among brothers each centred his *familial* and *jural* concerns on his own family and household, but also the Taita view of brothers
as *jural* rivals. They were dangerous to each other precisely because they

were equivalent. They became less dangerous to each other later in life when (or if) they were all married and had sons. Then they could not inherit from one another, nor could one brother's sons share in another's estate. If a man did not leave any sons behind him, his property went to an heir or heirs chosen from among his brothers' sons. Thus elderly brothers settling down near one another had survived the worst years of rivalry.

The sorcery beliefs mentioned above treated of the conflict inherent in the brother–brother relationship as conceived by Taita. *βutasi* attended to their rivalry as it focussed on the property interests respecting which they were competitors. Divination could attribute a man's misfortune to transgression of the inheritance rules, attempts to cheat a brother, etc. But it treated such actions as *kurashana*, quarrelling together, as offences against the parents. Offences of this kind lay at the heart of rituals directed to the ancestral dead, along with the latters' demand for proper funeral and post-funeral observances and, later, for offerings. *Jural* rules exacerbated rivalry among brothers. When they failed to overcome that rivalry with *familial* concern, their angry parents visited on them *jural* wrath, not *familial* love.

2. *Brother and sister*

A man's sister, when she married, went to live in the house of another man of the same generation, but the brother continued to show diffuse concern for her well-being while having a *jural* interest in the survival of her marriage as a contractual arrangement. The dual nature of the brother–sister relationship was manifested in the derived relationship of the man and his sister's children, for he, as mother's brother was their 'third parent'.

A married sister claimed honour in her brother's house partly because bridewealth received at her marriage had helped him to marry. His wife had to be especially courteous to her if she were the linked sister whose bridewealth heifer had actually borne the one making the marriage possible. The brother also accepted a special degree of responsibility (after the father) for repayment of bridewealth should his sister be divorced. However, all brothers who shared rights in the herd to which other bridewealth gifts contributed shared the duty to repay, for they had 'eaten' her bridewealth animals.[20]

Brothers were to an extent super-ordinate to sisters in that they replaced the father and the father's brothers as her senior agnates. Since they continued the exchange relationship established by him with their sister's affines, she was responsible to them in much the same way as she was to their father for the proper carrying through of the relationship. They, by

virtue of being the closest males of her agnatic line, assumed responsibility
for her behaviour as a woman-given-in-marriage, even as they looked out
for her welfare in her conjugal home. This aspect of the brother–sister
relationship can be seen as derived from the parent–daughter relationship.
As legitimate sons of the parents, men inherited, assumed *jural* responsibility and continued contractual relationships entered into by the father.
They assumed resultant duties, including duties towards their sisters, each
of whom could claim use-right in one of the inherited fields. Women, as
legitimate female offspring, brought in bridewealth with all the social gains
entailed; their doing so was their main resultant duty towards their
brothers. As siblings, brothers and sisters were equivalents; as male and
female offspring their *jural* rights and duties were different, but balanced.

The brother–sister relationship also displayed balanced expectations.
On the basis of his brotherly (*familial*) interest in her welfare, a man was
expected to look out for his sister's welfare on all occasions and, especially,
to see that she and her children were well treated by affines. He should be
willing to bring a public accusation against her husband for persistent
ill-use of the woman or children. And to do so would mean asserting the
primacy of his concern for her as dear sister over his (*jural*) property
interest in the survival of her marriage and its bridewealth arrangements.
On the other side, Taita regarded a sister as the person who could be most
relied on for affection and concern. With the wife, the affinal (*jural*) aspect
of the role too much obtruded itself, while the mother was a senior with
whom it was hard for an adult son to be on terms of easy, relaxed friendliness. With male agnates, rivalry as actual or potential heirs and co-heirs
interfered with spontaneity, while no non-agnate had shared the intimacy
of life together in the same domestic family. A sister was of a man's own
generation; she had grown up with him and she had no claim on his
property should he die. The courtesy a man was required to show was
not incompatible with friendliness. Hence a Taita man was supposed to
look to his sister as the one person to whom he could turn when he was in
trouble, and she was an ideal confidante.[21]

That brother and sister were thought of as expecting much affectionate
concern from one another, coupled with the fact that their interests in the
jural system only partially overlapped (and then not in terms of rivalry)
was shown in ritual. Their hearts could not injure each other. It was in
the next generation that the derived relationship with the sister's children
ritually bore the fruit of a man's *jural* super-ordination over his sister.
Then, whether living or dead, he could be named by a diviner as responsible for the barrenness of a sister's child (or illness of the child of sister's
child) if bridewealth for his sister had not been completed. That was the
negative side of his position as 'third parent' to his sister's sons and

daughters. His mystical anger treated them as nothing but the offspring of a brother-in-law instead of dear sister's children, his closest junior non-agnates whom he was supposed to love and protect throughout his life. On their part they had to observe a curious taboo against touching the head of mother's brother lest he grow grey prematurely. It does not seem too far-fetched to see this as a displaced incest avoidance. The head, as has been mentioned, stood for the total person in ritual and had a host of associations with selfhood and continuity. That touching had sexual connotations is self-evident but also indicated in myth. Causing premature ageing might be thought of as a diluted threat against the person's life. Hence the ban on touching the mother's brother's head carried the suggestion of dangerous incest between siblings, explicit formulation of which Taita also left to myth.[22]

3. Sisters

Since women could not inherit, sisters were not bound together by common interests in property as brothers were, nor by the maintenance of an affinal exchange relationship such as that linking brother and sister. At marriage each went to the house of a different non-agnate (or distant agnate), since sororal polygyny was forbidden. For each, her duties as wife and mother in her conjugal home and her enduring obligations as daughter in the parental home claimed her time and attention. Towards her sister a woman had few formal duties of a *jural* kind.

Though a pair of sisters could not be the wives of one man, they were often the wives of men who themselves were related. To the general preference for marrying within the neighbourhood there was added the feeling that siblings of both sexes should live near one another and be married to people who 'knew their ways'. Therefore it was not uncommon to find sisters, married to men who were cousins to each other, living in nearby villages or perhaps even the same village. Thus women who during their girlhood shared the work of house and field as companions and helpers of their mother continued to share many of the same activities. They continued to rely on each other in many ways, tending each other in times of illness and childbirth, helping with a daughter's initiation and marriage, sharing agricultural tasks and so on.

For all such mutual helpfulness, sisters were supposed to depend on the *familial* obligation to show generalized and diffuse concern. Perhaps the best illustration is provided by the fact that when a woman died leaving a small child her sister was the proper person to take care of it. It was said that if the father were to marry again his new wife might well resent her predecessor's child and treat it badly. Women of the father's own lineage might take such a child, but though they would have an interest in their agnate's offspring, they would lack real affection for a 'stranger woman's' child. The mother's sister could not be suspect on these points. To the contrary, the care she gave, thought to be based on the bonds of affection between herself and her dead sister, would be loving and generous. (We have seen a Taita man shocked into numbness by the death of a mother's sister. When I remarked that she was not his 'real' mother, he answered, 'They're the same, they are all mothers.') In short, the *familial* aspect predominated in the sister–sister relationship. In the *jural* system there were virtually no significant cleavages of interest between sisters once they were all married. Prior to that time they were under an obligation to observe the courtesies due to seniority and marry in order of their birth, a rule often flouted. Their primary *jural* involvement was with their respective affines and with parents and brothers, not with each other.

One result in *βutasi* was that diviners did not cite sororal anger as the source of a woman's misfortunes, nor did they name quarrelling among sisters as an offence against the parents for which one sister was paying. The only case of such sororal anger that came to our attention was that of a woman who, during her sister's difficult labour, searched her heart and found there was a hidden resentment that had been aroused originally by the junior sister's having married before her. Along with their emphasis on the *familial* aspect of the sister–sister relationship, Taita spoke of a related belief. It consisted in the attribution to sisters (perhaps largely by men) of so strong an affective bond that they were dangerous to other persons. Sisters were so close, it was said, that even were one to learn that the other was a sorcerer she would not turn against her. Their mutual affection was supposed to be carried over to the next generation, for the children of sisters were supposed to be ready to help each other at all times. They were 'matrikin in sorcery' (*βamwanoama βa βusaβi*). One would help the other to do evil against those with whom she was involved in *jural* obligations. The love of sisters for each other was seen, therefore, as undermining other relationships in which *jural* aspects were more pronounced.

The conceptualization of the sister–sister relationship is critical, supporting as it does the view that the inter-connections of *jural* and *familial* aspects of family relationships lay at the core of the system of domestic anger-removal rituals. There were few ways in which the action of one sister towards another could suggest the stripping down of their relationship to *jural* essentials, for the latter were minimal. For brothers, the tension between *familial* and *jural* aspects was prominent, with prescribed amity counterposed by rivalry. That tension, a product of the equivalence of brothers, was read back into the responses of the living and dead parents who were the source of fraternal equivalence. For parents and children, the working of hearts' anger and consequent ritual action was marked by the asymmetry of *jural* authority combined with the dependence of off-spring on parental love and care. The husband–wife relationship showed the effects of asymmetry on the *jural* side welded to the pervasive image of women as both giving and withdrawing nurturance, love and life itself.

Examination of each of the relationships in the family shows that differential authority played a part within a larger pattern. Family relationships differed according to the particular combination they displayed of *jural* and *familial* aspects or components. Thus the authority of parents over children, husband over wife, and (to a more limited extent) brother over sister, was related to the way in which the mystical anger of hearts could take effect. But that occurred in the context of treating relationships as if they could be reduced to their *jural* aspect; as if, once the relationship were so reduced by one party's default, the other angrily attacked the *jural* remnant. The conceptualization of women as life-giving and life-threatening also makes sense in this context; indeed, relationships involving women display most clearly the varied weightings of *familial* and *jural* aspects. A woman as wife could be the source of anger that killed her own children as the *jural* assets of the husband who had withdrawn from the *familial* side of the relationship; and the food she cooked could become dangerous to him if he, to whom she jurally owed the duty of cooking, was angry at her. In contrast to the complex joining of the *jural* and *familial* in the conjugal relationship, the sister–sister relationship was dominated by the *familial* aspect and so women as sisters seldom harmed each other by heart's anger. The threat to others of their closeness, expressed in terms of possible support in sorcery, was the counterpart to the danger of brothers committing sorcery against each other. That contrast points up the heavy weighting of *jural* concerns in the relationships of brothers and of father and son, where also parental (especially paternal) authority showed itself in *βutasi*.

Outside the range of the nuclear family and the mother's brother as 'third parent', the individual hearts of living kin usually could not injure each other. The exceptions occurred when more distant kin actually became members of the same domestic group and therefore shared the intimacy of family life. An interesting variation on the general theme is found in the capacity of a young man's heart to injure the paternal uncle should the latter, having taken charge of his dead brother's widow and children, misappropriate property of the deceased that he should have held in trust for the heir(s). The dead man himself could be identified in divination as demanding a sort of ritual fee when the levirate went into operation. But it was his heir who, as rightful owner of his property,

could visit mystical rebuke for wrong-doing. The affair was treated in
βutasi as if the heir attacked his father's brother as mere senior agnate,
one guilty of unfairness to him, not as the close 'father' who should have
cared for him as his own son.

Another possibility in cases such as the one mentioned above was for
divination to show the heir's father's father as angry at his surviving son
on account of misbehaviour toward another son's heir. Paternal grandfathers and grandmothers were also angered by 'quarrelling' among their
grandsons, members of the inheritance group settling the last details of
the grandfather's estate (including repayment of debts derived from the
gifts made between brothers). Patrilineal first cousins could thereby be
called upon to perform *kutasa* on each other's behalf in the course of
placating their common grandparent. More remote agnates seldom had such
direct involvement in patrimonial property. On this account the inheritance
group marked the outer limit of participation requiring primary *kutasa* of
agnates on each other's behalf in rituals focussed on the dead. Beyond the
limits of the three-generation segment within the small lineage, agnates
joined in such rites out of courtesy and good will. Matrilateral kin could
be involved in placating close ancestors angry at failure to complete their
own or their daughter's bridewealth. Finally, since the ancestral dead of
both sexes – parents, grandparents and, more rarely, great-grandparents –
demanded offerings from time to time, agnates and matrikin participated
in those rituals of *βutasi*. Beyond the limits of the small lineage (and the
same degree of relationship among persons connected through a woman)
agnates participated on the basis of personal friendship or as a result of
the affinal and matrilateral ties so often coincident with agnatic relationships. Members of a great lineage took part in the retirement or completion
ritual, *Ox of milungu*, but within the network of kin and affines having
the ritual's subject at its centre. *All* their hearts *together* could injure the
subject; anyone recognizing himself as harbouring anger had to cast it
out in addition to doing *kutasa* with the others of his sex and age-group-
ing. Members of a great lineage and the sons of female members looked
also to the shrine centre for their common and individual welfare.
Whereas the skull repository was related especially to the internal aspect of
their relations, focussing the attentions of persons having common agnatic
descent, the *Mlimu* shrine centre marked out the great lineage in its external political aspect as one lineage among many. Members also joined in
rituals benefiting the entire community. Within the locality neighbours,
like kin outside the family, could not harm each other as individual
persons by means of the heart's mystical anger. They were important to
each other's welfare, as the next chapter shows.

5

GROUP WELFARE AND THE GREAT MEDICINES

No ritual united all Taita as participants, nor was there one in which all communities or lineages were represented. No ritual was supposed to benefit the entire country in a specific way. The custodianships of *Mlimu* shrine centres and the offices of Defender and Rainmaker were distributed throughout Taita by virtue of their attachment to lineages and neighbourhoods. Men who held ritual offices within groups or who owned individual shrines occupied positions in a status system cutting across the boundaries of descent and local groups, a matter of political organization lying outside the scope of this discussion. Such men, the elders, were not arranged in a Hills-wide hierarchy, nor were shrine assemblages so arranged; elders from various parts of the Hills did not cooperate in any national rites.

Within any local community a shrine assemblage marked each lineage as one among many, in a system of patrilineal descent groups as these were organized into neighbourhoods, for a *Mlimu* shrine assemblage underwent partition (over some years) when one part of a great lineage split off to become part of another local community. At the same time, participation in the affairs of any one lineage shrine centre was not exclusive to the members of a great lineage. A diviner could direct someone to make an offering to the *Mlimu* of his mother's brother's people. Given the high frequency of marriages within the neighbourhood, mother's brother's people and their *Mlimu* were usually close at hand. Through such offerings made by offspring of the women of a great lineage the latter showed itself bound to others in the locality.

The elders of a neighbourhood engaged in a vast amount of cooperation in the performance of religious and other rituals. Those who qualified for participation in the affairs of their own lineage shrine centre were allowed to share also in the affairs of other *Mlimu* in the neighbourhood. Specifically, consecration of a new building to house the shrines, and installation of a new custodian, required the attendance of elders outside the great lineage as well as of those within. Also, custodians often called on non-agnates to give assistance at rites performed under their direction and to bear witness to the correctness of their acts. In theory, any elder from any part of the Hills could serve in that capacity; in practice, only the elders of neighbouring great lineages (all of them likely to be matrikin and/or affines, in any event) were allowed the privilege.

A network of ritual ties emerged within a neighbourhood, apart from rituals explicitly registering the unity of groups. There was also a series of group-related religious rites; but it must be pointed out that for some of them the 'group' to which they pertained changed with the shifting of relationships in other areas of activity. I must add also that some of these rites, performed very infrequently, did not take place during fieldwork or else we were unable to attend them. Others were no longer performed at all.

GREAT LINEAGE (*Kichuku Kibaha*) RITES

As has been made clear from earlier chapters, Taita did not practise an ancestor cult in which offerings to the founding ancestor of a great lineage were made on behalf of all his descendants. Tendance of ancestors was the concern of agnates as members of segments of shallow depth and narrow span, more especially as members of inheritance groups descended from a common grandfather. Those rituals overlapped with the body of anger-removal and placation rites carried out by members of families with their complex ties of agnation, matrikinship and affinity. Still, offerings to ancestors required performance of *kutasa* 'in the direction of' the *lineage* skull repository and, therefore, all the members of a great lineage took notice of their common patrilineal descent in the course of ritual performances.

The *Mlimu* shrine assemblage bore upon the fact that, however members of a great lineage might be enmeshed in a neighbourhood, they were nonetheless a property-transmitting group whose members had at least a theoretical claim on each other's land and cattle in the event of failure of immediate or close heirs. As described in Chapter 1, the male house-holders of a great lineage formed the dominant element in that tract of territory where they had their homesteads and the bulk of their cultivations, and they shared a tract of plains land. The great lineage was a social group with a corporate identity; the regular, 'ordinary' *Mlimu* offerings by individual persons were indirectly related to lineage unity in the jural sense. Direct emphasis on the welfare of the entire lineage as such occurred in sporadic new-fire rituals which may have ceased to take place by the time of fieldwork.

One kind of new-fire rite was described as occurring every 'two or three' years, but that is not to be taken literally, for Taita used the phrase for any class of rites held only occasionally. All rituals of this kind were prescribed when many calamities in a great lineage – or in the neighbourhood in which it was embedded – were attributed to a single cause.

Revelation of the cause might come from a Seer who announced what must be done; or from a long series of inauspicious *βula* readings, showing disaster for a great lineage by way of the sign for its Number. The 'real' (*tiƙi*) new-fire rite was held when revelation or divination assigned blame for general misfortune or its portent to the need for rekindling the hearth fires throughout a great lineage. For the rite, lineage elders assembled at *Mlimu* every day for seven days to drink beer and perform *ƙutasa* for the general welfare. (As in rainmaking, the speeches of *ƙutasa* took the form of wishings – on this occasion for prevention of disaster – without any direct reference to or addressing of *Mlungu*.) Outside the building housing *Mlimu* they built an altar and, in the fire set under it, medicines from the lineage Bag shrine were burned for the welfare of lineage people and livestock, especially the latter. Twice a day the lineage Bell was rung outside *Mlimu*, and this shrine also had its strength renewed by being laid on the altar for fumigation.

On the seventh day all hearth fires of the great lineage homesteads were put out and scattered. A new fire was built in the *Mlimu* house, using the wood of *iti*, a 'strong' tree of the plains border. Household fires were then kindled anew with brands from the fire in which medicines from both peaks and plains were burned. People and livestock were supposed to pass through the smoke in order to benefit from the medicines. On the final day, the presiding elders took down the altar and dismantled it, throwing the parts away on waste ground. (It may be supposed that the 'seven days' referred to in informants' descriptions of this ritual corresponded to the seven movements of the sun, both risings and settings, followed in the rituals we observed.)

Special steps were taken also when an old shrine centre became unfit for use and a new one must be built. In theory, a new house for the shrines should be built in a single day and mudded by women past child-bearing. However, we saw two such new *Mlimu* houses standing half built throughout our stay in Taita. One was to replace a building which was obviously in an advanced state of decay, while the other was to house a shrine assemblage whose shelter had already fallen apart completely and which had been removed to a portion of the custodian's wife's kitchen. In neither case was the custodian very anxious about the matter and both said that the shelter would be completed 'when there was time for the work'. There was agreement, though, that when a new *Mlimu* house was completed, a fire should be kept going in it for seven days, to dry it out; the custodian, observing sexual abstinence, should sleep by the fire every night during this time. A fire was built in the *Mlimu* house also when a new keeper was installed, but elders of other as well as of his own great lineage attended and they contributed medicines to be burned in the fire.

Thus the installation of a new custodian was not the occasion for an exclusively lineage celebration.

The rite in which a new fire was kindled both in the *Mlimu* and in the domestic hearths was the only one which can be pointed to as truly a rite performed on behalf of the great lineage and one in which all its members should have participated. For it, one of the rules stated that on the day of rekindling the fires 'all strangers' (*βagenyi βose*) must be excluded from the villages. However, without seeing the performance it was impossible really to assess the statement.

NEIGHBOURHOOD RITES

1. 'Figi' rites

The great defensive medicine of *Figi*, as has been noted, necessitated the observance of a set of rules. It was incumbent on everyone to observe those rules, for failure to do so not only brought misfortune to the offender, but it caused the *Figi* to become ineffective or to turn ferociously on the very community which it was supposed to protect.

Thus the curing rite performed by a Defender to restore the health of a person who had been 'seized upon by the plains' because of an offence against the *Figi* can also be looked on as a rite performed on behalf of the community for whose benefit the *Figi* must be kept in good working order. The same is true of those rites in which the Defender and the Rainmaker cooperated to cool the plains when a quarrel had occurred there, lest drought threaten the country. In another rite, the immediate aim was to restore the potency of the *Figi* to ensure its continued functioning.

For the latter rite, the prescription followed the usual pattern: a series of misfortunes or evil portents was attributed to the weakening of the *Figi*, and the Defender had to supervise its strengthening. The community concerned consisted of neighbouring great lineages, who shared one another's herding territories by mutual consent.

The time during which the rite could be performed was governed by the winds, for, it was said, when the winds were blowing towards the portion of the uplands above where the performance was held, the curses pronounced would be blown back upon the very people for whom protection was sought. *Figi*-renewal which was to have taken place at Paranga in the summer of 1952 was delayed because of quarrels between the Defender and his congregation until seasonal change in the wind made it too late to hold the performance that year; therefore only an outline of the procedure is available.

The rite was supposed to last for the usual 'seven days'. Participants should have included the Defender himself and also those men who actually had herding shelters in the vicinity of the *Figi*, though other men of the same great lineage took part also. Women were excluded, a feature which sets this rite off from most others in Taita. The *Figi* regulations were the only features of the Taita ritual system known to us which put women under this kind of ban. The emphasis was not on notions of impurity and contamination, however, but on the association between childbirth and menstruation on the one hand and strife on the other. In theory, every man who took part should have furnished a goat to be slaughtered, and the Defender himself should have provided the first offering. Sometimes it was said that every participant need not contribute a goat but that one animal ought to be killed on each day of the performance. (It was over just this matter of the apportionment of expenses that the quarrel mentioned above occurred between the Defender and his congregation.) Quantities of beer were needed too, and in theory the wives of all the participants were to contribute beer for each of the 'seven days'.

The performance itself consisted partly of the pronouncement of curses (with appropriate use of medicines) on the enemies against whom the *Figi* should act. To this end, a mixture was prepared from the Defender's own ('hot') medicines, together with the stomach contents and blood of a goat. This *kioro* mixture was sprinkled about the vicinity of the buried *Figi* by the Defender himself, who pronounced all the evils which would befall all the enemy tribesmen, wild beasts, sorcerers, and thieves who might try to approach the Hills from the plains or who might try to escape the Hills after evil-doing. The rest of the performance consisted of joint meals of goat meat, beer drinking, and the joint performance of *kutasa*. Prayers were recited together for the prosperity and safety of the homeland, the herding territories and the stock; more curses were pronounced against all possible enemies of the people and their country.

During the entire 'seven days' certain rules must be obeyed; meat and beer were to be divided into as nearly equal shares as possible, but no one should murmur that he had been slighted. Everyone attending should be offered meat and drink, but a man with a pregnant wife or a child just cutting its teeth must not accept; all portions should be consumed and nothing taken home. Above all, there must be no quarrelling lest the prayers be ineffectual and the curses be brought down upon the people themselves. Indeed, all the rules can be subsumed under the general statement that anything which might be productive of strife or which was associated in any way with strife, bloodshed or pain must be avoided. Finally, when leaving the scene of the rite, a man should not look back over his shoulder, for fear of carrying with him the curses which had been pronounced.[1]

In some areas the Defenders performed other rites alone or together with the neighbourhood Rainmaker twice a year before the rains were due. Curses were pronounced against enemies, that they might be 'seized upon by the plains', but officiants also pronounced blessings on the plains-border gardens. Only a few of the latter needed to be sprinkled with medicines in order for the entire area to benefit: according to one Defender, 'the plain understands' (*nyika yatambukilwa*).

In the larger-scale rite outlined, in which the Defender was the central figure, the emphasis was placed on his performance of a specialized task on behalf of the community. The features of greatest importance, in addition to this one, were those having to do with joint participation by those persons supposed to benefit from the rite. They performed as equals of one another, they must avoid any behaviour even reminiscent of strife, they must share in common meals and beer drinks; they joined in pronouncing curses against their common enemies and blessings on the community of which they were members. Strikingly, cursing outsiders went with blessing those who were truly Taita.

2. Rainmaking

Besides cooperating with the Defender to cool the plains after the most serious offence against the *Figi* – quarrelling on the plains when the rains were due – and besides helping with the seasonal blessings of the plains-border gardens, Rainmakers took part in and supervised the more complicated rites of *kunyesha-vua*, 'causing the rain to pour'. Performances were held before the rains were due and they did not always wait upon the instruction of a Seer. Instead, they could be undertaken after consultation between a Rainmaker and his fellow elders. As to the role of the Rainmaker on these occasions, it will be seen that his was not an overtly dominant part. He was responsible for the correct performance: for the correct assignment of the various tasks and for seeing that they were done properly. At the same time, he was very much the man 'doing the work' of rainmaking on behalf of the people, and his own behaviour had to be most circumspect, lest he be censured by them.

The rite took place in one of the small rainmaking groves called *kinyesha-vua*. In one of these groves there could be no cutting of trees for firewood (though brush was collected), but there was a little clearing in the centre. Thus rainmaking rites took place in a cool, shady place, the very opposite of the sun-drenched homestead terrace where so many other rites were held. A rain grove sometimes was set on top of a hill in an isolated spot, but the preferred location was near where two or more main paths crossed.

If a rainmaking rite was held at the direction of a Seer, the latter set the month for the performance, and consultation among the elders set the day. The Rainmaker and other elders (his agnates and other kinsmen and men from the neighbourhood also) gathered in the grove. The man whom the Seer had ordered to supply the animal of offering came too, though usually someone else actually led in the animal. As the morning wore on, more and more men drifted in, but the performance did not wait upon their arrival. Since participants from the various great lineages of the neighbourhood took part, the Rainmaker waited until elders from each of them arrived, but no one elder acted as representative of his *kichuku kibaha*. In any event, the Rainmaker always wanted at least one other elder to act as his assistant, bear witness to his correct performance and accept some of the responsibility.

Small boys came too, to play among or sit next to the elders, their grandfathers. Women, the wives and kin of the male participants, gathered outside the grove by the pathside. Before settling down there, however, each married woman brought into the grove a calabash of beer which she poured into a single large pot placed there; if she had no beer to contribute she paid ten or twenty cents, for all the married couples taking part must contribute something.

The Rainmaker had brought with him a packet of twigs from four special trees and bushes, gathered by him or at his direction from the peak of *Yale*, where mists often hang thickly and where, according to Taita, the rain falls first. The Rainmaker slashed the twigs with a knife, then gave them to a boy who took them to the bank of the nearest stream and crushed them between two stones. Another boy was sent to the stream with the Rainmaker's gourd to wash it under a little waterfall or in a swiftly flowing part of the stream. The Rainmaker then put the crushed twigs and their leaves into the water brought back in the gourd, reciting:

We proclaim well-being. May the rain fall. May we eat, and may the women and children be filled. We ask that all foodstuffs may prosper. May those foodstuffs which have been lost to us [i.e. given up since the coming of Europeans] return to the land. May the grass for the herds spring up, and may the stock thrive and bear multiple offspring. Indeed, thus we say.

The Rainmaker then moved the gourd of medicines three times around the head of the animal of offering; the latter should be a sheep. Then three times he forced some of the medicines into the sheep's mouth. A man chosen by the Rainmaker then stunned the sheep by battering it on the head with a rock. (This man might or might not be a member of the Rainmaker's own lineage; there was little effort made to distribute specific tasks among members of the various lineages represented.) When the sheep was unconscious, its mouth and nostrils were held closed and, when judged to be dead, it was skinned, then butchered and the blood collected in the skin.

After the usual herdboy's portion was set aside, the carcass was divided into two parts, one for the men and one for the women. By this time two cooking places had been set up, one in the grove for the men and one where the women had gathered outside. On this occasion more care was taken than ordinarily of the rules for distributing meat among sex and age-status groups. Thus women could not be given the tail, brains or small intestine; young men should not eat any of the liver, but old men should do so.

Next the entrails were prepared for *βula* examination and the elders performed *kutasa* over them, saying:

We say, may this sacrifice we perform here bring well-being to the country. May the rain fall, may it not tarry. We say, may the streams fill with water, may the channels defy fording. May the baobab put forth watery fruit. May the people thrive and may the stock thrive and bear plentifully. Indeed we say thus, that it may come to pass.

It was said that this and the other prayers and invocations during rain-making were addressed to *Mlungu*, even though Creator's name was not mentioned.

The *βula* was then examined, the *Mtalo* (Number) signs being taken to stand for entire great lineages: if the *mtalo* signs for all participating lineages were auspicious, the offering had proved generally efficacious for the entire neighbourhood making up the Rainmaker's congregation. The *mtalo* sign for Nine referred, of course, to all the women, particularly those of child-bearing age, while the signs for the 'paths' or fates referred to the future of the community. Leading the examination, the Rainmaker recited the signs and, if they were good, he pronounced, 'We are filled with food (*Daguda*).' The others inquired, 'Is it true? (*Ni loli?*)' and he answered, 'Yes, there is no hunger at all (*Hee, njala yasia puta*).' A full caecum was noted with the pronouncement that the women would bear many children in the year to come.

The two portions of meat (for men and for women) having been put to cook, the Rainmaker sent a small boy with a gourd to get more water from the stream. To this water the Rainmaker added the stomach contents of the sheep, with a prayer for blessings. Over the gourd, he placed a covering made of the *mvumu* twigs which were to be used for sprinkling the mixture. The gourd of *kioro* was then set aside.

Late contributions of beer were added to the pot, which had now been set in the centre of the circle of men, elders sitting together, their juniors a little distance off. A little of the liquid from the gourd of *kioro* was squeezed into the pot of beer, a round of beer was served out, and *kutasa* performed with the recital of a prayer for an increased beer supply:

We say, may the sugar cane spring up as of old.

At this point the man who supplied the beast of offering brought a large horn (*lwembe*) such as every *Mlimu* house contained and it was doctored with a little of the *kioro* mixture; another prayer for rain was said meanwhile. (The horn used was probably from the *Mlimu* house of the Rainmaker's own great lineage, but I neglected to make certain of this.) Presently the horn was blown several times in the grove. Then general beer drinking ensued, though performances of *kutasa* might occur intermittently. The conversation became general, but the use of Kiswahili was forbidden because it was the 'language of money' (*lwaka lwa pesa*) and foreign to the long-term relationships among Taita and with mystical agents. Quarrelling and shouting were also forbidden, lest the efficacy of the rite be endangered.

While the beer drinking went on, the horn was taken out of the grove and blown again, then it was blown several more times at the nearby crossing of the paths; blowing the horn was considered an honour bestowed on the man who had provided the offering, in recognition of his gift. The blowing of the horn itself proclaimed the performance of the rite and announced the beginning of the *mdumba*, the 'seven days' ban on agricultural work.

When the meat had finished cooking, it was distributed within the sex and age-status groups. Everyone must eat his share sitting down. Before eating, each must take a sip from the gourd of *kioro* mixture; but then general feasting and drinking went on. More of the *kioro* mixture was wrapped in maize husks (by the Rainmaker and others) and tied into little packets for distribution to women who wanted to bury them in their fields as fertility medicine. Switches of the *yandu* bush were also cut and distributed to people to put in their water pots when they returned home, the pots having been left full of water when the owners left to attend the rite, in the hope that the rains would bring them a copious supply of water.

Without joining in the meal and beer drink, two men went out to sprinkle *kioro* in the fields. They were not elders but middle-aged men whom the Rainmaker and the others considered responsible persons; they did not have to be agnates of the former. One man carried the gourd of *kioro* and the aspergillum of *mvumu* twigs, while the other went ahead, collecting samples of the foodstuffs remaining in the fields: pieces of cane, cassava, sweet potatoes, yams and bananas were gathered into a basket. (Because of the staggering of planting throughout the year for certain foodstuffs, in addition to the main plantings, there were always some standing crops.) The man with the *kioro* sprinkled a bit of the mixture about, and both men recited:

We say, may the country be well, may it be oozy like a clod of swampy earth. May all the various foodstuffs return. May the rain fall night and day. May the earth be fertile and bring forth its fruits.

As in other similar cases, treatment of a few fields sufficed for all in the vicinity: a block of land was chosen in which various people from all the lineages in the neighbourhood were currently cultivating, and so a sort of representative sample received treatment on behalf of all. The foodstuffs which the men collected they took to the Rainmaker or an assistant of his. The collectors themselves could not keep them for they had 'stolen' them from the gardens of other people, and they would fall victim to any anti-thief medicines which might have been hidden there.

It was usual for a rainmaking rite like the above to be followed by the performance of the dance known as *mbeka*. This dance, danced at the crossroads all night long, constituted for an observer one of the most enjoyable of Taita festivities. After the sun had gone down, groups of people gathered along the pathside and outside nearby homesteads. Men talked about various affairs; women discussed their own concerns. Girls gathered in groups to play at riddles, small boys flitted about or hung about their elders. At last the master of the dance arrived, an older man known locally for his skill as a dancer. A couple of paraffin lamps were hung on nearby trees and the dancing (*kuvina*) began. Married men and women danced *mbeka*. The participants arranged themselves in two lines, men and women facing each other across an open space; the rest watched and everyone sang. The master of the dance started by dancing about for a bit in the central space; then he danced over to the women's line until he was opposite one woman who must then leave the line. The couple danced opposite one another, without touching, as they moved about within the open space. After a time the man danced back to the line of men, whereupon the woman chose another partner. When she ultimately danced back to the line of women, he chose another woman and so on, until dawn. Pelvic movements lent an erotic note to this dance which, however, was extremely restrained and dignified.

Taita said that they enjoyed dancing *mbeka* very much, but they also said that it was work. It celebrated a successful offering (and would not be performed if *βula* had been inauspicious), but it was also itself a part of the task and its faithful performance was supposed to benefit the country. Sometimes a Seer ordered the performance of the *kinyandi* dance which was performed (not only for rainmaking, but on many occasions) during the day and by youths and maidens. Occasionally the daytime dances were taken over by the women afflicted with the ailment known as *saka* which dancing was supposed to relieve. At other times, too, rites more simple in nature than that described above were ordered by Seers.

During the *mdumba* period of restrictions on garden work, all participants had to observe sexual abstinence. Above all there must be no quarrelling. Peace must reign in the land and it was of utmost importance to observe all the moral and customary rules.

In preparation for the last day of the period, which ended the rite, women brewed beer again, and, in the brewing of it, the wife of the man who supplied the offering animal should take the lead. On the final day, the Rainmaker and a few assistants of his own choosing gathered on the bank of a stream having a falls or rapids, taking a calabash of beer with them. The Rainmaker shook the remains of the *kioro* mixture into the swiftly flowing water while the others performed *kutasa*. All recited:

This mixture for asperging we pour away. May the rain fall that the waters may rise. May the earth ooze and may foodstuffs be plentiful.

Returning to one of their dwellings, the men then held an ordinary beer drink.

The foodstuffs gathered by the men from the gardens which they asperged were given by the Rainmaker to the women who prepared beer for the 'pouring away' (*kudia*) of the *kioro*. The ban on work in the gardens was now lifted; the great horn was blown to notify people that now they could return to their fields and work vigorously in preparation for the coming rains.

3. *Crop-furtherance rites*

The rites directed towards ensuring a good harvest differed in degree of elaborateness and in other respects, from one performance to another. The differences resulted in part from the pronouncements of Seers who announced when it was necessary to hold them. A Seer announced what must be done, when it ought to be done (roughly), who ought to participate and whom the 'ancestors of long ago' had chosen to supply the necessary materials. Sometimes a Seer issued instructions only to men of one *kichuku*, who then performed a very simple rite, with a common meal and/or beer drink following a performance of *kutasa* including prayers for a good harvest and for general well-being and prosperity. On other occasions large numbers of people were drawn in as participants: hence the shifting nature of congregations for these rites.

Usually it was twice a year that Taita performed a rite that was at once a crop-furtherance and a first-fruits rite, the combination being made possible by the Taita cropping system. For localities in the middle zone, Seers might order one performance for November or December, when the main crop of *mngulu* bean began to bear and when people awaited the main maize harvest, which came a bit later. Another performance could be prescribed for some time in May, when another crop of *mngulu* was beginning to bear preceding the ripening of the maize in dry, low fields. Thus the rite was at once a first-fruits observance with respect to the bean crop and a crop-furtherance rite respecting maize and certain other crops. For residents in the other zones revelation adjusted the schedule to suit the different agricultural cycles.

This variety of crop-furtherance *cum* first-fruits rites was called *Mnavu* after the leaves of the *mngulu* bean, these leaves being used by Wataita as a vegetable relish. It was also called *Kutambula minavu*, 'to let loose the bean leaves'. The remote ancestors, via the Seer, sometimes chose not to order an animal offering, but if they did demand one, the man to furnish it was also designated. The wife of this man also had a leading part, for she must direct the brewing of beer on the day before the rite, though the work and expense were actually shared among the women participating. The wife must also spend part of the night preceding the performance cooking a large pot of bean leaves which had been gathered during the day from her own garden or from several neighbourhood gardens. Ordinarily, the leaves were pounded, mixed with maize and other foods, etc. For *Kutambula minavu*, the leaves were simmered slowly in water.

In the morning, her husband went out with one or two men of his own choosing to visit several gardens in the vicinity. The gardens were again selected according to convenience, though some individuals requested that theirs be visited: again the actions performed in a few fields were considered beneficial to a wide area. What was done was simple enough. The men walked through the garden breaking off a few bean leaves and throwing them on the ground; as they did so, they prayed for a successful harvest and they also prayed that the new food would taste good to the people and would lie well in their stomachs without making them ill. General well-being, health and prosperity were also mentioned.

In the afternoon people gathered for the main performance, which should be held in a public place and not at a homestead. If a sheep was offered, it was killed by strangling or by battering it on the head. *βula* was examined to see whether the future of the country would be good and, hence, whether or not the offering was acceptable. *Kutasa* was performed by all the men with prayers for the prosperity of the country (*izanga*), and again the hopes were expressed that the food would taste good and nourish the people without making them ill. Everyone there received a portion of the cooked bean leaves served out in little wooden basins (*fuβa*) and a little of this was spat out at *ķutasa*. Throughout, the man who supplied the offered animal acted as the distributor of meat and beer, while his wife served out the bean leaves: they had to perform services for the rest.

A *ķioro* mixture was made from the sheep's stomach contents and blood, together with some of the cooked bean leaves. The following day two unmarried youths used it to asperge a few gardens representing all those in the neighbourhood.

If revelation so ordered it, as was usually the case when there was an animal offering, there was a seven-day restriction on garden work and on the picking of bean leaves. If the restriction were ignored, it was said, the rite would be ruined: the harvest would fail and any food from it would give people pains in their stomachs.

Some Taita said that in addition to *Mnavu* there were formerly other rites which protected people against illness caused by new food, but that no one bothered to perform them any more. As the Christians would ignore the restrictions involved, the rites would be ruined invariably, so there was no point in bothering. To this lapsing, Wataita sometimes attributed the allegedly greater frequency of worm infection in their children as compared with pre-European days. Certainly most Christians did not observe the various restrictions on agricultural work following rainmaking and crop rites, but these nevertheless continued to be performed. A *Mtasi* breaking the *mdumba* restrictions was brought before neighbourhood elders and fined a chicken or a pot of beer. Failure to pay brought mystical punishment. Such a person was *mlui*, 'unclean' (*ķulua* = to be dirty; *ķulusha* = to soil) like one breaking a rule of kinship behaviour.

It must be noted, finally, that the crop rites were not thought of by Wataita as belonging to a category wholly apart from rainmaking rites. Crop and first-fruit rites were also said to help to ensure good rainfall during the coming months.

The first part of this chapter described rites having to do with the unity of a great lineage: the new-fire observances. As against this concern with the unity of a descent group, other rites had reference to local groups. Thus *Figi*-renewal rites were clearly associated with the neighbourhood in which constituent great lineages shared the use of plains territories. Each of these constituent lineages did not normally have its own Defender. The rainmaking rites held in a rainmaking grove also concerned the neighbourhood, in which constituent great lineages shared the services of a Rainmaker. The latter also cooperated with the local Defender in blessing the plains fields or cooling them after transgressions against the

Figi had increased their mystical heat and threatened drought. Though members of the Rainmaker's own great lineage might be dominant at rainmaking rites, members of the other great lineages also attended and the rite was supposed to benefit the 'whole country', i.e. the neighbourhood. The wishings included in the speeches of *kutasa* during rainmaking did not ask that rain and the good things dependent on it should be restricted to the neighbourhood. They asked for those good things of life legitimately sought by all Taita, but within the context of the widest action group.

For those crop-furtherance rites in which people of various places participated at the direction of a Seer, the situation is more difficult to assess and to describe accurately. I have classed these rites among 'local-group rites' but this is to imply a more precise correlation than was found in fact between participation and membership in a bounded local group. The same people did not always participate together on successive occasions. The distribution of Seers affected the situation since it was they who apportioned expense and labour and determined the participating groups. Not every one of the functioning neighbourhoods had a Seer of its own and the distribution of Seers did not follow any system of larger, more inclusive local units. Further, as has been mentioned, the territories of Seers were not necessarily exclusive and some Seers operated in overlapping territories. That meant that a Seer could occasionally prescribe for local groups of which he was not a member. But a Seer did not always prescribe for the same combinations of people. A minor crop-furtherance rite might be ordered only for certain villages occupied by members of one great lineage. For more elaborate rites, a wider area would be designated, comprising a single neighbourhood, occasionally more than one. In the fifties there was some tendency for a Seer to follow administrative boundaries and so to order a performance by people in a particular sub-Location or sub-Locations. In any event, the emphasis was on locality and not on participation according to great lineage membership. The area within which a Seer prescribed was also affected by the degree of prestige which he or she had managed to acquire. It is conceivable that one Seer, given appropriate circumstances, might acquire sufficient prestige to be accepted by everyone in the Hills, but this had never happened so far as we know.

No shrines were involved in rainmaking and crop rites. Shrine assemblages had nothing to do with the fertility of the soil, the bringing of rain to the land or successful harvests. Instead, animals were offered to Creator at the direction of remote ancestors, the 'people of long ago', communicating through Seers. It was not the ancestors, but Creator who sent the rains and caused the earth to be fertile. Creator held back the rains when angry, or sent locusts or plague. Thus Creator could bring upon humans those great misfortunes which reduce a people to a piteous state or scatter them afar. When Creator's anger was not aroused, when offerings proved acceptable, the rain would fall 'day and night' and the earth would bring forth its fruits. The people were 'filled with food' and there was 'well-being for humans and for stock'.

The primary aim of rainmaking and crop-furtherance rites was supposed to be the assurance of the earth's fruitfulness, so that humans would have an abundant food supply. It is important to note, then, that neither land nor the foodstuffs growing on it were productive, in the traditional way of life, of individual wealth. The rites stressed things and activities which were not the focus of economic differentiation. They aimed at securing things which human beings everywhere want: long life, health, the perpetuation of their kind, prosperity. Taita wanted certain of these goods in a particular form: they desired many children, but particularly sons to carry on the agnatic lines; they wanted prosperity not only in the form of an abundant food supply, but also in the form of numerous cattle, sheep and goats. It was by means of these specific good things that Taita were differentiated from one another as members of different great lineages and also as rich men or poor. Nevertheless, it was neither for the continuation of any particular lineage nor for the wealth of any individual that the rites were held. Just as all the fields of the 'country' benefited, so well-being was sought for all its inhabitants. The prayers asked for the fecundity of all the herds.

In order to realize the common welfare which the rites sought, a common effort had to be made. This included on the one hand, participation: attendance, contributions of beer to the common pot, the sharing of food and drink, participation in *mbeka* or other dancing and observance of the *mdumba* period of restrictions on garden work and sexual activity. It included also the common effort to maintain peace, to avoid raising or pursuing matters which might initiate quarrelling. True, it was a feature of all Taita rites that quarrelling, or even shouting which sounded like quarrelling, was supposed to ruin the performance. On most other occasions, however, only the welfare of an individual or a small group of individuals was affected. Here it was the welfare of an entire community that had to be protected. There had to be peace in communities as in families and within individual persons. Common themes ran through all performances of *βutasi* even though variations distinguished one kind of ritual occasion from another. The last chapter explores both common themes and regular variations in the elements of ritual.

6

RITUAL ELEMENTS AND RITUAL EFFICACY

Performances of the same ritual of *ßutasi* differed from one another to some extent. Circumstances might make it impossible to meet all the requirements considered necessary to an ideally correct performance. At least equally important, Taita conceptions of efficacy did not require rigidly fixed and supposedly unvarying repetition either of verbal formulae or of movement and gesture. The timing of religious and other rituals often depended on the convenience of individual participants and the availability of objects and materials to be employed. The state of inter-personal relations and of current political alignments could also affect the course of ritual events. Once a religious or other ritual began, the sequence of acts might not follow precisely as they had on a previous occasion. Still, *ßutasi* was a *ritual* complex, in which any given rite displayed a highly ordered sequence consisting of acts of bodily movement and speech, employing material objects and substances and directed toward an agreed-upon end.

At the centre of any religious rite was, of course, the act of *kutasa*. *Kizongona*, ritual slaughter of an animal for offering and the sharing of meat, came next in Taita conceptualization as fundamental to religious life. Other actions, especially those involving the manipulation of other material objects and substances, introduced complications to many religious performances. In this chapter I discuss the elements of Taita religious ritual: the bodily movements and verbal acts, the material objects and substances manipulated. I am concerned with the meanings of the ele-ments of religious ritual as they can be discerned both in their relations to each other and to features of non-religious life. The aim is not an exposi-tion of realities that ritual elements allegedly 'symbolized' or 'stood for' but rather of *what realities they recreated and made present*. Rituals are *events* of which one must ask, 'What has happened?'

As already shown in earlier chapters, the central and defining act of Taita religion, *kutasa*, combined bodily movements and speech: the taking into the mouth and spraying out of liquid and the uttering of *malombi*, the whole carried out with the body lowered in a squatting position.

Particular performances of *kutasa* varied in determinate ways. The liquid taken in and sprayed out differed according to the sex and status of the performer, with women using unfermented cane juice and men, depending on whether they were or were not elders, using ordinary beer, aged beer, beer of the altar, or beer to which honey had been added. What liquid would be used by elders depended in addition on the specific end of the total ritual, this in turn being connected with the mystical power involved. In the domestic rites of angry hearts, which I consider the core of *βutasi*, only the sex distinction operated, provided that cane juice or beer were actually available. Emergencies gave rise to the situational variant in which only water was used and to the (possibly only hypothetical) use of saliva alone.

The utterances forming part of the total act of *kutasa* were as necessary as the bodily movements. Spraying out liquid without the pronouncement of *malombi* simply would not count as *kutasa*. The descriptions of various religious rituals show how greatly *malombi* could vary from one occasion to another, depending on the circumstances of actual or potential misfortune as combined with the identification of the responsible mystical agent. The speeches of *kutasa* in rites concerned with living angry hearts tended to include specific references to the causes of mystical anger – to those injuries to the rights of persons, those failures to meet *jural* and *familial* obligations which were supposed to arouse wrath. With respect to typical contents, the speeches addressed to the ancestral dead overlapped those concerned with living hearts on the one hand and those addressed to shrines on the other. Since ancestors maintained concern with the kinship behaviour of their living descendants, *malombi* addressed to them might mention the transgressions supposed to arouse ancestral anger, in this way resembling speeches dealing with living hearts. In other respects some *malombi* to ancestors were like those to shrines in noting the 'desire' for installation and the demand for offerings. But there was contrast, too, between addresses spoken to ancestors and those directed to shrines: shrines were sometimes addressed as though they were responsible *for*, not responsive *to*, unharmonious kinship relations – that happened when the latter were seen as a misfortune suffered by a shrine owner whose dependents, whether animal or human, were not in satisfactory condition. Speeches at routine rainmaking rites, as shown, consisted of the expression of wishes made in the presence of Creator, and they excluded reference to circumstances other than the hopeful anticipation of the community.

On any given occasion, different performers might utter *malombi* showing quite different emphases, depending on the relationship of the performer to the subject of the rite and on the multiple diagnoses given in *βula*. A good example is provided by the shrine bestowal rite in which the *malombi* of the presiding elder focussed only on the shrine, while the subject's mother also referred to quarrels that aroused her own anger (see pp. 69, 73).

Some *malombi* were marked by the greater oratorical skill of their speakers. As in jural proceedings and political debate, so also in *malombi*, Taita admired the ability to produce forceful yet mellifluous speeches, well delivered. Most fittingly, men, especially middle-aged and elderly men, elaborated their *malombi* with figures of speech and special constructions. Certain metaphors were common property, amounting almost to clichés. For example, blessing a woman or a couple to have many children, in the speech of persons of both sexes and various ages, wished for them that they might 'bear the herder and the herded, the rhinoceros and the elephant', that is, male and female, son and daughter. (A male was supposed to be like a rhinoceros because that animal attacks blindly whether or not it is under attack, while an elephant, at least in Taita thought, will only counter-attack, and then only when its young are endangered – 'like a woman'.) Skillful elders used a variety of similes and metaphors in an overall pattern of parallelism: the *malombi* of rainmaking given on pp. 128–32 illustrates the favoured style.

Taita religious utterances did not include self-abasements, thanksgiving or praise: exclusion of such aspects of prayer, so common in many other religious systems, both scriptural and non-scriptural, reduced the 'worshipful' aspect of Taita religion. Yet seriousness and even solemnity pervaded the actual pronouncement of *malombi*. The latter term, as has been indicated, covered a variety of utterances: the speaking of wishes for beneficence; supplication for specific good things and, especially, for the turning away of the wrath of a mystical agent; the calling down of blessings upon the subject of the rite; the explicit casting out of anger from the heart of the speaker. The last named, indeed, underlay the entire body of *malombi*, as stressed repeatedly. Whatever the variety of *malombi*, the speaker took responsibility for the state of his own feelings, affirming beneficence towards the subject of the rite, and, in so doing, nullifying any anger or resentment that might be unknown to others and perhaps not even present to his own consciousness. The addition of *magemi* clinched the matter (as shown earlier) by subjecting the speaker to his own conditional curse against 'any sorcerer ensorcelling here'. Whether the speaker explicitly or implicitly cast out or nullified anger, his utterance was, in effect, 'I hereby refuse to appropriate wrath to myself. If I am angry at this person, I cast away anger, I act beneficently towards him.'

The whole of any *malombi* was a speech event, made up of a number of speech acts. Some of the latter might describe or mention aspects of the state of affairs occasioning the ritual performance. But the central speech acts, the wishings, petitionings, blessings and explicit castings-out of anger did not merely describe the state of the speaker's feelings, they seized upon those feelings, and managed them in acts of benevolence. The Taita religious actor, when he performed *kutasa*, did not merely *talk about* his feelings, he *acted*, refusing wrath in favour of love. His utterances were *performative utterances*.[1]

Insofar as Taita speakers, in the course of uttering *malombi* also described or mentioned features of the state of affairs, they spoke truly or falsely. That is, someone acquainted with the relevant persons and events could assess their statements as either being in accord with 'the facts' or not being so in accord. But those speech acts that were performative utterances, the *actual* refusals to appropriate anger, were not either true or false, but felicitous or infelicitous, valid or invalid: the utterances either 'came off' as genuine or valid acts of refusal to appropriate anger, of substituting love for wrath, or they failed, being non-genuine, invalid.[2] To perform a refusal of anger, whether in the form of wishings, supplications, blessings or explicit castings away of anger, was no more true or false than performing acts of greeting, thanking, adjudicating or promising. But like all other performative utterances, the rejection of wrath was successfully carried out, was genuinely or validly an act, only by meeting specifiable felicity or validity conditions.

One of the most important conditions set by the Taita's own theory of *malombi* was that of *sincerity*. According to that theory, the validity of *malombi* as rejections of wrath depended, not on the mere pronouncement of the words, nor yet only on the joining of the words to the proper and necessary action. The speech had to come 'from out of the heart'. It was not necessary that the speaker explicitly declare sincerity, as was done by the shrine-owner's mother (see p. 69), for an insincere utterance of *malombi* would not only *automatically* fail in validity, but would automatically fail to be efficacious. The latter is an important point: it must be remembered that in religion valid performative utterances, those that are successfully accomplished acts, also are supposed to have real effects in the world. So in *βutasi*, efficacy depended on validity and, in retrospect, a failure of efficacy could be interpreted as stemming from non-validity, itself the result of failure to meet the sincerity condition. Even in prospect, a judgement concerning a failure of efficacy might be based on assessing the actors as incapable of carrying out *kutasa* validly. That was the case when speculative participants judged that the couple whose children had died of maternal anger would find themselves going through the whole procedure over again (see p. 96). Onlookers who knew their circumstances believed that the couple's bad relationship made it impossible for them to act validly to reject wrath and thereby to perform *kutasa* efficaciously. But whatever the specific case, the sincerity condition was put into operation also by means of *magemi*. Willingness to pronounce the *magemi* was supposed to guarantee the sincerity of *malombi*. Insincere *malombi* combined with conditional curses would subject the speaker to dire consequences and so the practice of adding *magemi* was supposed to deter people from insincere attempts at *ḵutasa*. Conditional curses seem not to have had a sincerity condition; but in any event, each participant was subjected not only to his own conditional curse, but to the curses of the other participants as well.

Another condition for the validity of *malombi* and, therefore, of the total act of *ḵutasa*, had to do with the social relationships among participants. What I have been calling *primary ḵutasa* was that performance of *ḵutasa* that was *required* in order for the rite to be said to have been done. In the rites attending to the anger of living hearts, *ḵutasa* had to be performed by the offended person whose mystical anger had caused misfortune. Only that person could successfully complete the act of rejecting the wrath that had done the damage. In the tendance of the ancestral dead, only a male householder himself or, depending on the circumstances, his seniormost male agnate sharing descent from the offended shade could do *primary ḵutasa* validly. As seen in Chapter 4, the performer of *primary ḵutasa* did not always have to be only one individual, for the large body of kin and neighbours who did *ḵutasa* in the *Ox of milungu* rite did so of necessity on that occasion and not, as otherwise, by way of assisting the main performer. In shrine-acquisition rites the role of elder, particularly of presiding elder, entered into the conditions of performance, while in the tendance of a personal shrine only the owner's *ḵutasa* was valid. In like manner, the keeper of the lineage shrine assemblage performed *primary ḵutasa* when an offering was made, and no rainmaking rite could occur without the neighbourhood Rainmaker doing *primary ḵutasa*.

Another way of putting the matter is to say that proper social entitlement was one of the conditions for the validity of *malombi*. In this phrasing, 'social entitlement' does not stand only for occupancy of a formal office; it refers to the actor's occupancy of a role, his or her *standing* in a specified social relationship to the subject(s) of the rite. Thus, 'entitlement' refers equally to the qualification of the Rainmaker to do *primary ḵutasa* at rainmaking rites; to the qualification of a senior agnate to do *primary ḵutasa* on behalf of one suffering ancestral rebuke from the shade of the paternal grandfather; and to an angry wife whose 'husband's child' was ill on account of her wrath. The required *malombi* would not be completed as genuine acts unless the persons with the right social entitlements pronounced them. Genuinely completed *malombi*, as acts, made for genuinely completed acts of *ḵutasa*.

The validity or felicity conditions of sincerity and social entitlement were linked in complicated ways with numerous other conditions, including those set by the conventions of the Taita language. But of greatest importance here, sincerity and social entitlement, as conditions, linked up with the conditions set by 'facts' about the world. For Taita, facts about the world included the existence of mystical entities among whose properties were proneness to anger and responsiveness to human speech. The *malombi* part of *kutasa* also had to meet the conditions set by those facts: living human beings, speaking sincerely and with the proper social entitlements, addressed or spoke in the 'hearing' of mystical entities. The properly entitled speakers carried within themselves hearts that could be mystically dangerous under some circumstances, hearts that had to reject anger sincerely. The living persons pronouncing *malombi*, performing *kutasa*, were not the ordinary creatures of a secularized world, but persons with their own mystical endowments, their hearts figuring in the roster of mystical agents. That fact points the way to the basis for the connection between validity and efficacy. *Kutasa*, including *malombi*, formed the basic means of interaction among human beings in their capacity as mystically endowed beings, and also the means of acting towards mystical entities other than living human hearts. Human hearts and other mystical entities shared a world in which, as a matter of 'fact', anger and the rejection of anger had effects on the life and well-being of humans, livestock and crops. Given mystical causation as a feature of the world, sincerity and social entitlement linked not only to conventional acts but to 'natural' processes. Fulfillment of the conditions for validity was necessary in order that practical, 'natural' results should be achieved.

This means that the outside observer who does not share the traditional Taita view of the world should not offer, as complete, interpretations that explain away without doing anything else. The sincerity required of speakers of *malombi* cannot be adequately understood *only* as part of a disguised attempt at psychotherapy through a purging of the emotions. Nor is the requirement of proper social entitlement justly treated *only* as part of a complex of 'symbolic' statements about the social order. It must be continually borne in mind that Taita *βatasi* were sacramental realists for whom *something really happened* in the course of religious rituals. Those rituals, for them, were not only theurapeutic or socially symbolic dramas, but actions consistent with and made necessary by processes and events extending beyond the human person and the social universe, into physical and biological events.

Nevertheless, the outside observer has to move beyond insiders' views in trying to understand some of the ways in which belief in the efficacy of ritual might have been supported. The persuasiveness of religious and other ritual surely varies among participants as well as for a single actor on different occasions and at different times in the life cycle. Even without a systematic enquiry into the connection between participation and inner conviction or alleged conviction, it was apparent that βatasi responded to ritual differently. The man who abstained from ritual slaughter and livestock offerings (on the grounds that they only served to mask a lust for meat among the living) shared a deeply serious attitude with an aged elder saddened by his ancestors' refusal to enable him to be a skillful diviner. Men like these found many kin and neighbours in whose lives religious action united with thoughtfulness and expressions of conviction. For others, religious concerns sat more lightly. Much depended on the nature of life circumstances and the stage of the life cycle, but marked individual differences showed also. The man who frequently divined for himself on account of mishaps viewed by others as trivial (as when a succession of maize-cob milk bottle stoppers had gone missing), aroused laughter by his readiness to suspect mystical influences; another, careless of his wife's concern over an ill child, earned himself a reputation as a man both hardhearted and foolish. It appears that most βatasi believed religious rituals to be necessary, but that persuasion did not involve them in devout forms of piety.

Religious rituals are related in a special way to the sources of persuasiveness guaranteeing rituals in general. Whether performances are ceremonies aiming only at 'conventional' consequences – for example a change in social status – or whether they aim at influencing mystical agents, ritual acts are completed within the framework of the total ritual event or performance. That is seen especially in the performative utterances characteristic of ritual speech. In a court, adjudication and sentencing are completed as conventional acts within the framework of the legal system and the courtroom proceedings. So also in religious ritual, religious acts are completed; their completion does not wait upon the 'success' of the ritual, i.e. realization of its aims. To reiterate a point already made: *in* (not merely 'by means of') the utterances of ƙutasa, participants performed the *act* of refusing to incorporate anger. They performed this act either separately, using conventional phrases in which they explicitly cast out anger; or they performed it implicitly in the course of performing the acts of wishing, petitioning and urging mystical agents, or in the act of blessing the subject. *Religious performers really did something: they did not only talk about something.*[3] Their really having done something was not dependent on whether a sick person recovered or a poor herd began to prosper. Paralleling religious ritual everywhere, in Taita any one act of ƙutasa was an element in an ongoing complex of interaction. *Ultimate efficacy* depended not only on completion of the felicitous or valid religious act but on mystical response to it as well. Over time, mystical responses made for the realization of the practical aims of only *some* rituals. But, given that religious action was, as everywhere and at all times, a matter of long-term interaction, no single religious performance had to bear the weight of concern with 'success'. No one ritual stood or fell by itself.

To say this is to say that only in a restricted sense and to a limited extent does persuasiveness attach to particular religious acts. Insofar as valid acts are completed within the framework of the ritual event, ritual persuades that something has been accomplished. Indeed, from the observers' point of view also, something has really happened: living human beings have accomplished their part in one sequence of interaction. In the main, persuasiveness attaches to the whole complex of religious ritual as interaction. At the same time, long-term religious interaction relies on living human actors performing valid acts completed within the frame of a single ritual event.

A major source of the persuasiveness of the entire complex of religious ritual lies in the bonds between religious acts and the social order. As pointed out above, one of the most important validity or felicity conditions for acts of *primary kutasa* was proper social entitlement. More widely, proper social entitlement was a condition for validly performing any religious act, even one suitable only for a marginally participating person. That requirement yielded a feature of religious life familiar from a variety of small-scale societies: religious roles matched those in other domains of social life; the ritual system mapped the system of relationships among persons similar or different from one another by virtue of sex, age-status, position in the system of descent, kinship and marriage, residence and citizenship. Should one choose to emphasize that aspect, ritual action among *βatasi* could certainly be seen as a 'circuitous dramatization' of the social system;[4] other analyses of Taita religious ritual as 'social drama' might certainly be profitable.[5] However that is not the present enterprise. My point is this: that social entitlement as a condition for validity brings into the heart of ritual the persuasive powers of the social order. In societies such as that of pre-Independence Taita, a sophisticated but non-machine technology is united to a personalistic system of many-stranded social relationships. That personalistic system of social relationships dominates the activities and processes through which adaptation and survival occur.

That is, the social order is in a quite direct sense a major component of the ecology: the Taita land use system and the body of rules governing rights in property played that part. As an intricate and effective device for living in the world, the social order of a small-scale society is truly powerful. Ritual conformity with the social order is, therefore, only part of the story. Social entitlement as a condition for the validity of ritual acts makes those acts (for participant believers) *part of* the total device for living in the world, partaking of the power of the whole. This being so, it is misleading, or at best, inadequate, to speak of religious and other rituals as 'mirroring' the social order, as though the social order were the 'really real' and the ritual order a less substantial reflection of its points and contours.

The ritual domain and other domains inter-penetrate in the constitution and actions of persons simultaneously endowed with such 'ordinary' social capacities as rights over property and with mystical capacities and relationships. In Taita religion, a woman did not merely 'reflect' her social role as mother when she performed *kutasa* at the shrine acquisition of her son. A Taita mother was a *kind of person*, part of whose very constitution consisted in her capacity to injure through the mystical anger of her heart a son on the threshold of elderhood. A Rainmaker was not only one vested with a high-status office as a rich householder-citizen of his neighbourhood. He was a certain kind of person, a man who 'knew' the medicines of rainmaking and was thereby mystically endowed with capacities used on behalf of the community. For traditional Taita, social endowment and mystical endowment were inter-connected aspects of personhood. In performing valid religious acts, therefore, actors deployed linked features of their total selves. When they brought their mystical endowments to the fore in religious rituals, *βatasi* perforce brought also the non-mystical capacities to which the mystical was linked. In so doing they displayed and used the authority and persuasiveness of the total system of relations among persons.

The 'authority' and 'persuasiveness' of the system of inter-personal relations need not be thought of as something external to the experienced selfhood of actors.[6] Socio-ritual endowments, taken into the self, are experienced in the course of the life cycle. The 'kind of person' someone is changes; the religious system, along with the entire socio-ritual system, unfolds in the course of the life cycle as a moral career. For Taita religious actors, perhaps the most important feature of the process was the requirement to treat themselves as they treated others, as beings at once capable of mystically dangerous anger and susceptible to the mystically dangerous anger of other living humans, the ancestral dead, shrines and Creator. Everyone started life in the infantile condition of susceptibility to mystical anger as an extension of the parents, particularly the father. Everyone who reached the age of sense developed the capacity to harm some of the people closest to him through anger. Everyone who reached full adulthood by achieving parenthood experienced both susceptibility to a wider range of mystical influence and the extension of his or her own mystical capacities and endowments. The overall course and shape of the moral career differed as between men and women. Nonetheless, everyone was divined-for on account of mystical anger outside himself and everyone was at times identified as bearer of the anger damaging to another living person.

Everyone had to speak the phrases in which the act of rejecting wrath, of refusing to incorporate anger, was performed explicitly or implicitly. Everyone had to subject himself or herself to the conditional curses of *magemi*. Taita religion thus required that every adult person acknowledge himself to himself and before others, as one endowed with a mystically dangerous heart. It required that every *Mtasi* take responsibility for anger and resentment harboured in the heart. It required persons to acknowledge themselves as bearers of dangerous feelings of which they hitherto might not even have been aware.

Taita religious ritual therefore, like the rituals of other religious systems, effected what can be called the *presentation of the self to the self*. Probably the most extreme example is given in the case of the woman supposed to have been responsible, through her anger at her husband, for the deaths of her own three children and the serious illness of a fourth. Divination and ritual presented her to herself, as well as to others, as one capable of destroying her own precious children. The requirements of *kutasa* demanded that she speak in such a way as to acknowledge her anger and its damaging power; the sincerity condition required that she perform the act of anger rejection in a truly 'heart-felt' fashion – she must sincerely refuse to incorporate wrath, casting it away. Although most religious rituals did not require self-presentation in this extreme (and probably very painful) fashion, all required persons to take responsibility for dealing with their own actual or possible maleficence. All religious rituals involved persons as participants in an ongoing system of inter-action in which sentiments had real effects. The living human participant was not merely a passive sufferer from the wrath of non-human mystical entities, but was actively engaged in the exchange of mystically effective feelings.

Evidence that this aspect of *βutasi* really entered Taita experience of themselves was to be seen in Taita concern for the nature of other people's feelings and the management of their own. Assessments of the state of other persons' feelings was a regular feature of discussions following meet-ings and other social events. While most Taita exercised great restraint in the open expression of powerful anger, many seemed very ready to take offence at real or imagined slights, whereupon their sulky, resentful demeanour would be noted by others. The anthropologists' need to learn the language was not infrequently discussed in terms of the importance of speaking freely so as to assure others of our good feelings: we were also instructed to avoid certain gestures that Taita believed to be signs of unspoken anger. It is likely that acknowledgement of one's own anger and concern with other angry mystical entities were reinforced by daily attention to feelings and that daily attention to feelings in turn contributed to the impact of religious action. In this way also, the persuasiveness of religious ritual took strength from the non-religious.

Of at least equal importance was the fact that the need to perform *kutasa* was not routine. Unless someone was desperately ill, rituals were often delayed because people were reluctant to slaughter livestock and might not even have an animal readily available, and they did not always find it convenient to brew and offer beer. But sooner or later, recurrent or continuing misfortune required performing the ritual. Sometimes religious rituals took place in life-and-death crises. At the very least, religious rites were performed in a context of concern with important matters. They were associated with attempts to restore or realize the good things of life for individuals and for families or other groupings. These serious concerns lent their own weight and persuasiveness to the action as something that needed to be done. Besides, the very form of *kutasa* associated it with an activity of prime importance for individuals and social groups: eating. I turn now to that association as it appears in the 'oral idiom' of Taita thought and practice.

Bodily movements and speech were both necessary for completion of the act of *kutasa* as it stressed potential incorporation and actual refusal to incorporate. In the bodily movements, something potable or edible was taken into the mouth and spat forth, ejected from the body. In *malombi* speeches, anger that might otherwise be retained in the heart was cast out in a refusal to incorporate it. Focus on the incorporative aspect of eating was linked in certain ways to the destruction of what could be incorporated or refused. Outside ritual action, the Taita judged various things partly in terms of how easily they were 'eaten' and so destroyed without much benefit to the 'eaters'. Money was the prime example of that which was inevitably, in the Taita view, 'eaten in a day', easily disposed of in ways that left little to show for it. Money went primarily for trade goods – tea and sugar, clothing, enamel dishes, things treated (especially by men) as having little worth, because non-durable and non-reproducing. Such things were, literally, consumer goods, things easily 'eaten', in contrast to livestock that reproduced itself.[7] These formulations gave shape to the notion of profitless incorporation summed up in the proverb, 'Beer is not food but merely urine.' Some things were not worth incorporating in large quantities, not only because they were not worth much in themselves but because they interfered with more worthy things. To some extent, the 'spitting out' of anger in *kutasa* treated wrath as something of

no worth, something that interfered with the more beneficial sentiments
on which life and well-being depended.

The widespread African use of 'eating' as a metaphor for sexuality
and for conquest was not prominent in Taita. True, in girls' initiation,
ritual defloration took place in the guise of being 'eaten by the hyaena
(or lion)'.[8] But otherwise the oral idiom and sexuality were more indirectly connected (p. 183, n. 17). As for triumph or conquest, Taita spoke
of one person's 'surpassing' or, literally, 'leaping over' (*kuchumba*) the
other. Far more strikingly, Taita associated oral incorporation with guilt
and innocence seen as bound up with feelings, intentions and the actions
springing from them.

Juridical rites, as noted elsewhere, involved the eating of medicines
together with appropriate oaths in the form of conditional curses. The
rite of making a blood pact partnership, *mtero*; the rite of administering
the oath medicine *mugule* to supposed perjurers and sorcerers; and the
rite of searching out sorcerers by means of *mwalola*, all required the
participants to take in *and swallow* medicine having powers mobilized by
the words spoken in part by the subject himself. The man who remained
innocent of wrong-doing towards his pact partner feared no more from
mtero than the man innocent of perjury or sorcery feared from *mugule*.
The guilty suffered death, for the medicines found out guilt from inside
the person who had incorporated them. *Mwalola*, the search medicine,
showed this most clearly. The guilty person retained the medicine as he
had retained his wrong feelings and his secret knowledge. The innocent
vomited the *mwalola*. Indeed, the effects of search medicine on the
innocent amounted to a sort of involuntary *kutasa*: ejection from inside
the person of something dangerous. *Kutasa* itself might be thought of as
a voluntary vomiting up of dangerous feelings.

Beliefs and practices concerned with sorcery showed an elaboration of
oral concerns and the use of the oral idiom. Sorcery could be performed
in a number of ways, but the supposedly most common mode employed
harmful medicines secreted in the victim's food and, of course, mobilized
by unconditional curses. Frequently, according to Taita, the victim could
not properly digest his food because it turned into something that could
be felt going round and round inside him. Should a timely antidote
enable the victim to vomit, the ensorcelled food showed itself black and
hard.[9] Sorcerers thus caused other people to incorporate involuntarily
something dangerous: sorcery spoiled the eating for its victims. The
sorcerer himself, instead of refusing in the normal way to incorporate
anger, had stored up wrath and the secret knowledge of the ways in which
he had acted from that wrath. A sorcerer could not tell the truth about
either his feelings or his deeds and might only go through the motions of

performing *kutasa*: hence, the need for *magemi*, the conditional curses forming part of most religious performances. The word 'truth' (*loli*) had multiple meanings, standing for *inter alia* 'factual' truth and also genuine expression of feelings. People who perjured themselves could be as dangerous as sorcerers – indeed, lying (and other wrong actions) could be called sorcery; and sorcerers lied or dissembled. In juridical ritual, the potentially fatal *mugule* oath medicine was administered to those whom *βula* had shown likely to be one or the other. *βutasi* required persons to be truthful in both of the senses mentioned. Religious action thus stood in opposition to both destructive anger and deceit.

The associations between *kutasa* and oral incorporation formed part of a wider complex of associations with bodily processes and activities. A sorcerer, as I have indicated, had a wrong relation with eating. But sorcery was also associated with wrong kinds of elimination and wrong kinds of sexuality. Defecating in the wrong places, notably in the house, on the plaza surrounding the house or on a path, could be the deliberate work of a sorcerer using his faeces as bad medicine. At the very least, an adult who did that sort of thing showed himself anti-social and, therefore, likely to commit sorcery by other means. In a similar fashion, the acts considered by Taita to be sexual perversions could be either labelled sorcery in themselves or taken as signs of the sorcerer's nature. By contrast, the true *Mtasi*, the non-sorcerer, the 'normal' person, had the right relations with eating, elimination and sexuality. The nature of someone's control over and use of bodily functions carried implications for the state of his feelings and his relations with other persons. 'Abnormal' relations with eating, elimination and sexuality suggested, to Taita, that the individual 'did not love people'. His actions affronted others, demonstrating his contempt, his lack of caring for others. Thus someone defecating on the path left the filth where others might step on it; a man who persisted in 'abnormal' sexual practices endangered his wife's fertility. Above all, wrong relations with food and eating signalled angry feelings and possibly hostile actions towards others. Taita called a traitor an 'eater in two places': someone who dissembled, making other citizens think that he and they shared food in good fellowship. Treachery could be conceptualized in this way precisely because eating with someone was supposed to show good will. Being associated with good will, right eating was for Taita a primary medium of social interaction. As an act at once intimately private and socially malleable, eating lent itself to linking feelings inside the person with relations among persons.[10] In the same oral idiom, *kutasa* brought angry feelings out from inside the actor, helping to improve relations with other persons and person-like agents.

Since the bodily movements and the speech of *kutasa* together made up

the performer's refusal to incorporate (or 'eat') anger, the relationship
between the components needs some attention. The suggestion that the
speech component of religious or other ritual 'describes' what the bodily
movement accomplishes cannot be taken seriously.[11] To speak of 'describing' in this context would reduce ritual speech to the predicative and
referential, neglecting its action aspect. At the same time, assertions to the
effect that bodily movements and speech simply constitute equivalent
messages in different media cannot stand in the absence of extensive
empirical findings.[12] The concept of performative utterance offers help.

A Taita speaker, like a speaker of English, has available to him a wide
range of devices for showing how his speech act is to be taken, whether
he is making a statement – and doing nothing in addition to that – or
whether he is performing the act of warning or threatening, promising,
forbidding, judging, betting, vowing or whatever. Like the speakers of
other languages, the Taita speaker can use an explicit 'performative verb'
(by saying, 'I state', 'I warn', 'I vow', etc.) or he can use one or more
conventional devices such as tone of voice, idiomatic phrases or conventional circumlocutions. That is, a speaker can choose among various
'illocutionary force-indicating devices'.[13] Features of the total speech
situation also contribute to showing what act is being performed in uttering.[14] Accordingly, the participant in *βutasi* could use a range of devices
to show what he was performing: an explicit rejection of anger, or an
implicit one joined to acts of wishing, blessing, supplicating or urging.

Futility attends the search for a single kind of relationship between
ritual speech and bodily movement. However, attending to the above
feature of *malombi* helps to relate speech and bodily movement in some
ritual acts. It is clear that in some total ritual acts one of the components
functions as a force-showing device that indicates how the other component is to be taken. Movement, through an explicitness of 'body
language', can show how a highly formulaic utterance is to be taken: what
act is being performed. Or an explicit utterance may show how a formulaic
gesture is to be taken: what it accomplishes. Or speech and gesture can
function as mutual force-showing devices, each 'spelling out' what the
other does. The physical spitting out showed how the *malombi* were to be
taken, whatever their specific form: as acts of truly *rejecting* the incorporation of anger. At the same time, the *malombi* showed that the physical
spitting out was neither ordinary spitting for 'practical' purposes nor yet
the spitting done as a deliberate rudeness, but the act of rejecting (by
ejecting) *anger*. In *ƙutasa*, then, the two components of speech and bodily
movement functioned mutually as force-indicating devices, each showing
how the other was to be taken in contrast to other speech acts or bodily
actions.[15]

Kutasa presented a connection between feeling, speech and oral incorporation. The link appeared also in the idiom referring to thoughtful, deliberative speech as *kuja malago*, 'chewing words'. More directly relevant to *kutasa*, feeling resentment or anger could be spoken of as 'hiding words in the heart'. In *kutasa*, such 'words' were rejected in the speech of *malombi* and ejected in the bodily spitting out. This requires some discussion of the importance of eating for Taita religion.

Any religious ritual among the Taita entailed commensality. In the simplest rites dominated by the central acts of *kutasa*, participants always shared the beer and cane juice after the completion of anger-rejection. They did so as persons with 'coolness' in their hearts who were therefore at peace with one another. In the rituals that included *kizongona*, commensality formed part of a far more complex sequence of ritual actions.

The modes of killing animals for religious rituals distinguished *kizongona* both from ordinary 'practical' slaughter of animals for feasting and also from the use of animals in certain juridical rites. Killing animals (usually chickens) for food required the most convenient and expeditious methods. For administration of *mugule*, the oath against sorcery and perjury, chickens and goats had their throats cut: bloodshed and *blood itself as shed through killing* were intrinsic to the rite. In *βutasi* (apart from the *Seso* rites) correctness demanded that the animal be killed *bloodlessly*; or at least that it be made unconscious before the blood-shedding knife came into use. The choice between strangling and battering into unconsciousness depended on the nature of the animal and the end of the ritual, as did the practice of rubbing the beast's nose and mouth with medicine leaves or stuffing vegetation into the mouth and nostrils. Slaughter and use of an animal in a religious ritual by no means precluded the usual beer drink. Pieces of flesh and most of the internal organs, roasted on skewers, provided small quantities of meat to be shared out among participants who also drank beer or cane juice together.

Examination of *malombi* shows that in those religious rites that included *kizongona*, Taita *offered* the animal to a mystical agent. They told the mystical agent that they were *giving* a goat or ox or whatever, and they urged the mystical agent to *eat* it. Similarly, they offered beer and urged the mystical agent to drink it. Absolutely no evidence presents itself, either in what Taita did or said in religious rituals or in what they said about their practices, that *kizongona* was 'sacrifice' in the sense of vicarious offering. Taita did not offer an animal victim in place of a human victim except in the most general sense: the human victim of mystical anger hoped to be released from misfortune by offering *kizongona*. Insofar as the anthropological use of that term *sacrifice* has been (unfortunately) invaded by the notion of vicarious offering, it is inappropriate to the Taita situation. That is why I have referred to animal *offering*. In *kizongona* Taita *offered a gift* that was specifically a *gift of food*, as in offering beer they presented a gift of refreshment.[16] Pathside offerings to ancestral dead made the point most clearly; *malombi* on other occasions indicated the same. Since participants shared meat and beer, the offering of food gifts to mystical agents entailed commensalism among living humans – who themselves possessed mystical attributes. In religious rituals angry mystical agents were placated with gifts of food, and commensalism drew human participants together in mutual good will. In this way religious events resembled other contexts of Taita life in which gifts, including food gifts, and commensality were tied to the creation and maintenance of good fellowship.

In the Taita view, the most desirable forms of exchange contrasted with market transactions in being personalistic, entailing long-term relations of mutual interest and concern. Among forms of exchange, gift giving ranked high; and among gifts, food held a special place, especially food shared among persons. The true mutuality supposed to characterize personalistic exchange, gift giving and food sharing depended (in Taita thought) on good will. In being tied to ideas about how good will is kept, lost or re-established, the giving of food meets with the doctrine of hearts. An exhaustive account of Taita exchange and commensality would go far afield. Yet even without such an account, non-religious exchange and commensality can shed light on Taita religious rituals.

Preference for personalistic as against market transactions dominated the exchange of land and livestock. The outright purchase of livestock for 'cash-in-hand' (*pesa mkononyi*) found little favour. Men preferred to arrange the transaction known as *kifu*, 'belly', whereby one party contracted for the offspring of a pregnant cow owned by the other. Some *kifu* transactions stretched over many years. Even after completion of the exchange, the cow's owner could make a request of the recipient of the calf on account of the favour he had shown by agreeing to the transaction in the first place. Or the man who had received the calf might request another favour of the mother cow's owner on the grounds that the original favour showed friendliness that could be relied on again. Any single *kifu* transaction, including that of bridewealth, became part of a network of long-term exchange relationships. Other transactions also entailed the assumption of long-term involvement and Taita viewed them as evidence of friendliness likely to be shown on other occasions too. On that account alone gift giving could not be set wholly apart from other personalistic transactions. In the Taita formulation any non-market transaction entailed an element of gift giving in the sense of a favour or favours conferred. *Kizongona* therefore cannot be thought of as a 'buying off' of a mystical agent with a payment of meat. Rather, transactions that persons accustomed to a market dominated economy think of as sales and purchases, in Taita bore the marks of gift-like transfers sharing some important features with religious offerings.

In pre-Colonial times poor men attached themselves to the households of rich elders, serving as herders in exchange for their keep. Although remnants of the practice survived in the period of fieldwork, another established practice was preferred. A man in need of livestock went to a richer man offering a small gift and asking a larger one. If the richer man did not wish to 'give' anything, he refused the *douceur*. If he accepted the latter and gave the supplicant what was wanted, he did not expect a quick return. On the contrary, the recipient, if much poorer than the donor, repeatedly asked for more. He counted among those owing the richer man respect, service, hospitality and support in disputes. The richer man (who was also likely to be considerably older than his supporter) in turn accepted a long-term, diffuse obligation to look out for his follower. Transactions arranged between men of modest and roughly equal resources entailed mutual support and concern. Whether dictated by need or by the customary expectations based on kinship or affinity, clothing and other purchased goods, money, hens, seed grain and other items changed hands in a welter of small gifts among which transactions in land and livestock stood out as carrying special political implications.

Taita had a ready response to questions about 'giving' (*kuneka*); when the parties differed greatly in resources or were by definition of unequal status (elders and juniors), the richer or socially superior one was said to 'get his person' (*wapata mundu wake*). The other party was said to 'get his great one' (*wapata mbaha wake*). For those equivalent in wealth and status, each could be said to 'get his person'. In either case, Taita expected long-term mutual concern to prevail between them.

In all exchange relationships (exclusive of straight market transactions), demand for a final settlement signalled the desire to end the relationship. Should the recipient of a gift make a quick and equivalent return he left himself open to a charge of pride (*βuŋeti*) as one unwilling to accept favours from another. When givers of *kifu*, mutual-aid partners, 'great ones' or exchanging friends demanded immediate settling-up they threw the emphasis on indebtedness rather than on mutuality. To Taita that indicated either growing remoteness or anger that must be soothed if the relationship were to continue. Ideally, each occasion of giving and receiving demonstrated good will. The things given and received were not only goods in themselves; their passage showed willingness to enter into and maintain long-term mutuality. In *βutasi* the anger of a mystical agent, felt in misfortune, signalled that something had to be put right in the relationship. The placation of anger with an offering of livestock and/or beer aimed to restore good feeling. Equally important, living human participants rejected and ejected anger from themselves. *Kizongona* and *kutasa* joined to re-establish the mutual good will of long-term relationships. Commensalism created and demonstrated that good will.

On a great many occasions in Taita life, a beer drink and perhaps a feast of meat and other cooked food rewarded services, insured future ones, bound participants as witnesses and, in general, contributed to good fellowship. Giving and sharing food bound people together in the web of exchanges mentioned above, all underlain by the assumption that kin, affines and neighbours were related to one another in mutual concern, and not merely engaged in self-seeking. Indeed, by Taita definitions, merely to offer to share food showed amity, while refusal to eat with someone showed hostility. Given that food and drink had to be won by much effort and were often in short supply, sharing had a practical importance. But Taita considered it enough that a man, receiving a visitor just as he was finishing a meal, offered to share the remaining scraps. It was enough that someone hurrying through a hamlet on the way to the fields should stop to accept a mouthful of food from a neighbour dining out under the trees. Refusing to feed or refresh others, as well as refusal to eat or drink with them, Taita took as a sign of selfishness and of 'not loving people'.

Food giving and eating together constituted a vital part of the life of households, villages and neighbourhoods. Those who most often gave each other gifts, including food gifts, also ate and drank together on numerous occasions and expected to continue doing so. Food giving and commensalism, then, occurred in contexts in which people assumed, hoped for and avowed continuing amity and mutual concern. Certainly in any society assumptions, hopes and avowals are often not matched by real feelings. Taita did not merely hold that assumption tacitly, they made it a central theme in their religious life. In that religious life, the central act employed an oral idiom, being always associated with commensalism and often with an offering of food or drink.

Religious giving and sharing of food conformed to the Taita standards for personalistic transactions. They could not be once-and-for-all payments for release from misfortune. True, *malombi* asked that the sufferer recover and enjoy all blessings. But Taita did not expect any one religious rite to bring everlasting good; but to the end that present misfortune be lifted, present anger must be placated. There could be no assurance that the same shrine, ancestor or living person would not be angry another time. There was also no assurance that the present victim of mystical anger would not again fail or be judged to fail in his obligations. Living humans, mystically endowed, stood to each other and to mystical agents in continuing dialectic relationships. On religious occasions, offerings and commensalism, together with *kutasa*, were supposed to be at least potentially efficacious and not merely correctly symbolic of social relations. Efficacy depended on assuaging the anger of mystical agents and rejecting anger from the hearts of living human actors. The basic religious act, *kutasa*, was joined with feeding, eating and gift giving. Together they declared the good feelings without which neither individuals nor communities could survive. In this manner, Taita based their religious life upon the most fundamental of human experiences.[17]

Religious building upon the fundamental human experiences of eating and giving means also building upon the basic social experiences: upon experiences within the family and, ultimately, upon the mother–child bond of free gift and nurturance on one side, acceptance and dependency on the other. I do not mean by this that the whole of Taita religion should be thought of as nothing more than a projection of family relations or of the mother–child relationship. It is true that in the view presented in Chapter 4 and elsewhere, the domestic rituals of *βutasi* are central to the religious system as a whole. However, even in the domestic rites, fundamental – even universal – experiences and themes have been elaborated to suit a wider scheme of relationships and values. Perhaps the most striking is the critical importance for domestic rituals of the jural rights and obligations deriving from agnation and affinity. That accords with the way in which the wider social order penetrated and shaped Taita family relations. But that wider social order was shaped in turn by the particular values Taita attached to familial ties. The familial scheme of relationships was set within and inter-penetrated with the wider system of jural-political relationships.[18] So also with religious ritual: eating and giving permeated all of *βutasi*.

More elaborate themes and more extended actions suited wider relationships and more ramifying concerns, drawing together bodies of more remote kin, neighbours and the politico-ritual leaders among them. Shrine rites and communal rituals included a variety of acts and objects not found in most domestic rites. I turn now to the features that accounted for much of the greater complexity of non-domestic rites.

Like a ritual forming part of any other ritual system, any Taita religious or other ritual can be seen as made up of many elements. In the course of studying a ritual system one might record all of the elements recognized by participants as significant and differentiated bodily movements and utterances as well as material objects and substances.[19] A 'laundry list' of elements would of course not suffice, for the relationship among the elements carries the weight of meaning. One kind of relationship among ritual elements is that of temporal sequence: no matter how informal people's conduct may be, rituals embed rules according to which some elements must come before, with or after others. Another and more important kind of relation among elements is that of their occurrence in *sets*. One such set occurring in Taita religious rituals was made up of the liquids used in *ƙutasa*: saliva, water, unfermented cane juice, ordinary sugar cane beer, aged beer, beer of the altar and honey beer. Rituals and parts of rituals differed from one another in drawing different elements from this set. Several aspects are important:

a. The list of elements is not an artefact of the anthropological imagination; each element functioned as a unit recognized as such by Taita.

b. Taita recognition and specification of the elements was bound to a rule or a body of rules for determining when it was appropriate to use one rather than another element from the set. For instance, the rules operated that saliva and water were emergency liquids in differing degrees; that when liquids other than saliva and water were available, women should use unfermented cane juice unless they were past the age of childbearing, when they could use ordinary beer if they chose to do so; that the choice of fermented liquids used by men should match their age-statuses while according also with the nature of the mystical agent addressed and the aim of the rite.

c. Entire sets of ritual elements commonly differ from other entire sets according to degree and kind of boundedness. For example, an outsider might see no reason why Taita should not have done *ƙutasa* with tea, since it was a popular drink and had been made part of many ceremonialized occasions, notably those connected with marriage. But tea could not be used for *ƙutasa*. The element set comprised of liquids used for *ƙutasa* was bounded by a rule that also bounded the set of languages used in *βutasi* and the set of participants. That rule excluded (at least in theory) all that was 'foreign' from the rituals of Taita religion. Swahili or English words and phrases were not supposed to be used; strangers were not supposed to participate; and tea or other 'foreign' liquids could not be used in *ƙutasa*.

d. The boundedness of a set and also the rules for selecting elements from it can be seen in terms of one or more coordinating concepts or principles relating the set to general aspects of reality. This means that the use of only one or some elements from a set never makes the other members of the set irrelevant to an understanding of what happens in a given ritual. On the contrary, the part played by the element or elements used in one ritual is to a considerable extent a function of their *relation* to the absent elements, the latter being selected on other occasions for other rituals or other parts of the same ritual. For example, the selection of a fermented beer to use in *ƙutasa* excludes the selection of unfermented cane juice in the same ritual or the same part of a complex ritual. What is important is the *contrast* between what is selected and what is excluded, in this case the contrast between fermented beer and unfermented cane juice. For liquids used in *ƙutasa*, a major coordinating concept was the distinction between the sexes, seen by Taita as 'naturally' entailing different relationships to mystical entities and different moral careers. Another, related concept had to do with differences of age-status among males as intrinsic to the social and religious career.

Two or more element sets may be connected through one or more coordinating principles. Thus the principles of sex distinction and age-status distinction run right through Taita ritual, entering into the significance of many different elements in many sets. Further, the principles relevant to the liquids of *ƙutasa* are cross-cut by another distinction having to do with the 'cleanliness' of various creatures: Taita regarded the honey bee as the 'cleanest' of all animals and hence beer with honey in it was fit for high-status elders.

e. The elements of ritual can be said to have 'meaning', but not in the sense that they are 'symbolic of' or 'stand for' some reality not present in ritual itself. An element used in a given ritual 'refers' primarily to the total set of elements, including the absent members. Selection and use of particular elements does not so much 'represent' as *present* reality through and in ritual action. For Taita, the 'natural' social, moral and ritual differences between the sexes were not 'represented' by their use of different liquids for *ƙutasa*. That aspect of reality was *acted, recreated* and *made present*.[20]

Besides the set of liquids used in *ƙutasa*, other element sets have been mentioned repeatedly and some have been discussed. The total set of persons-in-relationships required to do *primary ƙutasa* was large and complex, but the rules governing selection were determinate and the set was bounded. I have treated this aspect of the personnel engaged in religious ritual in terms of various aspects of the Taita doctrine of hearts and also in terms of the validity conditions for the performative utterances of *malombi*. Descriptions of rituals have included mention of the various locations where rituals or portions of rituals were held: they made up another set. The animals used in *ƙizongona* made up a set given special recognition by Taita when describing given rites as composed of *ƙutasa* and *ƙizongona*. It should be clear from earlier chapters that the personnel and the locations of rites could not be randomly related to one another. Neither was either one randomly related to the selection of a particular animal for *ƙizongona* or to the choice of one or more kinds of liquid for *ƙutasa*. On the contrary, *who* performed *primary* (and other) *ƙutasa*, *where*, with *what* liquid, and offering *which animal* were closely related, bound as they all were to the subject and purpose of the ritual in relation to one or more mystical agents. Various element sets were partially independent insofar as they presented different aspects or 'facts' of Taita reality. But they were connected with one another in actual rituals, as they combined to present the world's complexities. Ritual might be thought of as being like a piece of music scored for many parts. Each chord is made up of notes selected from sets of possible notes, the whole being governed both by the melodic potentialities of each instrument and the demands of harmony among them.

An ideal combination of description and analysis would specify all the elements of a ritual system; their membership of sets, the rules for selection and combination; and the operative principles and concepts coordinating members of each set with each other and with the members of other sets. To do so would be to produce a work having something in common with the books of liturgical 'recipes' available for the rituals of scriptural religions, but one which, if satisfactory, would be more rigorously analytical than those. Here I can discuss only some aspects of some sets. They have been chosen because, first, they account for a large number of features occurring in the more complex of Taita religious rituals and, second, because they are ordered by principles or concepts of key importance. No further examination is given to the personnel doing *kutasa* or other religious actions or to the bodily movements and speech of *kutasa* and other actions. (The movements of *βutasi* included anointing, aspersing, circumambulating, changing the elevation of the body and parts of the body, moving objects in relation to each other and so on. Many of these followed well-nigh universal modes of ritual movement. Discussion of them could not be isolated from considerations of personnel and material objects or 'sacra'.)

Taita used the following animals in *kizongona*, offering: chicken, goat, sheep, ox. The order given accords with a principle entering into selection of one animal rather than another for particular rituals: chickens could be used only for 'little affairs' (*malago matini*) because they were the cheapest animals, while an ox suited only 'great affairs' (*malago mabaha*), requiring a considerable outlay in money or small stock. Goats and sheep were intermediate in price.[21] Choice of one animal rather than another also and more importantly depended on another consideration, that of how relatively 'clean' (*ielie*) an animal was considered. Goats and sheep, though alike in money value, differed in relative cleanliness and found different uses in religious ritual. Chicken and ox, vastly different from one another in price, also had different places in the scheme of relative cleanliness, the latter being less clean than the former, as goats were less clean than sheep. To call animals 'more clean' and 'less clean' suits Taita judgements according to which none of the animals used as *kizongona* was clean or unclean in an absolute sense. If Taita had been persuaded to name an animal they considered entirely unclean, they probably would have named the hyaena, which they looked on with a disgust not wholly determined by its penchant for raiding their livestock shelters on the plains. (After all, leopards also had raided stock enclosures and Taita considered them fearsomely dangerous but not unclean.) The fact is that notions of absolute cleanliness and uncleanliness played almost no part in Taita thought and action. The creature (*nyamandu*) held to be most clean was the honey bee. It was the object of Creator's favour, Taita said, because it could eat even carrion and ordure, turning them into honey. Clearly feeding habits as such did not determine the degree of cleanliness so much as the creature's own ability to transform food into something desirable. Chicken and sheep produced chyme, *mafumba*, used in the preparation of beneficent accessory medicines. This partly processed grain and grass, taken from relatively more clean animals, Taita reckoned good and relatively more clean in itself, whereas goat's chyme was less clean and was sometimes mixed with dangerous medicine, as in rites to strengthen the *Figi*. Another consideration also differentiated between goats and sheep. Sheep went quietly to the slaughter, letting themselves be beaten on the head; goats struggled and screamed, and, like oxen, required strength and determination to strangle them. Chickens, though resistant, yielded quickly. The emphasis on bloodless killing for *kizongona* can be seen here, in the greater relative cleanliness attributed to those animals for whom death at human hands need not involve an assault resisted by the creature itself. The linkage was made by way of the association between being clean (*ielie*) and being cool or peaceful (*sere*).

The use of a sheep for the consecration of a Stool attended to the fact that although goats and sheep cost the same in money, sheep were rather rare in Taita and more highly prized than goats. Thus the three major shrine acquisition (or bestowal) rites for Bag, Stool and Bell required a goat, a sheep and an ox respectively. The choice of animal for shrine consecration thus accorded with the relative rank of the shrine. But the other principle, that of relative cleanliness, determined the use of a sheep in the installation of an ancestral skull. That rite consecrated part of the deceased's body, 'revivifying' it through the use of sheep's chyme as a clean and 'lively' substance (see p. 84).

Offerings as against consecrations displayed an odd-seeming pattern. Oxen and goats served as offerings to living human hearts, the hearts of ancestral shades and shrine medicines. Creator received sheep and Cursings (*Seso*) required chickens unless another animal had been specified by the person whose suicide created the Cursing. It might be thought that the scope of a mystical agent's influence or the scale of grouping for which it served as a reference point might determine the offering selected. Ancestors, lineage shrines and personal shrines as well as the hearts of the living directed their anger and their benevolence towards particular categories of persons. In contrast, although rainmaking rituals were held by local communities, Creator affected all Taita and all of mankind – *Mlungu* did not serve as a reference point for any sectional identities or loyalties. Cursings made for inconsistency in this possible scheme, since suicides tended to direct their anger at their own lineages, while convicted sorcerers and thieves might curse the entire neighbourhood. The pattern of offerings also eliminates the hypothesis that relative cleanliness of the offering was correlated directly or inversely with the relative proneness to anger of the mystical agent. However, this second formulation, though inadequate, is nearer the mark.

Taita offered the less clean animals to those mystical agents that themselves were, or were most like, ordinary living human hearts, rather easily prone to anger and resentment, but also subject to relatively easy placation. Those mystical agents also conferred benefits on individuals and social groupings; in particular, shades and shrines exercised general beneficence and shrines conferred specific goods. Creator and Cursings stood alike at a distance from ordinary human hearts. The supra-human Creator, though mighty in wrath when aroused by moral rottenness, was slow to anger, more 'cool' than human hearts, while *Seso* Cursings were exceedingly 'hot', angry in an arbitrary way. The 'ordinary' mystical agents, human hearts and agents similar to them, fell within the scope of concern with the jural norms governing particular social relations. Living hearts, ancestral shades and shrine medicines were, so to speak, part of the social order. In contrast, Creator and Cursings stood on the borders between society and non-society. Creator was beyond human society, yet was concerned with the basic morality underlying its very existence. Cursings were produced by the anger of suicides and executed criminals, persons who had been cut off or had cut themselves off from human society. These 'extraordinary' mystical agents could not be placated in the ordinary way. Rituals directed to them included the offering of one of the more clean and cool animals as suitable for their extraordinary qualities. But whereas a cool and cleanly sheep matched the coolness of Creator, a cool and cleanly chicken counteracted the extreme heat of a Cursing.

Which of the more clean animals was offered to an 'extraordinary' mystical agent was a matter of the scope and importance of the ritual: the 'big affair' of rainmaking for a community demanded a sheep and the 'little affair' of placating a Cursing on behalf of an individual called for a chicken. Similarly, 'ordinary' mystical agents received goats or oxen depending on the scope of the ritual, with oxen reserved for acquisition of a Bell shrine, for *Ox of milungu* and for offering the *Ox of settling the earth* (for a deceased parent) and certain major juridical rituals. In selecting an animal for offering, then, Taita first applied the rule according to which the more clean animals were used for the 'extraordinary' mystical agents and the less clean animals for 'ordinary' mystical agents. Then they applied the second rule, according to which that animal was offered whose value accorded with the relative 'bigness' or 'smallness' of the ritual occasion.

In many religious rituals in Taita the presiding officiant or his delegate asperged humans, animals, farm fields or objects with *kioro*, the 'mixture for spreading and sprinkling' (*kuora* = to spread or sprinkle a substance on someone or something). This fact calls attention to the importance in *βutasi* of accessory (that is, non-shrine) medicines, now to be discussed. Taita made use of a large number of vegetable, animal and mineral substances in religious and other ritual, including real or alleged sorcery rites. The total set of ritual medicines was in principle unbounded, for outside religious and juridical rites, those who used either beneficent miscellaneous medicines or sorcery might discover or learn about new medicines from outsiders. As to medicines used in religious rituals, the boundary was set by the contrast between religion and sorcery as judged in particular instances by religious experts. Observing from the outside, I believe that in fact the total set of medicines used in Taita religion changed over time and that it was for practical purposes not bounded. At any one time, however, the proliferation of accessory medicines in religious ritual had been restrained by the watch that religious leaders kept on each other. One of the dangers besetting elders was that of being accused by a political enemy of using sorcery medicines instead of good ones; that provides an explanation for the requirement that all religious rites must be held during daylight hours, out in the open air and in the presence of witnesses. It seems likely that innovative additions to the body of accessory religious medicines would have been limited by the fear of arousing suspicion. Just what made some substances candidates for the 'sorcery' label, excluding them from the roster of religiously suitable medicines, can be seen only by considering the substances and materials themselves and then moving on to Taita notions about how the various medicines could be brought into operation. In the following brief discussion the structure of sub-sets cannot be fully expressed.

Some materials and substances functioned as the *ingredients* of medicine applied to persons, animals, fields and objects in various ways, including asperging, anointing, feeding and fumigating. Others found use as *instruments* or parts of instruments: materials and objects used for containers, aspergilla, altars and what I call 'barriers' and 'carriers'.

What was available for use as ingredients and instruments depended in part on Taita modes of discriminating among the things in the world, classifying them and using their properties. In general, ingredients and the instruments used to contain or apply them were matched according to notions of inherent 'virtues' or properties as well as convenience. Once again the boundary-creating distinction between Taita and foreign came into operation, for ideally nothing of foreign provenance was supposed to be used, though in fact a few objects of external manufacture were permitted.

Ingredients included a very large number of plants and plant parts as discriminated and classified by Taita. Roots, stems and leaves were commonly used, especially the last. Plant materials went by the general name of *mudi* (pl. *midi*), 'tree' or 'plant'; in some contexts, indeed, *mudi* was synonymous with 'medicine' (*ßuganga*). Gourds, calabashes, leaf packages, tubes made from rolled leaf and leaf cups contained the ingredients. Taita held that plants and their parts possessed inherent properties, some of which were determined by the places where they grew. In Taita phraseology, each plant had its own manner of growing, its own habitat, its own properties; it had its own 'path', 'way' or 'habit' (*chia*). Plants found on the high peaks, where rain first fell, had the intrinsic property of 'coolness', matching their habitat; in like manner, 'hot' plants grew on the hot, dry plains. The hot/cool distinction was of prime importance, for hot plant medicines could be used to harm, while the effects of cool plant medicine were peaceful, soothing, healing. As one would expect, the hot/cool distinction corresponded largely, though not entirely, to the sorcery/religion distinction. Sorcerers tried to harm their victims by using hot medicines and religious celebrants chose cool medicines except when performing legitimate acts of anti-sorcery and related rites such as strengthening a *Figi*. Some but not all plants were also distinguished from one another according to whether they were 'sour' or 'sweet'. Others were noted as especially hard and durable or as soft and perishable. Some plant parts entered the roster of medicines by virtue of their resemblance to what was being treated or averted: that held less for the medicines of religion than for non-religious beneficent medicine and sorcery. For example, a beneficent medicine used against certain grubs infesting gardens was made from pods resembling the pests in colour and form.

Taita employed no category coextensive with our category 'mineral'. Red ochre and white chalk, mixed with sheep's fat and used for ritual painting and anointing, clearly fell outside their categories 'trees' (or 'plants') and 'animals'. The same was true of stones, used as instruments: for stunning animals used in offering and, in juridical rites, as 'barriers'. Water was an important ingredient of many medicines, and here the important distinction was between moving water from waterfalls and rapids, and still water.

The instruments and ingredients of accessory medicines cannot be treated entirely apart from the other uses of vegetable, mineral and animal materials in ritual. Stool shrines had to be made from a hard, durable wood; the Bell shrine was just like an ordinary iron cow bell. Of much greater interest in relation to accessory medicines are the human and animal parts and products. Enshrined skulls and the arm bones in lineage shrine centres were human parts figuring in religious ritual. Of human body products, saliva was used in emergency *kutasa*. Domestic animals did not figure in the materials of shrines, but some wild animal bones and skins were supposed to be among the components of central lineage shrines. Domestic animals contributed their stomachs, entrails and the contents of the latter to divination. Semen, menstrual fluid and milk were absent from all licit ritual medicines, although human milk was supposed to be a non-ritual curing medicine for snake bite. Human body parts and products could not be used as an ingredient in licit ritual medicine with the exception of human blood in two juridical rites. Each man entering a blood pact ate a bit of meat smeared with his partner's blood taken from a small cut over the breastbone; and the oath-medicine against sorcery and perjury contained the subject's own blood and was drunk by him and rubbed into cuts over his joints and breastbone.

Numerous parts and products of domestic animals were used in ritual, especially religious ritual. As noted previously, animals killed for religious offering had to be rendered unconscious by bloodless methods, the blood being later collected for use in the offering and ritual meal. Such blood was *mnyoo* as against ordinary shed blood, *paga*. Religious ritual made no use of either kind of blood in accessory medicine, but the oath medicine against sorcery and perjury also contained the *paga* of chicken and goat, along with the subject's own blood as mentioned above. Shed blood of humans and animals was associated also with sorcery ritual. Over against the juridical (licit but non-religious) and sorcery (illicit) ritual uses of blood, stood the religious use of the chyme of animal offerings as a primary ingredient of the 'mixture for spreading and sprinkling' (*kioro*). Ox urine was used in the medicine applied to a new Bell shrine and its owner. Ingredients did not include the dung of livestock, but the dung of hyrax, associated by Taita with the prospering of goats, was used in the medicine applied to a new Stool shrine.

Taita much prized the fat of the fat-tailed sheep as a condiment, pouring it over cooked plantains and other dishes. In religious ritual this fat appeared as an instrument for binding together some of the plant, mineral and animal ingredients used in the Bag shrine medicines. The hides of

goats and cattle, used in making clothing and beds, in religious ritual
supplied thong bracelets, coverings and 'barriers'; hides were also instruments for segregating some persons and objects from others.

The selection of ingredients and instruments for particular rites depended on several coordinating concepts. Themselves inter-related, the
concepts also brought accessory medicines into line with the other materials
used in ritual. If one starts with blood as an ingredient of accessory
medicines, its absence in religious ritual contrasts with its presence in
juridical rites and sorcery. But the most significant contrast is that between
the religious use of blood collected from an animal killed or rendered
unconscious bloodlessly and the use in other ritual of blood shed in the
course of killing. Blood used in religious ritual was, so to speak, 'non-
violent blood'. The blood used in juridical rituals was human blood shed
by a living, conscious person submitting to the knife, and animal blood
as the product of an assault: as the animal's throat was cut the blood was
collected in a calabash. (Alleged) sorcery also employed shed animal blood
which the evil-doer sprinkled around his victim's homestead while uttering a curse. The contrast, then, was between the peacefulness of religious
ritual, the licit violence of juridical rites and the illicit violence of sorcery.
In this connection, it is significant that the human arm bone forming a
component of (some?) lineage shrine assemblages was not supposed to be
the product of violence but (in Taita terms) of peaceful offering of a
human being. One account of a shrine arm bone held that the lineage
founder offered his own daughter in order to secure his descendants' life
and well-being (though to what mystical agent is quite unclear) whereupon her arm bone became part of the shrine assemblage. In contrast, the
most powerful of all sorcerers' instruments was held to be a human corpse's
arm bone decorated with beads and wire and used to strike the victim as
the sorcerer pronounced a curse. Here, too, sorcery was associated with
illicit assault in contrast to religion.

Another coordinating concept intertwined with the contrast between
peaceable and assaultive modes of obtaining blood and bone. It had to do
with the processes and products of change and transformation. Taita
probably had chosen the skull and one of the long bones as those
portions of the human body used in religious ritual partly because of
the enduring quality of bone. The skull was associated with enduring
personal identity also because of being recognizable (in theory, at least)
from its conformation and dentition, and it had contained the major sense
organs and the brain, associated with speech, 'rationality' and social
maturing. In addition, for proper enshrinement, human skulls and long
bones had to be 'revivified' by treating with chyme. The arm bone used
by a sorcerer was the relic of a corpse; religiously used human bones were

associated with life. Chyme, blood and urine from offered animals had life and conferred life because they were drawn from the animals immediately after non-violent killing, but chyme was most of all taken by Taita to be a vehicle of ongoing life processes. That the other contents of the digestive tract of livestock had the same nature can be seen from the fact that each full portion of intestine noted in divination was an auspicious sign. Contrastingly, human faeces were associated with sorcery both because sorcerers allegedly used faeces as evil medicine and because sorcerers did not properly control their body functions.

The concept of body products as being either vehicles of life processes or relics of death found a counterpart in the use of plant ingredients, further complicated by modes of preparation. Freshly picked green plants, particularly those growing on the moist peaks, epitomized vegetable life, the rain it depended on and the lives of animals and men depending on it in turn. Rotten vegetable materials were good for nothing – I know of no suggestion that even sorcerers would use rotten plants, devoid of all intrinsic virtues. Whatever the virtue of a plant, it could be preserved, fixed, by slowly heating and charring the material, whereupon it was ground up, mixed with other ingredients (including fat) and stored in horns or small gourds. Good plant parts properly prepared, then, were 'lively' after the fashion of chyme, even though charred and, consequently, black.

The third coordinating concept drew the others together and linked them to other aspects of religious ritual. Using what might be called an 'alimentary model' of the relationship between humans and their livestock, it involved seeing all parts of the livestock digestive tract as useful to man and as contrasting with man's own alimentary canal. The throat and some intestinal parts of offered animals went to elderly men and women. The stomach served as a balloon-like cushion on which to rest the intestines and their mesentery, spread out for haruspication. Chyme, as has been stressed, was pre-eminent among animal body products seen as embodying life processes, and even faecal matter, while still within the animal's body, was good. Actually, though Taita disapproved of people who did not keep their homestead plazas swept clean of dung, they did not consider the latter filthy in itself. (Cow dung was not only not objectionable, but, as for farming people throughout the world, both good in itself and a sign of other good things. A Taita proverb that advised giving everyone his due said, 'Even the herd-boy gets his slice', slice referring here to a cross-section of cow-pat.) On the contrary, it was associated with auspiciousness, life, peace and, therefore, with relative purity or cleanliness. The human alimentary canal was seen very differently, as exhibiting polarity. Saliva, used in emergency *ƙutasa*, was in any case mixed with the liquid taken into the mouth in performance of *ƙutasa*. Along with the liquid, it served as an instrument for rejecting anger. Taita did not treat saliva as positively good, and some uses of saliva were rude, but it was not in itself dirty. The faeces produced by the lower end of the human alimentary canal were filth *par excellence*. In this way, humans, livestock and also plants eaten by men and herds were made part of a chain of being, about which Taita were quite explicit. Livestock ate grasses and leaves; transformation of these foods was seen in the chyme, the embodiment of life processes. Human beings not only ate their own vegetable food as well as the flesh and blood of their herds, but ritually 'consumed', that is, put to their use, as medicinal ingredients, all parts and products of the livestock alimentary canal. What had passed through the human alimentary canal was totally without any good, a catabolic relic useable only by sorcerers. Thus the upper part of the human digestive tract, in *kutasa*, was connected with the rejection of anger, with non-violence, and life; the lower part was associated, in sorcery, with angry violence and death. The good body products of livestock, along with good vegetation, became ingredients of the beneficent medicines of *βutasi*. They effected and presented, in ritual, the incorporation of livestock and plant life by man with whose life and well-being livestock and vegetation were identified.

Among wild animals, the hyrax supplied a medicinal ingredient for doctoring the Stool because its dung, commonly found in upland places where goats browsed, had on this account an association with the livestock prospered by the Stool. So far as my information goes only a few small wild animals supplied components for the great lineage shrine. Use of wild animal parts for their potency in serving the sectional interests of lineages had a morally ambiguous quality for Taita who, in general, saw the wild and its creatures as alien and dangerous. Between those creatures on the one hand and man and his livestock on the other, were the domestic dog and cat, totally excluded from licit ritual of all kinds.

I now summarize the coordinating concepts accounting for the ritual occurrence and selection of animal parts and products. One principle contrasted the non-violent (i.e. 'bloodless') killing of animals for offering with the assaultive killing for other ritual and non-ritual uses. Body products derived from the two different modes of killing partook of the quality of the animal's death and thereby became eligible for use in peaceful religious ritual, licit (but 'violent') juridical rites and illicit sorcery. This principle was closely linked to the second, contrasting body products seen as incorporating ongoing life processes with those seen as the relics of death and catabolism. The third tied the first two to the conceptualization of a chain of being in which livestock having unpolarized alimentary canals (in the sense that products of all parts of the canal embodied ongoing life processes) incorporated vegetation and in turn were incorporated by the polarized human alimentary canal. The polarity of the human alimentary canal embodied the polarities of non-violence versus violence and of ongoing life processes versus the relics of death and catabolism. According to the fourth principle, socialized humans (i.e. non-sorcerers properly controlling their body functions and properly getting rid of their anger) stood, together with their livestock, over against creatures of the wild whose use was therefore morally ambiguous and ritually slight; between the fully domestic and the wild were the domestic cat and dog. The four interlinked principles or concepts might be summed up legitimately in terms of a contrast between culture and nature. However, it is not clear that such a formulation contributes anything more to understanding what Taita religion was about.

The complexity and inter-connections of the principles and concepts as actually used in ritual yielded a situation in which colours could hardly be monosemic. The white-red-black colour triad occurred, with built-in polysemy. For example, white chalk as an ingredient, identified by some Taita Bag owners as snow from the top of Mt Kilimanjaro, was a good, cool, clean substance. But the whiteness of a pale, bloodless mesenteric flap in haruspication spelled lifelessness. Whether or not red was desirable or undesirable was a function of its association with either 'non-violent' blood as embodying life processes or the shed blood of 'violence' (including the involuntarily shed blood of menstruation and childbirth). Hence blood in the mesenteric veins was 'good' but a red spot near a vein was a 'bad' sign of sorcery. The blackness of dung in the intestine was an auspicious sign in haruspication, but a black spot was a 'curse' linked with the badness of human excrement and of ensorcelled food.

Selection of an ingredient could not, therefore, be a matter of any simple evaluation of body products, but had to take account of processes and inter-relations. The resulting ambiguity of colours themselves was especially striking for black. Accusations of sorcery against elders almost always asserted that they had black medicines in their possessions. But, as I have noted, any vegetable ingredient could be prepared by roasting and charring the substance so as to preserve its virtue. Blackness could not in fact be used to distinguish bad medicines from good ones. That Government officers and missionaries were not aware of that fact made it possible for some Taita to implement their grudges against others in the guise of a concern to stamp out sorcery. The tendency of Europeans to associate the colour black with evil contributed to the practice. Actually, it is not correct to speak without qualification of Taita attributing significance to *colours* as labelled in English. In common with many other African people, Taita stressed the contrast between the dark of the night and the light of the day, a range of hues being associated with each, especially with the former.

Another range of hues was covered by a third term, sometimes suitably glossed 'red'. It is more in keeping with Taita conceptualization to use the labels, 'dark', 'light', and 'bright', recognizing the fact that black, dark brown and dark blue were all 'dark'; white, very light brown and buff were 'light'; and red, orange and yellow were 'bright'. Thus the colours black, white, and red were indeed important in Taita ritual, but the words used in referring to them were not colour terms corresponding to the English colour terms.[22]

The notion of process as affecting the use of various ingredients and having consequences for evaluating 'colours' was linked further to conceptualizations of the ways in which medicines 'worked'. Two familiar principles operated, that like produced like and that action taken upon a part affected the whole. Thus medicines made from plants found on the peaks produced 'cooling' effects akin to the coolness of the heights; animal products embodying life processes had life-enhancing effects. The part-whole notion is seen in the practice of sprinkling *kioro* on only some of the fields belonging to members of a lineage in order to insure that all their fields be affected by the 'liveliness' of the chyme and other ingredients of sprinkling medicine.

The use of magical analogizing[23] extended to matching instruments and ingredients, as when 'cool' medicines were mixed in a 'sweet' calabash and 'hot' medicines in a 'sour' calabash. In a special development of this principle, a number of substances and objects served as instruments with which to transmit the effects of medicines or to hinder their influence. Sheep's fat, used to bind together some medicinal ingredients, also helped to transmit the virtues of the medicines to the objects and persons treated. Another 'carrier' was smoke: in several religious rituals, plant medicines were burned beneath a little altar on which objects lay which, by means of fumigation, had the qualities of the medicines transmitted to them. Water, besides carrying medicinal virtues, also produced its own effects: water drawn from a waterfall or rapids embodied the qualities of dynamism and copiousness associated with rain, as still water did not. (Mist and drizzle were not kinds of rain to the Taita. The first was copious but not dynamic, the second was dynamic but not copious. Rain was both.) Sound also carried the virtues of medicines, as when a horn from a *Mlimu* house was doctored with rain medicines and blown at crossroads during a rainmaking rite. By contrast, stones prevented the transmission of medicinal virtues. Hence the stone on which a person swearing the *mugule* oath (pp. 38, 170) ensured both that the effects of the medicine would be confined to the subject and that nothing acting as an antidote could reach him from the ground where it might be buried. Hides acted as barriers but were also used to separate key participants in ritual from others present and to unite them with one another (as mother and child in the Bag curing rite, two men making a blood pact and the new Bell owner with the elders conferring it on him).

Properties of the entities treated with medicine required its application in particular ways. For the human body the joints and the breastbone were points of entry for medicines rubbed into cuts. The joints were also exit points for the blood collected in juridical rituals. Legs and arms were treated when the medicine was supposed to increase the subject's strength. An important part-whole relationship operated also, in that application of medicine to the head effected treatment of the entire person. The landscape also had its points of entry and exit at crossroads and at the passes leading from the plains to the hills.

Attaching importance to points of entry and exit was part of conceptualizing the human body and the landscape as having an inside to which and from which substances and influences could flow. *Vis-à-vis* the plains wilderness, the hill homeland was the inside to be protected from alien influences. The human body had also to be protected from attacks from outside by way of sorcery. As will have become clear from this and previous chapters, Taita gave much thought to the human body and the whole human person as having an inside from which and to which mystical influences flowed. The mouth was of course the primary orifice for entry from the outside, of food and of medicine, both good and bad. Faeces with a potential as sorcery medicine exited from the other end of the polarized alimentary canal. The mouth took in liquid and sprayed it out in *kutasa*. From the mouth also came the speech of *malombi*.

The capacity for speech connected the inner selves of human persons with the capacity of medicines, minimally personified mystical entities, to respond to speech. None of the medicinal qualities and processes discussed in this chapter could operate in the absence of the spoken word issuing in religious acts of *malombi*, in the conditional cursing of juridical rites or in the unconditional cursing of sorcery and execution ritual. The principles accounting for the selection of medicines were keyed into the conceptualization of the world as a place where mystical entities with person-like attributes interacted with living humans having mystical attributes. Human speech 'from the heart', i.e. from inside the self, was essential to religious action and interaction. Through it, feelings and intentions could be directed and consciously sent forth as active agents in the world. Medicines provide a test of this proposition. From 'our' point of view, the Taita notion that a man who had been bitten by a snake could be cured if a woman with milk in her breasts suckled him, displays an interesting 'magical' thought fraught with Oedipal suggestiveness. However, Taita insisted that the cure worked mechanistically, needing no words to set in motion the non-ritual curative virtues of mother's milk. On the other hand, *mbaro*, the execution medicine, again from 'our' point of view, was a virulent poison; yet Taita insisted that it could not take effect properly without the cursing by the Executioners' Society acting against an enemy of the people. The effectiveness or non-effectiveness in a mechanistic sense clearly was beside the point. What counted was the attribution in ritual to living human persons of the capacity to act on the world in 'heartfelt' speech as well as in bodily movement.

In Chapter 2 and, indeed, throughout the book, I have followed the Taita assertion that *βutasi*, the religion of *kutasa*, comprised a domain of action with its own cultural and social dimensions. The movement of this chapter shows the ways in which *βutasi* was defined as a domain by juxta-position with and in relation to other ritual. That concepts and principles cross-cut religious and other rituals can be seen in a concluding brief com-parison of the juridical ritual of *mugule*, the oath against perjury and sorcery, with rainmaking.

A person taking the *mugule* oath proceeded with other participants in the rite to an uncultivated spot near but not at a crossroads. Under the direction of the elder keeping the medicine (which was carried for him by an assistant), the subject removed all clothing except a waistcloth. A stone having been set in place as a 'barrier', a chicken and then a goat had their throats cut so that blood dripped on the stone and was also gathered into a calabash. The officiant also made cuts over the subject's joints and breastbone ensuring that his blood also flowed onto the stone and into the calabash. The subject then stood upon the stone while a red 'tarboosh' (fez) was placed on his head. The three kinds of shed blood were mixed in the calabash with the 'hot' *mugule* medicines to which still water was added. The male witnesses, sitting in a semi-circle around the stone, took out their knives and put them on the ground with their points toward the subject. The officiant rubbed *mugule* into the subject's cuts and then offered him the calabash of medicine to drink. In between three sips of the medicine the subject swore, 'If I am indeed a sorcerer (or perjurer), may I die before the next beans ripen.' The medicine, set in motion by the oath, killed the guilty and left the innocent unscathed.

Since the religious ritual of rainmaking has already been described fully, here I only summarize the key contrasts. The location was one of the rainmaking groves, the officiant the neighbourhood Rainmaker. Instead of a bloody assaultive killing of goat and chicken (yielding *paga*, shed blood), a sheep was battered into insensibility and then suffocated, yielding chyme and *mnyoo*, 'unbloody blood' of offering. *Kutasa* with beer and cane juice distinguished men and women participants, the presence of both sexes being required. The utterances were *malombi*. In this case prayers in the form of wishings were performed 'in the presence of' Creator, to whom offering ostensibly was directed. Men prepared *ƙioro* from cool medicines mixed with chyme and moving water (taken from a waterfall or rapids), and spread it on selected farm fields. The horn of a *Mlimu* house, doctored with rain medicines and blown at the crossroads, enabled the virtues of the medicines to be carried by sound. Peaceful cooperation had to be shown in a variety of ways, as by putting all beer contributions together in a single large pot. All actions were in keeping with the pervasive theme of peace within human hearts, peaceful relations within the community and the peaceful, cool aspects of the livestock, vegetation and rain on which humans depended. *βula* read from the sheep's entrails showed whether the ends of the rite would be realized. A married people's dance celebrated an auspicious reading and also contributed to a happy outcome. Figure 3 shows the contrasts between *mugule* and rainmaking.

At numerous points, the *mugule* rite and that of rainmaking exhibited 'differences that make a difference'. Were each Taita ritual to be compared, point by point, with all others, intricate combinations of similarities and differences would be revealed, showing how elements from various sets were selected and combined. The groupings of similarities and differences could be displayed as yielding the categories of ritual recognized by Taita themselves: *βutasi tiƙi* (religion in the paradigmatic sense); *sa βutasi* (non-paradigmatic religion, i.e. juridical rites other than the ritual of execution); *sa βusaβi* (execution ritual, that which was 'like sorcery' but not paradigmatically sorcery) and *βusaβi* (paradigmatic sorcery). Rites using beneficent medicines would be left as a residual category not labelled by Taita. The central acts of *ƙutasa* and *ƙizongona* would be shown to characterize those rituals that Taita called *βutasi* or *βutasi tiƙi*; and rites belonging to that group or domain would be shown to differ from one another in their selection of elements. The major distinctions between *βutasi* and other rituals would be those discussed in Chapter 2. As the comparison between *mugule* and rainmaking shows, juridical rites (*sa βutasi*) and *βutasi* proper were indeed parts of a wider ritual system with the same major principles operating throughout it. Even though not all alleged sorcery acts were carried out, sorcery rites have to be counted as part of the wider ritual order, along with execution ritual, for part of the meaning of licit ritual acts lay in their relationship to sorcery as supposedly performed.

The elements making up *mugule* differed from and sometimes formed simple paired contrasts with the elements making up rainmaking. For each rite, the significance or 'meaning' lay in the relationship among different elements and different combinations of elements. That is, the

Figure 3. Ritual elements: *mugule* and rainmaking

	Mugule	*Rainmaking*
Aim	Peace of community, by way of getting rid of a criminal	Realization of common good: rain, crops, fertility of humans and livestock
Participants	Adult males; women not required (unless subject a woman)	Males and females of all age-statuses
Location	Waste ground	Rain grove
Officiant	Keeper of *mugule* medicine	Neighbourhood Rainmaker
Utterances	Conditional curse (*magemi*) pronounced on self by subject	Prayers (*malombi*) in form of wishing for the good things of life for all
Movement joined to utterance	Subject drinks medicine; all others point knives at subject while officiant administers medicine *kuja mugule*	All men spit out beer, led by Rainmaker *kutasa*
Animal used	Goat, chicken	Sheep
Mode of killing	Slitting throat	Battering, suffocation
Animal killed in order	To supply shed blood	To offer (*ostensibly*) to *Mlungu*; to read *βula*
Medicinal ingredients	Shed blood, hot plant medicines, still water	Chyme, cool plant medicines, moving water
Medicinal virtues transmitted by	Drinking (by subject), rubbing into subject	Asperging, blowing of horn (transmission by sound)
Points of ingress	Mouth; joints	Representative farm fields; crossroads
Actions followed by	Waiting to see effects of *mugule*	Commensalism; dancing *mbeka*

meaning of bloodlessly killing an animal for offering depended on its contrast with the bloody slaughter of animals to furnish shed blood as an ingredient of hot medicine. The location of a *mugule* rite on a piece of waste ground took meaning from its being in an 'outside' place peripheral to current human use and so contrasting with the rain grove as a ritual centre focussing the hopes of a community for the good things of life. Blowing the *Mlimu* horn at the crossroads to transmit the benefits of rain medicines, and rubbing *mugule* medicine into the oath swearer's joints, together showed the human body and the social body as alike in having special points of ingress. So also for the other elements. In relation to each other, the elements of Taita ritual *presented* reality in action.

Though elaborate by comparison with domestic rites of *βutasi*, the same basic themes of wrath and love occupied the centre of the two rites compared. Both concerned community interests, the oath swearing focussed on eliminating criminals from the body politic, rainmaking rites seeking positive goods. Both presented connections between human feelings and action and the rest of the world.

EPILOGUE

Like the shrines, the accessory medicines discussed in Chapter 6 were especially abhorrent to missionaries who hoped to convert Taita to Christianity. But for anthropological purposes they are especially interesting, for they carry the exposition back to its beginning: to the organizing of the 'natural' environment by social and cultural forms and its transformation into a world permeated with social and therefore moral significance. It is still fashionable in some circles (mostly outside social and cultural anthropology) to assert that life in non-industrial societies is 'close to nature'. If the assertion implies, as it sometimes seems to, that persons in such societies are less thoroughly socialized than 'we' are, it is foolish. But there is one sense in which such a statement presents a truth: in a society such as traditional Taita society was, the 'natural' world was not entirely 'outside' human society, for it was credited with some limited, human-like characteristics, while features of the 'natural' world were read back into human persons and communities. The result was a total universe in which *both* mechanistic and mystical causes and processes were at work, linking humanity with the rest of the universe.

This exchange of qualities Taita achieved in various ways, among them being the use of what is for 'us' the metaphor of heat and coolness. For Taita, the hot/cool contrast was not only metaphorical, but constitutive of reality. This 'constitutive metaphor' is a common one which Taita put to use in their own special way in the context of a hill homeland surrounded by bleak plains.[1] The heat of the dry, game-ridden bush was equated with anger, and the coolness of the high peaks with absence of anger in a heart that was clean and at peace. Topocosm and psychocosm were structured in the same way, with the polarities of hills/plains and peaceful heart/ angry heart running through the ritual system. Other polarities were congruent: inside/outside; social/anti-social; Taita/non-Taita. What was bad to have inside the person, namely anger, had to be cast outside; its affinity was with the heat of the plains, with the anti-social acts of thieving, perjury and violence, and with dangerous alien influences. The good inside of the person whose heart had been purged of anger was linked to the coolness of the peaks, with proper behaviour and with being truly Taita. Communities had to purge themselves of sorcerers, the embodiment of heat, anger, violence and treachery, and to be filled with peaceful, right-acting and loyal citizens.

I emphasize again that anger in itself was not judged a wrong. It was anger held within, resentment unspoken, that was dangerous and had to be expelled. Creator's anger was *just* wrath. Ancestral shades *rightly* punished quarrelling among their descendants; they and shrines properly claimed tendance. Still, anger had to be cast out from living hearts and the anger of other mystical agents had to be turned away. Anger and the reasons for anger formed the Taita answer to the problem of evil, an answer that guided divination and religious ritual. Both rested on the assumption that birth, maturation, sickness and death, while having a mechanistic aspect, were also moral events in the lives of persons and communities and arose also from mystical causes.

What was the 'angry heart' that Taita supposed was so dangerous to others, particularly to members of the same nuclear family? I believe that the Taita formulation grasped the common human concern with the potentially dangerous psychobiological individual 'inside' the social person. Two aspects can be distinguished analytically and seen in relation to one another. I have noted earlier that the heart did not become effective until the young child reached the 'age of sense'. Significantly, Taita saw arrival at that stage of development as entailing both control over the self sufficient to permit the child to perform small tasks and also the ability to know when a parent mistreated him. 'Sense' thus encompassed both the carrying out of such obligations as a small child could manage, and the judging of others' performance in terms of their obligations to him. Now the ability to judge role performances according to shared standards of right and wrong is not an attribute of any social role or bundle of roles. It is presupposed by the demands and opportunities of any role and it cuts across roles in all societies. This faculty of judgement, closely related to notions about responsibility, is central to any conceptualization of the human person as one who both applies and is subject to social and mystical sanctions. (Thus in Taita both the hopelessly wicked and the hopelessly insane could be killed by authorized persons. But while the wicked were deemed responsible for what they did and so were punished, the insane were not considered responsible and their destruction was not punishment, but a measure taken in defence of the sane. Thus the wicked remained persons, albeit diminished ones, while the insane had ceased to be such.)

The Taita concept of the mystical heart combined the judgemental faculty with the persisting psychobiological nature of the individual who in his 'self-seeking' also transcends all social roles. Taita carefully observed all idiosyncracies, commenting on them by means of nicknames, songs and jokes, as well as in comments on and predictions of individuals' behaviour. When they discussed the relative influences of nature and nurture on the development of hearts as prone to be 'hot' or 'cool', they grappled with this universal problem of the relationship between the persisting individual and the social person. The official formulation combined the two. Insofar as the concept of the mystical heart pointed to the physical organ as the seat of the emotions, it attended to the psycho-biological individual subject to, but potentially recalcitrant in the face of, the shaping influences of society. But in presenting the human heart as acquiring effectiveness through socialization in the family, and as persisting after bodily death, the concept emphasized the development and persistence of the transcendent judgemental faculty. Thus the Taita concept drew on the emotional power associated with the psychobiological individual with his vast capacities for love and hate. It linked the effectiveness of those capacities to social growth.

Not surprisingly, the beginnings of that growth were seen as taking place in the early years of childhood, as boys and girls learned who they were in relation to their parents. The family continued to be the social field in which the heart's mystical power predominated. That accorded with the centrality of close kinship in the social order, in the structuring of social persons and in moral careers. Appropriately, as the mystical heart developed in both daughters and sons, so both wives and husbands had hearts that were effective (albeit in accord with their social differences), and both mothers and fathers became ancestors whose hearts affected their living offspring. Women as well as men could achieve *complete* personhood, for both acquired the judgemental faculty that was activated in their social relationships.

Men, as has been noted, developed fuller or, rather, more *elaborated* personhood, in the course of acquiring political and ritual roles closed to women. As in other societies, so in Taita, some people (mainly men) tended to obscure the difference between completion and elaboration of personhood. One stereotype of women presented them as flighty, foolish and irresponsible, in need of masculine guidance and control. That is, women were pictured as deficient in the judgemental capacity. Having less elaborated personhood, they were held to be also less complete. However, central religious doctrine and practice belied the mutterings of the everyday battle of the sexes, important as the latter was.

βutasi said that to reduce a family relationship to its *jural* essentials signalled an end to *familial* concern. In the idiom of hearts, the withdrawal of love was phrased as anger or heat. As impoverishment of a family relationship threatened its continuity, so anger in place of love could threaten the health and life of the family members. The oral idiom of *βutasi*; the ambivalent powers assigned to women as food-giving wives and mothers; and the linking of a man's ritual advancement to his father's death suggest that in Taita religion (as in others) the meeting between social and psychological processes took place in universal human concern with socialization, dependence and autonomy, and therefore with relations between succeeding generations. *βutasi* was a specific social creation and not merely a projection of psychological formations. Yet Taita religion seized and put into action universal capacities of the human psyche as shaped by life in Taita society.

The point is related to questions about religious change. One common opinion, especially outside anthropology, is that religions change or disappear in the modern world because they are vulnerable to the 'scientific world-view', a conclusion associated with identifying religion with 'belief'. Anthropologists, especially those more oriented to the study of action, emphasize the dependence of religious systems on the wider social action systems with which they are intertwined. It is still the case that anthropologists pay insufficient attention to the consequences of the fact that religious action is *interaction*, bringing together mystical agents with person-like qualities and living human beings endowed with mystical attributes. Attending to that fact raises the question of the vulnerability of religion to the demystification of the human person under various social conditions. We saw some evidence that a few young men, in process of detaching themselves from the old social order, rejected also the mystical attributes of the human person as presented in religious action. Whether the process of demystifying the human person has continued in Taita, and with what results, remains to be seen. At that time, most Taita acted as though, for the sake of life itself, anger must be cast out.

NOTES

Preface

1 See Sperber (1975). It is very likely that the exposition of 'meanings' given in Chapter 6 of this work is subject to some of the same strictures. However, my procedure requires the point-by-point comparison of ritual elements *as distinguished by participants within their action contexts*; that should eliminate some of the simplistic interpretations to which Sperber objects. (His propositions respecting psychology do not strike me as convincing or pertinent.)

2 My own early article on *saka* possession among Taita women is a case in point. Without changing the main thesis, I would now want to pay more attention to the points at which this 'ritual' performance touches on psychological formations. G. Harris (1957).

3 An extremely important contribution is M. Fortes' discussion of the response of anthropology to 'the challenge of psychoanalysis'. M. Fortes (1973b and forthcoming).

4 Fortes' discussion of the concept of the person among the Tallensi has contributed much to my treatment of the Taita situation. M. Fortes (1973a).

5 G. Harris (1976a).

6 J. L. Austin (1962).

7 G. Harris (1976c).

8 Personal communications. I. Schapera (1949).

1. Introduction

1 The people's own name for themselves was *βadaβida*, people of the Hills or mountain massif. *Daβida*, the name for their homeland used by people living on the central massif, became *Taita* or *Teita* to outsiders, who called inhabitants of all three mountain homes Wataita or Wateita. Under British rule the official name of the administrative district was *Teita*, a spelling that might have been taken over from the Germans, but *Taita* accords better with English pronunciation, given accepted orthography.

2 For the structure and inter-relations of ecological zones and settlement pattern, see A. Harris (1958).

3 The population has been described as having increased vastly over the last twenty years (personal communication). N. Humphrey (1946) assembled information on land and population for the Colonial period.

4 Sir Frederick Jackson (1930), p. 147.

5 R. Coupland (1938), pp. 391–2, 398.

6 A. Downes-Shaw (1885), p. v; John C. Willoughby (1889), p. 60; H. H. Johnston (1886), p. 215.

7   For instance, the principal distinctive feature of the Mbale dialect was (is) the occurrence of a voiced lateral fricative in positions where other dialects have a voiced alveolar fricative except in certain borrowed words pronounced alike in all dialects.

8   I use the past tense here for the sake of consistency even though the language and its dialects are unlikely to have changed drastically over a single generation.

9   Or trilingual if they also spoke Swahili, as many of them did.

10 J. A. Wray (1894) contains a mixture of dialects. Some of the missionaries believed that they could construct a single form of speech by combining features from various dialects and then persuading Taita to 'compromise' by using this 'unified' language.

11 Some narrators added, 'Whereupon *Mlungu* rested', paralleling the Biblical account in Genesis with which many Taita were familiar.

12 Taita often identified an individual as 'that dark woman' or 'that light man'. One Taita frequently began his explanations of Taita actions with the words, 'we dark people'.

13 Taita considered Kamba sorcery to be especially virulent.

14 *Daβida* is a steep upland massif; *mugongo* = high hill or mountain; *lugongo* = slope, mountainside or hillside.

15 A. H. J. Prins (1950a). That and other accounts by A. H. J. Prins (1950b) (1952, pp. 97–132) contain numerous inaccuracies resulting from the brevity of his stay in the Hills.

16 See A. Harris (1958), especially Chapter III.

17 Early visitors reported on Taita irrigation. See Joseph Thompson (1885) p. 79; C. W. Hobley (1895), pp. 550–1.

18 Taita men killed leopards with Taita-made short swords of soft iron.

19 M. Fortes (1945), pp. 242, 244, has remarked that the cessation of warfare had a disequilibrating effect on Tallensi society, indicating that 'equilibrium' as he uses the term is not synonymous with 'peace and quiet'. So also for Taita, imposed 'peace and quiet' appears to have resulted in some non-reversing changes.

20 G. Harris (1962), pp. 72–84.

21 Times of famine saw the mobilization of relations between fodder-rich and food-rich areas, with residents of the former seeking refuge in the latter; A. Harris (1958), pp. 143–51.

22 G. Harris (1962), pp. 77–8.

23 Allegedly by 'Arabs'.

24 The land use system was not understood by members of the Colonial administration, some of whom thought that the Taita made an unduly large amount of fuss over the alienation of relatively small pieces of land.

25 The permanency of rights in some kinds of fields and the possibility of sale varied from one part of the Hills to another to some extent.

26 For details and technical discussion see A. Harris (1958), Chapters V, VIII and X.

27 A. and G. Harris (1964), pp. 140–2.

28 I.e. a pair of brothers could not marry a pair of sisters, men could not exchange sisters and sororal polygyny was prohibited.

29 Defender and Rainmaker had to cooperate ritually. An idealized arrangement would have two lineages associated to form a neighbourhood, one supplying the Defender and the other the Rainmaker. Some neighbourhoods conformed to this model. Others had three lineages, with one lineage excluded from holding a community ritual office.

30 G. Harris (1962), pp. 81–2.

2. *The domain of religion*

1   The word *βutasi* belongs to a class of abstract nouns that includes also *βucha* (goodness), *βuloli* or *loli* (truth) and *βupoiye* (beauty, pleasantness).
2   The word *dini* was borrowed from Swahili.
3   As discussed later on, water or even saliva could serve in *ḳutasa* if necessary; some elaborate rites required taking in and spitting out small bits of meat or cooked bean leaves.
4   That which is *tiḳi* is paradigmatic of an entire class; that which is not *tiḳi* is a sub-class of the larger class and is less than fully paradigmatic of the class as a whole.
5   See Chapter 6.
6   See M. Fortes (1966b). As I use the word 'mystical' it has the same meaning as Fortes' 'occult'. What is mystical is what is 'hidden', what is not apparent on the surface of things.
7   Some missionaries mentioned disparaging remarks made by a few Taita Christians, the remarks turning on the use of beer in *βutasi* or on other real or supposed practices repugnant to those missionaries. A certain amount of mis-information was conveyed by Taita Christians whose command of English was less than total and whose understanding of *βutasi* was minimal. For example, someone might say that in girls' initiation ceremonies the novices were 'naked', meaning that they were bare-breasted. However, most Taita Christians spoke respectfully and even proudly of the religious heritage of their foreparents.
8   Anglican missionaries gave up an early attempt to maintain separate Christian villages. Christian families achieved some degree of social apartness by marrying among themselves. The insistence on the part of some Taita Christians that marriage with the child of one's godparent would be incestuous caused some difficulties.
9   *Kumanya* = to know legitimately and officially as a result of proper instruction; *ḳuichi* = to be acquainted with by hearsay or by uninstructed observation. In some contexts *ḳumanya* had the connotation of closely guarded knowledge of intimate affairs, e.g. a sorcerer's guilty knowledge of his victims and the harm he inflicted on them.
10 Apart, of course, from the basic fact that *βutasi* had no place for Jesus Christ as Son of God.
11 It would be unwise to depend heavily on this kind of linguistic evidence. The noun classes of Bantu languages are not so comprehensively regular as to be wholly reliable guides to solving semantic problems. See below on *milungu*.
12 Except for semantic tone, the Taita word for fig tree is identical with *Mlungu*. Having failed to notice the significant tone difference, some missionaries believed that *βutasi* called on Taita to 'worship fig trees'. Some Taita pupils at mission schools used to repeat this error.
13 *βarumu*, by a series of phonetic shifts, is the equivalent of Swahili *mizimu*.
14 I cannot think it advisable to gloss *milungu* as 'souls'.
15 As a shrine or relic does not 'contain' a saint.
16 We once asked an elder who did not know us well whether all lineages had *Chago*. While denying that he had ever heard the word, he slowly stroked his left forearm with his right hand.

17 Though I write of the ranking of personal shrines, it would be a mistake to think of Taita as having formal grades of elderhood.

18 *Pace* J. Goody (1961), p. 145, who refers to the 'undifferentiated' African category of medicine. I doubt that 'medicine' is a semantically undifferentiated category in any African language. The fact that English speakers can refer to both physicians and holders of PhD degrees as 'doctor' does not mean that the category 'doctor' is semantically undifferentiated.

19 Apparently certain rituals by means of which feuding groups made peace had been part of *sa βutasi*. Since feuding had ceased before the time of our field-work, we could not observe such rituals, nor were we able to get a coherent report of what took place. Other juridical rites were still performed and, therefore, observed.

20 When *mwalola*, the searching-out medicine, was administered on one occasion, it clearly had a drugging effect on the subject who had been accused of sorcery. He lost sphincter control and appeared dazed, although he was aware of the nature of proceedings. His responses to the crudely leading questions gave us the impression that he could have been persuaded to say anything the officiant desired.

21 An exception might have been putting the (evil) eye (*iriso* = eye) on someone, a concept not much discussed by Taita by comparison with sorcery. Taita mentioned only the hypothetical case of an old woman visiting a strange neighbourhood putting the eye on the local children for rudely taunting her.

22 G. Harris (1973b).

23 A person who had cursed another and who then refused to revoke the curse when the recalcitrant one made amends was guilty of sorcery.

24 The 'turning' of sorcery medicine on its owner, mentioned below, was an automatically acting property not indicating any capacity to demand tendance.

3. *Ritual and the moral career*

1 G. Harris (1973b).

2 G. Harris (1957).

3 One Taita man scolded my husband for 'allowing' me to stay on Sagala without him, saying, 'The flock needs the shepherd.'

4 Although I explained my gesture as a mere sign of fatigue, a Taita woman once instructed me not to sit with my hand under my chin, supporting my head. She said, 'Here in this country we say that someone has anger in the heart when he holds his head that way.'

5 It belonged to the category *mbingu*, 'protective charm' (*kuβinga* = to chase away).

6 One British Government officer was infuriated by the way in which young girls whom he questioned would insist that they were 'unable to know' their villages. Being unmarried, the girls lived in their parents' villages and, not knowing where they would be living as married women, they truly were unable to know the 'identity' of their villages; in Taita parlance, an unmarried girl had no village that could properly be called 'hers'.

7 G. Harris (1962), pp. 65–7.

8 A. and G. Harris (1964), pp. 129–34.

9 Physical violence was very rare in Taita. The few murders remembered (aside from those committed by the 'insane') had been of two kinds: one was patricide

by sons treated unfairly for many years; the other kind was the murder of a neighbourhood bully by one of his victims, whose action others condoned.

10 The one man whose *mwalola*-drinking we saw was a junior accused of sorcery by a senior after the latter had suffered a series of misfortunes.

11 Literally, 'truly, completely, from out of the heart'.

12 Something similar occurs at ordinations in the Orthodox Church when the congregation responds '*Axios!*' (Worthy!) to the questions of the ordaining bishop.

13 One old and much loved elder stopped trying to divine when he concluded that his ancestors 'did not agree' for him to be a diviner.

14 This man lived very close to the spot where a prominent English clergyman commiserated with us for coming to 'people who have lost all their old customs'.

15 I cannot claim to understand why British Government officers sometimes said that 'Islam is the proper religion for black men.' Only one or two Taita thought so.

4. The hearts of kin: anger-removal rites

1   In literal usage, the opposite of a heart that was 'hot' (*ya modo*) should have been 'cold' or 'cool' (*ya mbeho*). *Mbeho* also meant 'chill' and 'wind', and was not used for hearts. The hot/cool contrast was clear, nevertheless, for *ngolo sere*, 'peaceful heart' or *ngolo ielie*, 'clean heart', were expressly lacking in heat.

2   There was said to be another exception, but I never heard of a specific case. If two men had *ßuturi*, livestock-keeping arrangement, and the one 'keeping' livestock for the other became angry at his partner, the livestock could sicken and die.

3   The action of an angry heart resembles Zande witchcraft, but was not witchcraft in the sense of morally blameful and abnormal mystical capacity to harm others; see E. E. Evans-Pritchard (1937).

4   Unknown Taita of speculative bent constructed a concept akin to that of limbo to deal with the problem posed by those baptized children of *ßatasi* who predeceased their parents.

5   Only the cranium was installed, not the jaw.

6   A number of skulls were removed some decades ago by an archaeologist holding the mistaken belief that they had ceased to be of any religious interest. Those Taita skulls are stored now in the building where I am writing this.

7   Barrenness was not officially accepted as a cause for divorce; neither was failure to bear a son or to rear a child to adulthood.

8   The tree was that named in the *Mraru* chant occurring in Bell bestowal and *Ox of milungu* held for a man.

9   They were not married 'completely'. For details see G. Harris (1962), pp. 65–7.

10 A. Harris (1958) provides details.

11 As in other Bantu languages, *Kidaßida* used (uses) the active form *kuloßua*, to marry, of the husband and *kuloßolwa*, 'to be married', of the wife. *Kuloßuana* = to wed each other.

12 Functional equivalents include public approval accorded the counter-measures taken by injured parties. In Taita those seldom included physical violence.

13 I believe that one reason sociologists fail to make use successfully of anthropological findings lies in their own tendency to confuse *jural* and *consociational* aspects, to fail to explore the relations between the two aspects, and to treat

interaction itself as the source of jural norms. One result is the eternal search for 'attitudes' that supposedly have an explanatory value.

14 Taita not infrequently passed judgement on 'Europeans' in these terms.

15 For details, see A. and G. Harris (1964).

16 My use of the terms *jural* and *familial* in 1955 and at the present is related to but not identical with M. Fortes' use (1969); our formulations developed in parallel from similar views of kinship. In proposing the distinction between the *jural* and *familial* aspects of relations among members of the nuclear family, I referred to the *familial* as a special case of the 'associational' aspects of relations in all communities of interacting persons. I have changed 'associational' to 'consociational'. See G. Harris (1955), note 151, p. 381.

17 'Drinking tea together' was a mid-century Taita euphemism for sexual intercourse. When Alfred Harris and Mwanyasi wa Tandara made a blood pact they stipulated that they would not drink tea with each other's wives.

18 G. Harris (1973a).

19 See M. Fortes (1974) for similarities and differences in the Tallensi situation, and for the general discussion.

20 It was usually necessary to manage patrimonial animals so that the brothers shared by appropriating in turn the calves borne by sisters' bridewealth heifers when they matured.

21 Taita said, however, that should a man have any illness affecting his genitals, his mother was the right person to care for him.

22 G. Harris (1976b and forthcoming).

5. Group welfare and the Great Medicines

1 On other occasions it was far too dangerous to walk close to a *Figi*. However, the *Figi* could be tricked into allowing one to pass nearby. That was done by pretending to go back towards the Hills, then sitting down and taking a little snuff as though one were at home. The *Figi* then 'believed' that the man had gone, whereupon he could turn around quickly and slip by. Minor *figi* protecting homesteads were less potent.

6. Ritual elements and ritual efficacy

1 In his perceptive review of *How to Do Things with Words*, Hymes considers that from Austin's work 'there emerges a conception that answers to the *grammatical* in reference-based grammar, the *appropriate* in cultural behaviour generally'. He makes the extremely important point that the usefulness of Austin's ideas for anthropologists depends on attending to 'the total speech act in the total situation'. D. Hymes (1965).

Philosophers of language and linguists have explored and expanded the problems raised by Austin. M. Fürberg (1971), John R. Searle (1969) and the papers edited by P. Cole and J. Morgan (1975) – especially those by Ross, Searle and Wright – provide discussions useful to social anthropologists.

R. Finnegan (1969) is the first anthropologist to publish ethnographic data analysed in terms of basic Austinian notions; S. J. Tambiah (1973) has incorporated Searle's refinements (John R. Searle, ibid.); M. K. Foster (1974) makes more sophisticated use of the expanded concepts of speech event, speech act and performative utterance. E. Goody (1975) uses Austin's and Searle's ideas as points of departure for an exploration of the nature of questions.

In an earlier article on magical speech, S. J. Tambiah (1968), in referring to Biblical accounts of creation, misrepresents the latter and, in so doing, passes over some of the more spectacular among the performative utterances occurring in the Bible. He asserts that God is shown creating the world by means of naming, citing Genesis 1:5, 'And God called the light Day and the darkness he called Night.' Earlier in the Biblical account, however, we are told that 'God said, "Let there be Light", and there *was* Light' (Genesis 1:3). That is, God issues a *command*, a performative utterance that *does* (commands) as it says. *God's command creates Light*, which he *later* names *Day*; God is also shown creating the beasts and fowls and *later* presenting them to Adam for naming. In the Bible God's performative utterances have the peculiar character of being always valid or 'felicitous': His commands are always validly or felicitously commands, His promises are always valid, felicitous promises. (That does not mean that men always obey the Deity's commands or keep their side of mutual promises.) As God's performative utterances are always felicitous, so also when God *talks about* something, what He says is always true. The Bible provides a very large number of examples of performative utterances. So do the rituals of Scriptural religions: for example, the Words of Institution in the Christian Eucharist ('Take, eat. . .') and the Sh'ma ('Hear, oh Israel. . .). Prayers display many kinds of performative utterance other than commands, as in 'Blessed be the Name. . .', 'Forgive us our trespasses. . .', 'May that which is in this Cup. . .', etc.

Jef Verschueren (1976) provides an updated bibliography and terminological guide.

2　Much of the literature continues to use Austin's original terms, 'felicitous' and 'infelicitous', but 'valid' and 'invalid' also occur. Though they may not intend it, users of the latter set of terms bring their usage into line with venerably aged discussions of ritual by liturgical theologians.

3　See Max Black (1963).

4　S. F. Nadel (1951), p. 138.

5　E.g. V. Turner (1968).

6　See M. Fortes (1973a), pp. 314–17.

7　See G. Harris (1957), pp. 1051–4.

8　For alleged ceremonial defloration, see G. Harris (1955), note 94, p. 167.

9　I was once told that I might be a victim of sorcery after I complained of vomiting blackened food.

10　See M. Fortes (1966a), especially pp. 16–17.

11　Dom Gregory Dix (1945), Chapter VI, has an historically oriented discussion of the relationship between speech and movement in the Christian Liturgy; it is well worth anthropological attention even as it exhibits the difficulties in understanding the relationship between speech and movement.

12　E. R. Leach's (1966) formulations are too facile. Birdwhistell notes that 'speech and movement (are) both infra-systems in a multi-modal communications system'; but he shows that an understanding of the relations between the two is very difficult to come by. R. Birdwhistell (1970), p. 127 and the whole of Chapter 17.

13 John R. Searle (1969), p. 30ff.
14 See D. Hymes (1965) and note 1 above.
15 A similar view is put forward in Peter Donovan (1976); the latter, however, still hints too strongly at 'description'.
16 Human beings (e.g. drummers at a dance) and mystical agents given beer were *kutaiswa*, 'caused to be refreshed'.
17 After writing this I came upon the discussion of oral imagery in Wolff's treatment of 'needy man' in the Old Testament. H. W. Wolff (1974), Chapter II. I wish I had read it earlier.
18 The inter-penetration of *familial* and *jural* is shown by M. Fortes (1969); see note 16 to Chapter 4, above.
19 In many anthropological interpretations it is not clear whether elements or units are distinguished as such by actors.
20 G. Harris (1976a).
21 At the time of the fieldwork a chicken cost 2 shillings, goats and sheep 20 shillings each, an ox 120 and a cow 220. Few animals entered straight market transactions although some money was drawn into personalistic transfers. Money had come to be the measure of the relative value of various animals.
22 See V. Turner (1966); also Brent Berlin and Paul Kay (1969). S. Gill (1975) makes some cogent criticisms of the methods used by Turner and others to interpret colour symbolism.
23 See S. J. Tambiah (1968, 1973).

Epilogue

1 S. J. Tambiah (1968), p. 194, states that 'sensible properties...are given metaphorical values in the Trobriand scheme of symbolic classification'. It is not clear whether his use of the term 'metaphorical' provides for the fact that what may be a 'mere' metaphor to an outsider presents a constituent or dimension of reality to believers. Fernandez' term 'constitutive metaphor' recognizes that fact. J. Fernandez (1971).

BIBLIOGRAPHY

Austin, J. L. (1962). *How to Do Things with Words*, Oxford: Oxford University Press.

Berlin, Brent and Paul Kay (1969). *Basic Color Terms: Their Universality and Evolution*, Berkeley: University of California Press.

Birdwhistell, R. (1970). *Kinesics and Context: essays on body-motion*, Harmondsworth: Penguin.

Black, Max (1963). 'Austin on Performatives', *Philosophy*, vol. 38, 145, pp. 217–26.

Cole, P. and J. Morgan, eds. (1975). *Syntax and Semantics*, vol. 3, *Speech Acts*, London: Academic Press.

Coupland, R. (1938). *The Exploration of East Africa, 1856–1890*, Oxford: The Clarendon Press.

Dix, Dom Gregory (1945). *The Shape of the Liturgy*, 2nd ed., London: Adam and Chas. Black.

Donovan, Peter (1976). *Religious Language*, London: Sheldon Press.

Downes-Shaw, A. (1885). *A Pocket Vocabulary of the Ki-Swahili, Ki-nyika, Ki-taita and Ki-kamba Languages*, London: S.P.C.K.

Evans-Pritchard, E. E. (1937). *Witchcraft, Oracles and Magic among the Azande*, Oxford: The Clarendon Press.

Fernandez, J. (1971). 'Persuasions and Performances: of the Beast in Every Body and the Metaphors of Everyman', in *Myth, Symbol and Culture*, ed. C. Geertz, New York: W. W. Norton and Co., Inc.

Finnegan, R. (1969). 'How to Do Things with Words: performative utterances among the Limba of Sierra Leone', *Man*, vol. 4, pp. 537–52.

Fortes, M. (1945). *The Dynamics of Clanship among the Tallensi*, London: Oxford University Press.

Fortes, M. (1966a). 'Totem and Taboo', Presidential Address, *Proc. Royal Anthropological Institute*, pp. 5–22.

Fortes, M. (1966b). 'Religious premisses and logical technique in divinatory ritual', *Philosophical Transactions of the Royal Society of London*, Series B, Biological Sciences, No. 772, vol. 251, pp. 409–22.

Fortes, M. (1969). *Kinship and the Social Order: the legacy of Lewis Henry Morgan*, Chicago: Aldine Publishing Company.

Fortes, M. (1973a). 'On the Concept of the Person among the Tallensi', in *La Notion de Personne en Afrique Noire*, ed. G. Dieterlen, Paris: Editions du Centre National de la Récherche Scientifique.

Fortes, M. (1973b and forthcoming). 'Custom and Conscience in Anthropological Perspective', The Ernest Jones Memorial Lecture.

Fortes, M. (1974). 'The First Born', The Emanuel Miller Memorial Lecture, *Journal of Child Psychology and Psychiatry*, vol. 15, pp. 81–104.

Foster, M. K. (1974). 'When Words Become Deeds: an analysis of three Iroquois longhouse speech events', in *Explorations in the Ethnography of Speaking*, eds. R. Bauman and J. Sherzer, Cambridge: Cambridge University Press.

Fürberg, M. (1971). *Saying and Meaning: a Main Theme in J. L. Austin's Philosophy*, revised edition, Rowman and Littlefield.

Gill, S. (1975). 'The Color of Navaho Ritual Symbolism: an Evaluation of Methods', *Journal of Anthropological Research*, vol. 31, no. 4, pp. 350–63.

Goody, E. (1975). 'Towards a Theory of Questions', The Malinowski Lecture, revised mimeo draft, August 1975.

Goody, J. (1961). 'Religion and Ritual: the definitional problem', *British Journal of Sociology*, vol. 12, pp. 142–64.

Harris, A. (1958). *The Social Organization of the Wataita*, PhD dissertation, University of Cambridge.

Harris, A. (1972). 'Some Aspects of Taita Agriculture', in *Population Growth: Anthropological Implications*, ed. B. Spooner, Cambridge, Mass.: M.I.T. Press.

Harris, A. and G. (1953). *Some Aspects of Modern Conditions in Teita District, Coast Province, Kenya*, memorandum to the Royal Commission on Land and Population in East Africa.

Harris, A. and G. (1964). 'Property and the Cycle of Domestic Groups in Taita', in *The Family Estate in Africa*, ed. R. F. Gray and P. H. Gulliver, London: Routledge and Kegan Paul.

Harris, G. (1955). *The Ritual System of the Wataita*, PhD dissertation, University of Cambridge.

Harris, G. (1957). 'Possession "Hysteria" in a Kenya Tribe', *American Anthropologist*, vol. 59.

Harris, G. (1962). 'Taita Bridewealth and Affinal Relationships', in *Marriage in Tribal Societies*, ed. M. Fortes, Cambridge Papers in Social Anthropology, No. 3, Cambridge: Cambridge University Press.

Harris, G. (1973a). 'Furies, Witches and Mothers', in *The Character of Kinship*, ed. J. Goody, Cambridge: Cambridge University Press.

Harris, G. (1973b and forthcoming). 'The Bad, the Mad and the Spirit-ridden', paper read at the 72nd Annual Meeting of the American Anthropological Association, New Orleans; revised version forthcoming.

Harris, G. (1976a). 'Inward-looking and Outward-looking Symbols', in *The Realm of the Extra-Human: Ideas and Actions*, ed. A. Bharati, New York: Aldine (for Mouton).

Harris, G. (1976b and forthcoming). 'Initiation and Sibling Marriage in Two Taita Myths', paper read to the Staff Seminar, Dept. of Social Anthropology, University of Cambridge; revised version forthcoming.

Harris, G. (1976c and forthcoming). 'Speech in Ritual: Performatives and Persuasiveness', paper read to the Monday Seminar, Dept. of Social Anthropology, University of Manchester; revised version forthcoming.

Hobley, C. W. (1895). 'Upon a Visit to the Taita Highlands', *Geographical Journal*, vol. 6, pp. 545–61.

Humphrey, N. (1946). *Land and Population in the Taita Hills*, unpublished ms.

Hymes, D. (1965). Review of J. L. Austin, *How to Do Things with Words*, *American Anthropologist*, vol. 67, pp. 587–8.

Jackson, Sir Frederick (1930). *Early Days in East Africa*, London: Edward Arnold and Co.

Johnston, H. H. (1886). *The Kilimanjaro Expedition*, London: Kegan Paul, Trench and Co.

Leach, E. R. (1966). 'Ritualization in man in relation to conceptual and social development', *Philosophical Transactions of the Royal Society of London*, Series B, Biological Sciences, No. 772, vol. 251, pp. 403–8.

Nadel, S. F. (1951). *The Foundations of Social Anthropology*, London: Cohen and West.

Prins, A. H. J. (1950a). 'An Outline of the Descent System of the Taita, a North-eastern Bantu Tribe', *Africa*, vol. 20, 1, pp. 26–37.

Prins, A. H. J. (1950b). 'Notes on the Kinship Terminology of the Wa-Teita', *Man*, vol. 50, 235, pp. 145–7.

Prins, A. H. J. (1952). *The Coastal Tribes of the North-eastern Bantu* (Ethnographic Survey of Africa), London: International African Institute.

Report of the Kenya Land Commission (1934). London: H.M.S.O.

Schapera, I. (1949). 'Some Problems of Anthropological Research in Kenya Colony', *Memorandum 23*, International African Institute.

Searle, John R. (1969). *Speech Acts: an essay in the philosophy of language*, Cambridge: Cambridge University Press.

Sperber, Dan (1975). *Rethinking Symbolism*, trans. Alice L. Morton, Cambridge: Cambridge University Press.

Tambiah, S. J. (1968). 'The Magical Power of Words', *Man*, n.s., vol. 3, pp. 175–208.

Tambiah, S. J. (1973). 'Form and Meaning of Magical Acts: a point of view', in *Modes of Thought*, eds. R. Horton and R. Finnegan, London: Faber and Faber, pp. 199–229.

Thompson, Joseph (1885). *Through Masailand*, London: Sampson Low, Marston, Searle and Rivington.

Turner, V. (1966). 'Colour Classification in Ndembu Ritual', in *Anthropological Approaches to the Study of Religion*, ed. M. Banton, New York: Praeger. (Also in *The Forest of Symbols: Aspects of Ndembu Ritual* [by V. Turner], Ithaca: Cornell University Press.)

Turner, V. (1968). *The Drums of Affliction: a study of religious processes among the Ndembu of Zambia*, Oxford: Oxford University Press.

Verschueren, Jef (1976). *Speech Act Theory: a Provisional Bibliography with a Terminological Guide*, reproduced by the Indiana University Linguistics Club, Bloomington, Indiana.

Willoughby, John C. (1889). *East Africa and its Big Game*, London: Longmans, Green and Co.

Wolff, H. W. (1974). *Anthropology of the Old Testament*, London: S.C.M. Press Ltd.

Wray, J. A. (1894). *An Elementary Introduction to the Taita Language*, London: S.P.C.K.